Plant and Service Tours
in Operations Management

FIFTH EDITION

Plant and Service Tours
in Operations Management

Roger W. Schmenner

Indiana University School of Business

Prentice Hall, Upper Saddle River, New Jersey 07458

Acquisitions Editor:	Tom Tucker
Editor-in-Chief:	Natalie Anderson
Assistant Editor:	Audrey Regan
Editorial Director:	James Boyd
Production Editor:	Lynda Paolucci
Production Coordinator:	Cindy Spreder
Managing Editor:	Katherine Evancie
Senior Manufacturing Supervisor:	Paul Smolenski
Manufacturing Manager:	Vincent Scelta
Marketing Manager:	Debbie Clare
Cover Design:	Bruce Kenselaar
Composition:	Impressions Book and Journal Services, Inc.

Copyright © 1998, 1994 by Prentice Hall, Inc.
A Simon & Schuster Company
Upper Saddle River, New Jersey 07458

Library of Congress Cataloging-in-Publication Data
Schmenner, Roger W.
    Plant and service tours in operations management / Roger W.
Schmenner.—5th ed.
       p.   cm.
    Includes index.
    ISBN 0-13-257247-8
    1. Industrial tours. 2. Service industries—Management.
  I. Title.
T49.5.S36 1997
658.5—dc21   97-34761
                                             CIP

Prentice-Hall International (UK) Limited, *London*
Prentice-Hall of Australia Pty. Limited, *Sydney*
Prentice-Hall Canada, Inc., *Toronto*
Prentice-Hall Hispanoamericana, S.A., *Mexico*
Prentice-Hall of India Private Limited, *New Delhi*
Prentice-Hall of Japan, Inc., *Tokyo*
Simon & Schuster Asia Pte. Ltd., *Singapore*
Editora Prentice-Hall do Brasil, Ltda., *Rio de Janeiro*

Printed in the United States of America

10 9 8 7 6 5 4 3 2

ISBN 0-13-257247-8

*To the memory of
my mother,
Gwendolyn Jackson Schmenner*

Brief Contents

Contents

Preface

Many things in our lives help prepare us to be better students of business. We are all consumers. We all have to deal with financial matters and with other human beings. In addition, the business press writes on such matters all the time and in some depth. As students of business, then, we can readily bring these experiences and knowledge to bear in learning more about marketing, finance, accounting, and organizational behavior. Moreover, our past experiences with these business functions are likely to whet our appetites for their continued study.

For the study of production and operations management—the study of how businesses effectively deal with the management decisions surrounding the production and delivery of goods and services—the situation is different. In today's world, fewer and fewer of us have firsthand knowledge of factories or service operations. Manufacturing accounts for only about a fifth of the workforce even though regional scientists are quick to maintain its role as the "economic base" of most communities. The business press typically does not report on operations with the same intensity as it reports on other matters. Thus, while operations management remains a critical business discipline, it is less a part of our consciousness and of our everyday lives.

This book is designed to help remedy this deficiency. Each of the ten "tours" in this book introduces a particular kind of manufacturing or service process. All ten processes described are different in important respects; together they span the entire range of process choices and fall into two categories: manufacturing and service. The manufacturing tours describe the following types of processes:

- Job shop
- Batch flow process
- Worker-paced line flow process
- Machine-paced line flow process
- Continuous flow process
- Hybrid process (part batch and part continuous flow)
- Project

Included in the service tours are the following:

- Service factory
- Service shop
- Mass service
- Professional service

The models for each of these process types are drawn from actual operations as they were functioning in 1996 and 1997. Naturally, I am greatly indebted to the cooperating companies for spending a great deal of time with me discussing their processes and walking me around them, and also for reviewing and correcting my written descriptions of their operations.

Each tour consists of the process description followed by a discussion of the salient features of the process. The sequence of the tours highlights the differences among the processes. For example, the description of a continuous flow process (Tour A) is followed immediately by a description of a job shop, which lies at the opposite extreme of the manufacturing process spectrum. By playing up these contrasts, the unique features of each process may be kept more clearly in mind.

R.W.S.

Introduction

The Spectrum of Manufacturing and Service

Operations. For many people, mentioning the word brings on a rush of disagreeable feelings and sensations. Details. Pressure. Long hours. Inhospitable working conditions. Dull colleagues. For these people, a company's operating managers—usually typed as engineers who could not hack it in the "more creative" design aspects of the business—lead very unromantic careers. Moreover, operations is viewed as a dead-end job with no future in the upper layers of management.

This description is an exaggeration, of course, but it conveys some of the impressions that people hold about operations. This book is a crusade against that kind of stereotype of the operations manager. In fact, operations offers an exciting and dynamic management challenge that is as absorbing and rewarding as any marketing or finance can offer. A badly run operation can be a staggering drain on corporate profits and morale, as a number of even large corporations can attest; conversely, a well-run operation can be a competitive weapon every bit as potent as any in the corporate arsenal.

For many senior managers, the path to the top snaked through operations—even for those whose climb has been in so-called "marketing companies." Many others would admit that a tour of duty in operations was an important part of their general management education and background. The point is that operations is and rightly should be a key concern for most companies and one that all students of business who aspire to general management responsibilities ought to know about.

The importance of operations has been highlighted in recent years. Numerous articles have appeared in business periodicals stressing the need for young managers, especially those fresh from business schools, to seek out careers in operations jobs. The success of the Japanese has reinforced this view in many people's eyes, since the prowess of the Japanese is widely recognized to be in manufacturing.

Our standard of living today owes much to our forebears' ability to create wealth. Fortunately for us, because of their efforts, we have become better and better at transforming raw materials of all sorts into useful, high-quality products. So, too, have we become better at delivering an ever-expanding menu of services to both businesses and final consumers. We have, over the years, become increasingly efficient at these tasks—wasting fewer resources, satisfying customers more completely, requiring less physical exertion from ourselves, and frequently, although not always, being kinder to the environment in the process.

PART ONE: MANUFACTURING

The Spectrum of Manufacturing Processes

The factory tours in this book describe a rich diversity of technologies and approaches to a variety of the issues faced by manufacturing managers. The summary chapter at the conclusion of the tours compares and contrasts the processes in considerable detail. Suffice it here to present a much more "bare bones" discussion of five major types of manufacturing processes that one can engage in. They form a spectrum (see Figure 1–1).

1. The Project. The project—building a skyscraper, bringing a new product out of the R&D labs, making a movie—is sometimes excluded from consideration as a manufacturing process because, by its nature, it exists only to do a particular, unique job. This is not to say, however, that one project may not look very similar to another. Many projects, be they large buildings, new products, or movies, require much the same work to get them up and running. There are certain regularities present in a project, among them:

- Projects typically make heavy use of certain skills and capabilities at particular times and little or no use of those skills at other times.
- Projects can often usefully be seen as the coordination of part-time or subcontracted skills and capabilities (people, equipment, etc.). Skills and capabilities, of course, can be many and varied.
- The coordination of those skills and capabilities requires a lot of attention to planning and scheduling, and subsequently, attention to the control of that schedule, and any rescheduling or expediting that may be required. Great attention must be given to which tasks must be accomplished before others (a precedence diagram) and what the expected durations for those tasks are.
- The quality of any project depends greatly on the skills and care of the members of the project team.

2. The Continuous Flow Process. At the other extreme of the process spectrum lies the continuous flow process. Many high-volume consumer goods and commodities are made by continuous flow processes—oil refining, food processing, papermaking, lightbulb fabrication. The continuous flow process's most significant characteristic is how materials move through it—hardly ever stopping, moving constantly from one process operation to another. With a continuous flow process, one can estimate realistically how long it takes to transform raw materials into a specific product. Work-in-process inventories exist at well-defined levels and are low relative to the value of output the continuous flow process generates. Capital investments and automation, on the other hand, are often higher than those of other processes, especially when contrasted with the workforce employed. Layouts are frequently product-specific, typically with a straight-line character to them, as the products in the making go from one operation to another.

Continuous flow processes can be very productive and very profitable, assuming normal sales levels. Only when sales levels plunge is the profitability of the continuous flow process in jeopardy.

Project   Job Shop   Batch Flow   Line Flow   Continuous Flow

FIGURE 1–1 The spectrum of manufacturing processes.

3. The Job Shop. Lying next to the project in the process spectrum is the job shop. It is the most flexible process for creating a wide variety of products in significant quantities. (The project, almost by definition, does not produce in quantity.) Machine shops, tool and die shops, and many plastic molding operations are job shops, working to fulfill particular customer orders.

The job shop layout is often distinctly different from that of a continuous flow process; it groups similar equipment together, primarily because no single product generates enough sales volume to justify the creation of a product-specific array of equipment.[1] Often a job shop has a diverse array of equipment and capabilities to choose from.

The flow of material in a job shop can be complex and far from straight line in character. Materials can be routed in many directions and can loop back to the same equipment later in the processing cycle. With each order (job) capable of such complexity, it is absolutely essential that information on how the order is to be routed through the factory, what is to be done to it at each step of the way, and how much time and effort is actually spent on it, follow the job. The job shop lives by its information flows. This information is vital, because job shops typically bid for work. Without good information on costs, times (run times, setup times, labor content times), routings, and process steps, a job shop would be seriously disadvantaged.

4. The Batch Flow Process. One step toward the continuous flow process from the job shop is the batch flow process. The job shop and the batch flow process have a good deal in common. Their layouts are similar, with equipment grouped by function rather than by product.[2] The product is regarded as moving from department to department within the factory. A batch flow operation depends on information such as routings and process steps and tracks costs and times spent. However, batch flow processes typically have a set menu of products that they produce, frequently, in set quantities (lot sizes). The batch flow operation is thus somewhat more standardized than the job shop, particularly as it relates to routings and costs.

While the job shop usually operates to fulfill an outside customer's order by an agreed-upon due date and in whatever quantity is ordered, the batch flow operation usually produces in established lot sizes that move into an inventory from which further production or final customer orders are filled. Batch flow processes are commonplace, especially when one considers all the times "fabrication" must be done. Examples of batch flow processes include much of the chemical industry, semiconductor fabrication, apparel, much of the steel industry, and huge chunks of the metal bending, metal forming, and metal machining industries.

5. The Line Flow Process. Between the batch flow and continuous flow processes, along the process spectrum, lies the line flow process. In reality it lies closer to the continuous flow process because it presents some substantive distinctions from the batch flow. The line flow process is most popularly exemplified by the moving assembly line that one finds in the auto industry, but it is also found in a host of other assembly industries such as consumer electronics and computers.

---

[1]Sometimes families of parts or products can be identified and exist in enough volume to justify the creation of a manufacturing cell within the job shop. Such a manufacturing cell gathers various, often different, pieces of equipment together in a product family–specific configuration.

[2]Here again, the innovation of the manufacturing cell is applicable. Defining manufacturing cells for the batch flow process rather than the job shop is likely to be much easier to do because the identification of a family of parts of sufficient volume is easier.

In contrast to the batch flow process, the line flow process exhibits the following characteristics:

- A product-specific layout with different pieces of equipment placed in sequence ready to perform operations on the product. There are, of course, mixed model lines that can produce distinctly different models of the basic product, but the more diverse the products made, the less satisfactory the line becomes at producing those.
- The product moves readily from one operation to another so that there is little work-in-process inventory, nor is there a stockroom in the product's path. This also means that there is a great need to examine the "balance" of the process so that the different tasks to be accomplished take roughly the same amount of time to perform and have the same capacities, not just over weeks of time, but over minutes of time.
- The paperwork needs of the line flow process are less demanding than the batch flow. Routings are not needed and operations sheets can frequently be simplified, if not eliminated altogether. The need for tracking labor and machine inputs to particular products/parts also fades away.
- In contrast to the continuous flow operation, the line flow is somewhat more flexible, and generally less automated and more labor intensive.

As one proceeds across the spectrum from project to continuous flow, one tends to move from a highly individualized, flexible process to one that is much more inflexible in the products it can make but, at the same time, much more productive and efficient in how it makes them.

Hybrid Processes

The five process types introduced above—project, job shop, batch flow, line flow, and continuous flow—are all "pure." Many factories are combinations of two (sometimes more) of these pure processes. Popular hybrids are the batch flow–line flow hybrid (auto engines, furnaces, air-conditioning, furniture) and the batch flow–continuous flow hybrid (breweries, many high-volume consumer products whose raw materials are made in batches, such as photographic film).

In these processes the first part of the flow of materials looks like a batch flow process (often, this part of the process is labeled "fabrication") while the latter part resembles a line or continuous flow process (and this part of the process is labeled "assembly" or "finishing"). Importantly, the two portions of the hybrid are separated by an inventory, typically termed a "decoupling" inventory. The batch flow process acts to fill up the inventory with parts or semi-finished product, which then is drawn down by the line or continuous flow process for assembly or completion.

The reason the hybrid process is divided into two parts is that the batch flow process is not normally as nimble as the line flow or continuous flow process. The batch flow may not be as nimble because significant chunks of time may be needed to set up the existing machines for a different component of the finished product. This puts pressure on the batch flow process for longer runs than would be needed to match precisely the product mix and quantities produced by the line or continuous flow process, which normally can change over to other products more quickly. If the batch flow process tried to match the line or continuous flow process precisely (say, hourly or daily), it would lose a lot of time to setup and this downtime could rob the process of the capacity it needs to keep up with overall demand. Thus, the batch flow process does not attempt a precise match of the line or continuous flow process's product mix and quantity, but rather a quantity and product mix match over a much longer period of time, say weeks or months. The batch flow process then acts to replenish the decoupling inventory, while the line or continuous flow process acts to fill particular customer orders.

Much of the push toward just-in-time (JIT) manufacturing, it should be noted, can be interpreted as a remedy for this deficiency of batch flow processes. In essence, JIT tries to make the batch flow process operate with the efficiency of the line flow process.

Manufacturing Choices

Manufacturing managers are faced with a wide variety of choices, and how well they make those choices, in large part, determines how successful they and their companies are. These operations choices define, in essential ways, the study of operations management. The remainder of this book is devoted to exploring how these choices are made and how they can be made better. Three broad categories confront the manager: (1) technology and facilities, (2) operating policies, and (3) operations organization. Let us review these categories and choices in turn by noting a number of questions about them. These questions point to some of the alternatives managers face. Do not be discouraged if you do not know exactly what these questions refer to. The remainder of this book should clarify things for you. Rather, let these questions "wash over" you to give you a feel for what operations managers face.

Technology and Facilities

These choices frequently involve large capital expenditures and long periods of time. These are the big decisions that do much to define the type of process employed.

1. *Nature of the process flow.* Is the flow of product through the plant characterized as rigid, with every product treated in the same way? At the other extreme, is the flow a jumbled one, with products routed in many different ways through the factory? Or, does the flow of product through the process fall somewhere in between?
   - Are segments of the process tightly linked to one another, or are the connections between process segments loose? How quickly can materials flow through the process?
   - Is the process a "pure" one or is it a hybrid of different process types?
2. *Vertical integration.* How much of a product's value is a direct result of factory operations? Should production involve more (or less) integration backward toward raw materials or more (or less) integration forward toward customers? Can it involve more (or less) of either of these?
3. *Types of equipment.* Is the equipment used general purpose in design or special purpose? Can any special-purpose, seemingly inflexible equipment be linked together in innovative ways to yield production systems that are themselves more flexible than the equipment comprising them?
   - Is the equipment meant for high speeds and long runs, or not? How flexible is it for changeovers in products/models? How quickly and easily can such changes be accomplished?
   - What possibilities exist for linking one piece of equipment with another for balanced and quick throughput?
   - Is the equipment operator controlled or automatically/computer controlled? Is its performance monitored by operators or by computer?
   - Can the equipment be speeded up or slowed down to match production needs?
   - Does the equipment demand substantial nonoperation support (maintenance, repair, software, setup, tooling)?

- Can the company build or modify its own machines? Does it have close ties to equipment manufacturers?

4. *Degree of capital or labor intensity.* To what degree has the equipment and/or technology permitted labor value to be driven out of the product or service? How important could reduced labor value in the product be to costs, yields, or sustained levels of "production to specifications" (good quality)?

5. *Attitude toward the process technology.* To what extent does the company pioneer advances in process technology? Is the company a leader in that regard or a follower? How closely does it track other process improvements?
   - How committed is the company to research and development? What mix is sought between the two?
   - How close is the alliance between manufacturing and engineering? To what extent are efforts made to design products so that they are easily manufactured? How are design and manufacturing teams organized for new product introductions?
   - Are engineering change orders (changes to a product's manufacturing specifications) numerous? To what can they be attributed? How disruptive to the process flow are they?
   - What investments are made in manufacturing engineering and industrial engineering relative to product design engineering?

6. *Attitude toward capacity utilization.* How close to capacity (defined as best as possible) does the company desire to operate? How willing is the company to stock out of a product because of too tight capacity?
   - Does capacity generally come in significant chunks? What can be done to keep capacity well balanced among segments of the process?

7. *Plant size.* How big does the company permit any one plant to grow? To what extent are either economies or diseconomies of scale present?

8. *Plant charters and locations.* Does it make sense to assign different product lines, product processes, or geographic markets to particular plants? How do the plant locations chosen mesh together into a multiplant operation?

Operating Policies

Once the process technology and facilities have been selected, management must still decide on a host of features concerning how the process technology is used. Three broad segments of such operating policies present themselves: loading the factory, controlling the movement of goods through it, and distribution.

Loading the Factory

1. *Forecasting.* To what degree is the plant's output mix known with certainty before raw materials must be gathered or equipment or personnel assigned? To what extent must forecasts be relied on to determine which raw materials ought to be ordered and which equipment/worker capacity reserved, and how much of each?
   - How reliable have past forecasts been? Does manufacturing second-guess marketing's demand forecasts? Should it?
   - What techniques work best for forecasting requirements? Is there a long product pipeline that risks pipeline momentum problems and heightens forecasting needs?

2. *Purchasing.* Given the decision on the plant's degree of vertical integration, what does the plant make for itself and what is purchased from outside suppliers? How are suppliers chosen? What kinds of contracts (e.g., long-term or spot) are sought?
   - Is purchasing formally integrated with forecasting and/or order taking? How much visibility is granted suppliers about the company's expected future needs? Are orders on suppliers made through an MRP system (a special computer-based materials management system) or other informal means? Or, are formal purchase requisitions required?

- How important is supplier quality compared to price in determining how suppliers are chosen? How is supplier quality monitored? How well does this monitoring work? What supplier improvement programs, if needed, have been adopted?

3. *Supply logistics.* How frequently, from where, and by what mode of transportation do raw materials arrive at the plant? How sensitive are costs to changes in these factors?

- How readily can materials be received, inspected, and stored? Is supplier quality good enough to dispense with incoming inspection? Is supplier delivery reliable enough and frequent enough to be able to feed the plant's production needs without large raw materials inventories?
- How is materials handling accomplished within the plant? How much is automatic and how much is manual? What controls are used?

4. *Raw materials inventory system.* How much inventory of raw materials is held? What system is used (material requirements planning, reorder point, periodic reorder)? How does the inventory level vary with demand, price discounts, supplier lead time changes, supply uncertainties, or other factors? What triggers the replenishment of the raw materials inventory?

- How are materials controlled in the stockroom? Are records accurate enough to be relied on without ceasing production for physical inventories? Is all scrap reported?
- Are materials placed into "kits," or are they fed directly to the shop or line?

5. *Production planning.* Are goods manufactured to customer order or to forecasts, or are they manufactured to stock some finished goods inventory? Is inventory permitted to be built in advance to cover peak period demands and thus smooth out production, or does production try to "chase" demand, with little or no buildup of inventories?

- How are workforce needs planned for? How are model or product line changes planned for? How far in advance can changes be routinely made to the general production plan? How disruptive to the process is any expediting or rescheduling?
- Are routine allowances made for such situations?

Controlling Movement Through the Factory

1. *Production scheduling and inventory control.* What triggers the specific production of goods: orders, forecasts, or reference to a finished goods inventory? How do factors like the pattern of demand and product costs influence any trigger level of finished goods inventory? How are specific departments, lines, work centers, and the like scheduled? What factors of the process, the pattern of demand, or product variations and costs affect the schedule?

- What determines specific priorities in the jobs awaiting work in a department? How much expediting is permitted? How much rescheduling?
- What or who determines the specific priorities of work: an MRP system, foreman discretion, specific rules, simulation results?
- Does instituting an MRP system make sense for the plant? How much fluctuation or stability exists for bills of materials, vendor reliability on delivery, production cycle times? What levels of accuracy and integrity exist for inventory counts and records, for production/rework counts and records for scrap? What kinds of exception reports and follow-through stand to be most helpful?

2. *Pacing of production.* Is the pace of production determined by machine setting, worker effort, management pressure or discretion, or some combination? How readily can the pace be altered?

3. *Production control.* How much information, and of what type, flows within the production process, both from management to the workforce and from the workforce to management?

- How easily can product variations, engineering change orders, product mix changes, or production volume changes be transmitted to the workforce? How soon can management react to machine breakdowns, parts shortages, or other disruptions of the normal flow of product and process on the plant floor?

- How are machines, workers, materials, and orders monitored? What "early warning signals" are looked to? What remedies are routinely investigated?

4. *Quality control.* Does everyone in the organization truly believe that quality (performance to specification) is his or her job, not simply the function of a quality control department? What mechanisms and cooperative forums exist to assure that "work is done right the first time"? How closely linked are design engineering, manufacturing/industrial engineering, quality control, workforce training and supervision, maintenance, and production scheduling and control?

- How is quality checked, both of process and product? How many checks are made at different steps in the process? How much authority is given to quality control personnel?

5. *Workforce policies.* What are the skill levels required of various jobs throughout the process? How are they trained for? Is the work content of jobs broad or narrow? Is cross-training of workers desirable? How do workers advance in the factory (by job classification, different jobs, changes of shift) into management?

- How and how much are workers paid? Are any incentives, wage or otherwise, built into the process? How are workers' achievements and ideas encouraged and recognized?
- How does management feel about unionization? What actions concerning unions does it take?
- What is the age and sex composition of the workforce?
- What opportunities exist for job enlargement and job enrichment? Is there a place for quality of work life projects? How else can the workforce be encouraged to participate in the management of the operation?

Distribution

1. *Distribution.* What are the channels of distribution? How are they filled? What are the trade-offs between service and inventory costs?

2. *Logistics.* What are the benefits and costs of various geographical patterns of warehousing and distribution? What modes of transportation make sense? How should they be managed?

Operations Organization

As important as the decisions about the physical composition of the factory and the systems in place to guide and control the movement of materials are decisions on how the factory is to be organized.

1. *Operations control.* Are the major operating decisions retained centrally or dispersed to individual plant units? What kinds of decisions rest primarily with the plant?

- How is the plant evaluated? What biases might that method introduce? What are the specific measures for the various levels of hierarchy in the plant and throughout the manufacturing organization?

2. *Talent.* Where within the organization are the best people put? What talents are most prized for the smooth and continued successful operation of the process?

The Product-Process Matrix

Another useful way to visualize some of the similarities and differences among different types of production processes is to array the processes within what has been called the product-process matrix. This matrix is nothing fancier than a box, one side of which describes the varieties of product mixes that are possible and another side of which describes the process patterns (the ease of flow of product through the process) that are possible. Figure 1–2 portrays this.

Product Mix

Process Pattern	One of a kind or few	Low volumes; many products	High volumes; several major products	Very high volumes; standard product (commodity)	Challenges for Management
Very jumbled flow; process segments loosely linked					Scheduling; materials handling; shifting bottlenecks
Jumbled flow; but a dominant flow exists					
Line flow Worker paced					Worker motivation; balance; maintaining enough flexibility
Machine paced					
Continuous, automated, and rigid flow; process segments tightly linked					Capital expenses for big chunk capacity; technological changes; materials management; vertical integration
Challenges for Management	Bidding; delivery; product design flexibility		Quality (product differentiation); flexibility in output volumes	Price	

FIGURE 1–2 A product-process matrix.

As we can see in Figure 1–2, the mix of products handled by the plant may range from a one-of-a-kind item (such as a work of art or a custom-designed house) to a very standard product that is produced and consumed in high volumes (such as sugar). In between, a company can produce many different products, each at relatively low volumes, or it can cut down on the number of different products offered but produce higher volumes of each.

As we might expect, management faces different sets of challenges in bringing each of these different product mixes to market. For example, a commodity item undoubtedly has to compete on price. While there may be a limited number of grades of the commodity, the ability to offer the item at low cost is absolutely critical to company success, whether the company produces paper clips or paper.

At the other end of this product mix spectrum, the one-of-a-kind item is frequently purchased with scarcely a thought about price. Since it is a custom item, the buyer is likely to have contracted for it beforehand. Thereafter, the buyer typically becomes concerned about whether the product meets specifications and whether it can be delivered on time. These concerns place a different set of demands on the manufacturer. Instead of paying near-exclusive attention to product cost, the manufacturer must pay particular attention to product design flexibility, and delivery, as the manufacturer's success depends more on these features of the production system. Because most work is contracted for, management must be accomplished at developing bids for each, which entails thorough knowledge of costs within the factory.

In between these two extremes, management confronts somewhat different challenges. When many different products—each with low production volumes—are made or when fewer products—each with substantial production volumes—are made, product features such as quality or the ability to gear up (or down) rapidly in production become relatively more important than before. Product quality is a key element in differentiating one's product from others available, and is a chief reason why some products command price premiums. Flexibility in production volumes, while less evident to the marketplace than quality, is often a reason why some companies have been so successful—either beating their competitors to the market with seasonal, cyclical, or faddish products (for example, building supplies or fashions) or turning off production when the market for a product appears to have dried up. Depending on the situation, product design flexibility, price, and delivery can still be very important to the manufacturer; but it is likely that as product design flexibility or quality rises in importance, price falls in importance.

These then are the chief challenges that various product mixes pose for their managers. A corresponding set of management challenges derive from the process patterns depicted in Figure 1–2. As the matrix reveals, the process pattern varies from a very jumbled flow to a continuous, automated, and rigid production flow. The linking of segments of the production process varies from loose to tight. The process patterns in between exhibit varying degrees of rigidity, pacing, and process segment linking.

For the jumbled process pattern, the challenges to management include scheduling, routing materials efficiently, and coping with shifting production bottlenecks. At the other end of the process pattern spectrum, the continuous, automated, and rigid process flow demands increased attention to such items as capital expenses for large-scale capacity increases, technological change in the process, materials management, and vertical integration. Between the process poles, factors like worker motivation, balance of capacities for different process segments, and process flexibility become relatively more important.

The arrays of product mix, process patterns, and their respective challenges to management line the outside of the product-process matrix. Now to fill in the inside. As our brief survey of production processes has revealed, different process types follow different process patterns and are also better suited to particular product mixes. It is easy, then, to match process types to the appropriate position within the matrix, as Figure 1–3 does.

As is readily apparent from the chart, process types should fill out the diagonal of the product-process matrix, from projects and job shops in the upper left corner down to continuous flow processes in the lower right corner. Only by being on the diagonal do processes match properly the process pattern to the prevailing product mix.

Consider what it means to be off the diagonal. Suppose, for example, that a company tries to manufacture low volumes of many different products by using a continuous, automated, and rigid flow process that is typically capital intensive

Product Mix

Process Pattern	One of a kind or few	Low volumes; many products	High volumes; several major products	Very high volumes; standard product (commodity)	Challenges for Management
Very jumbled flow; process segments loosely linked	Project				Scheduling; materials handling; shifting bottlenecks
		Job Shop			
Jumbled flow; but a dominant flow exists		Batch Flow		*opportunity costs*	
Line flow					Worker motivation; balance; maintaining enough flexibility
Worker paced			Line Flow		
Machine paced		*out-of-pocket costs*		Line Flow	
Continuous, automated, and rigid flow; process segments tightly linked				Continuous Flow	Capital expenses for big chunk capacity; technological changes; materials management; vertical integration
Challenges for Management	Bidding; delivery; product design flexibility		Quality (product differentiation); flexibility in output volumes	Price	

FIGURE 1–3 The product-process matrix, filled in.

and vertically integrated. The match is clearly inappropriate because the process would have to be interrupted constantly and retooled often to permit the kind of product flexibility needed to produce low numbers of lots of products. Not only is the match inappropriate, but it is expensive. The purchase prices of the automated machines and the cost of product changeovers would be staggering, involving a great deal of out-of-pocket expense.

Being above the diagonal brings on costs of a different kind. In this case, suppose a very standard product consumed in great quantity were manufactured in a jumbled flow process pattern. Here again the match is clearly inappropriate, though not because too many dollars go out-of-pocket to buy expensive machinery. Rather, operating costs (e.g., labor, inventories) are much higher than they could be, which means that the profit margin on each unit of the product made is much lower than it should be. By not substituting specific special-purpose machinery for high labor input and general-purpose equipment, the company forgoes profits that it would otherwise earn.

PART TWO: SERVICE OPERATIONS

Distinguishing Service Operations from Manufacturing

Six of the ten tours described in this book deal strictly with manufacturing operations. The other four, however, reveal significant distinctions between service and manufacturing. Some of the management challenges for service operations parallel those in manufacturing, but others are unique.

What is a service operation anyway? The answer to this question is surprisingly ambiguous. We may know service operations when we see them but have difficulty describing them in general. Perhaps the term can be better understood as what it isn't rather than what it is. Some have tried to define service employment as nonfarming and nonmanufacturing employment; others have also excluded government employment. This approach includes operations such as hotels, restaurants, repairs, amusements, health, education, real estate, wholesale and retail trade, transportation, and professional services like law, engineering, architecture, finance, and advertising. Although these selections may be intuitively clear, there are still some definitional problems. For example, what about public utilities? Some public utilities companies have service in their name (such as Public Service of New Hampshire), yet in many ways power generation is more manufacturing than service. And is a company like IBM a manufacturing company or a service company? As in the old story of the blind men and the elephant, the answer may depend on what part of the beast you are touching. Surely there are aspects of IBM that are strictly manufacturing but other aspects that are service (examples are field repair and the sales force).

This ambiguity is growing. As technology advances, more and more labor will be driven out of manufactured products; that is, there will be less direct labor involved in manufacturing companies and more indirect labor—the kind of labor that is oriented to support services. Even now, some high-technology companies have overhead rates that are six to ten times the direct labor component, mainly because of the substantial indirect labor in these companies. The traditional management focus on direct labor is becoming less and less relevant. Service operations management affects more than just service companies per se. Furthermore, the service sector will continue to grow. About two thirds of America's gross national product is now accounted for by services; the same fraction applies to the percentage of the workforce employed in service jobs. These fractions can only rise. Similar trends are observed in other developed countries.

Characteristics of Service Operations

Most services share certain characteristics to a greater or lesser extent. It is helpful to understand these characteristics and how they separate manufacturing from service.

1. The service provided is often something that the consumer cannot touch or feel. It may be associated with something physical (such as the food we eat, the airplane we fly in, the life insurance policy), but what is valued about the service and may be the focus of management typically involves intangibles, such as ambiance, information, or peace of mind.

2. The service is often created and delivered on the spot, in many cases with significant involvement of the customer in the service process (consider salad bars in restaurants). Because the process is often more on display in service operations than in manufacturing, whether it functions well is critical. The process cannot be saved by a quality control check at the end; it has to live with its defects. Therefore, training, process design, and employee relations are especially important to service industries.

3. Because of the visibility of the service process in many instances and the intangibility of many services, operations management and marketing are more interdependent than in manufacturing. Marketing and operations have to work together in service companies; they cannot afford to be antagonists.

4. Frequently, the consumption of a service is nearly simultaneous with its production. Services cannot be inventoried for use later on. This fact has some serious implications for capacity choice and capacity management in a service business. The site, size, and layout choices for service industries are critical. The wrong site, a size either too large or too small, or a poor layout can dramatically affect the performance of a service unit. This concern for capacity is heightened by the irregularities in the pattern of demand over time (whether a day, week, or season). Demand irregularities place a tremendous burden on a service operation to be flexible. They also force services to manage their demand via prices or the kinds of services offered.

5. Many service operations, although by no means all, require little in the way of capital investment, multiple locations, or proprietary technology. For these services, barriers to the entry of competing firms are rather low. Service companies are generally very sensitive to the real—or even potential—entry of others and must react quickly to the competition's actions and threats. Many service operations also possess rather low barriers to exit; that is, the assets of a service organization can be sold easily (such as planes or trucks). Because firms can get in and out of the service business quickly, some service strategies can play for the "hit and run."

Service Operations Choices

Part I of this chapter opened by reviewing a whole series of operations choices faced by manufacturing managers. Service operations managers, of course, face a similar list of choices. Table 1–1 outlines some major ones.

A Spectrum of Services

Much as we have thought of manufacturing enterprises in terms of different kinds of production processes, we can think of service operations in terms of distinct "processes." It is helpful to view these different service processes in terms of a matrix that contrasts the labor intensity of the process on the one hand, and the degree of interaction with and customization of the service for the consumer on the other. This matrix is shown in Figure 1–4. The quadrants of the matrix roughly define four reasonably distinct service processes.

The Service Factory   Some service processes have relatively low labor intensity (and thus a greater fraction of service costs associated with the facility and its equipment) and also a low degree of customer interaction and customization. These can be characterized as service factories. Much of the transportation industry, hotels, and resorts, for example, are service factories, as are "back-of-the-house" operations for banking and financial services companies. The Burger King Restaurant in Noblesville, Indiana (Tour F) is an example of a service factory.

TABLE 1–1 Key choices for service operations

I. Technology and Facilities

Type of facility and equipment (Used by customers themselves? How? How attractive do they have to be? How are they used during a peak versus a nonpeak situation? General-purpose versus special-purpose equipment? Anything proprietary about equipment or its use?)

Layout (Job shop–like? Fixed position? Other?)

Location (How critical to attracting customers?)

Size of the facility

Geographic spread of any multiple facilities

Degree of labor intensity

Attitude toward capacity utilization (Facility for the peak demand or not?)

II. Operating Policies

A. Planning the operation

Forecasting (Extent required? Type used?)

Logistics and inventory system used for materials employed

Manpower planning

Schedule setting (Can service provision be "leveled" in any way?)

Demand management for peak and off-peak times

B. Controlling the operation

Labor issues—hiring, training, skill levels required, job content, pay, advancement, unionism

Accounting controls used

Checklists developed

Foolproofing designed into the layout and the equipment

Quality control audits and policies

What triggers provision of the service and the pace of the operation (Customer? Forecast?)

Production control (How does the information flow within the operation? What is on track? What is not? How can anything gone amiss be fixed? How can any changes be implemented?)

III. Operations Organization

What is kept at the individual unit level, and what is centralized?

Where is talent held in the organization?

The Service Shop   As the degree of interaction with—or customization for—the consumer increases, the service factory gives way to the service shop, much as a line flow operation gives way to a job shop operation when customization is required in manufacturing. Hospitals and repair services of all types are prime examples of service shops. Tour G of Ogle–Tucker Buick auto repair operation is an example of a service shop.

Mass Service   Mass service processes have a high degree of labor intensity, but a rather low degree of interaction with or customization for the consumer. Retail operations, retail banking, schools, and wholesaling are examples of mass services. The Lazarus department store at the Castleton Square Mall, characterized in Tour H, is an example of mass service.

Professional Service   If the degree of interaction increases and/or customization become the watchword, mass service gives way to professional service, as provided by doctors, lawyers, consultants, architects, and the like. Arthur Andersen's audit services in Charlotte (Tour I) provide an example of professional service.

	Degree of Contact with, and Customization for, the Consumer		Challenges for Management
	Low	High	
Low	**The Service Factory** Airlines, trucking, hotels, resorts and recreation	**The Service Shop** Hospitals, auto, and other repair services	Capital decisions, technological advances, managing demand to avoid peaks and to promote off-peaks, scheduling delivery of service
High	**Mass Service** Retailing, wholesaling, schools	**Professional Service** Physicians, lawyers, accountants, architects	Hiring, training, methods development and control, employee welfare, scheduling workforces, control of often geographically spread locations, start-up of new units, managing growth
Challenges for Management	Marketing, making service "warm," attention to physical surroundings, managing fairly rigid hierarchy with need for standard operating procedures	Fighting cost increases, maintaining quality, reacting to customer intervention in process, managing advancement of people delivering service, managing flat hierarchy with loose subordinate-superior relationships, binding workers to the firm	

*(Left axis label: **Degree of Labor Intensity**)*

FIGURE 1–4 A matrix of service processes.

Challenges to Management

Let us look at the challenges to management that are implied by labor intensity and interaction/customization differences. The service operation that is more highly capital intensive has to look carefully at (1) its capital decisions regarding land, facilities, and equipment; and (2) technological advances that may affect them. Capital-intensive processes often cannot easily augment capacity, so demand must be managed to smooth any demand peaks and to promote the off-peak times. The inflexibility of capacity also implies the scheduling service delivery is relatively more important for these process types.

For process types with high labor intensity, managing and controlling the workforce become paramount. Hiring, training, methods development and control, employee welfare, scheduling the workforce, and controlling what may be far-flung locations are critical. If new units of operations are contemplated, their start-up may become a problem; managing a group of such new units can be difficult.

What about the challenges to management implied by differences in the interaction with and customization for the consumer? Those service processes that have a low degree of interaction and customization face a stiffer marketing challenge. They must try to make the service "warm" and "exciting" even though they may not give the personal attention that a customer might want. Attention to the physical surroundings and the layout become more important. With a low degree of interaction and with little customization, standard operating procedures can safely be instituted. The hierarchy of the service organization itself tends to be the classic pyramid, with fairly rigid relationships between levels.

As the service takes on a higher degree of interaction and customization, management must deal with higher costs and more talented labor. Keeping costs down and yet maintaining quality becomes a challenge. Talented employees want attention given to how they may advance in the organization. The hierarchy of control tends to be flat, with much less rigid relationships between superiors and subordinates. Keeping workers bound to the firm rather than hopping from job to job becomes a challenge as well. Service firms with a high degree of consumer interaction also must react to frequent consumer intervention in the process.

Naturally, there are some gray areas as one passes from low to high on either dimension of this matrix. For example, while fast-food restaurants are probably best seen as service factories, the traditional restaurant is more problematic. Traditional restaurants offer a higher degree of interaction and customization for the consumer, and they are more labor intensive than fast-food restaurants. While they may be best characterized as service shops, they are fairly low in that quadrant, with at least some gourmet restaurants arguably characterized as professional services.

A Continuous Flow Process

International Paper
Androscoggin Mill
Jay, Maine

(Courtesy of International Paper)

The Androscoggin Mill, situated along the Androscoggin River in central Maine, was one of 25 domestic pulp and paper mills of International Paper. It was one of the largest, built originally in 1965 with significant additions in 1968 and 1977. The plant occupied 478 acres of land, had 20 acres under roof, and represented a replacement value investment of nearly $800 million.

The mill, part of International Paper's Pulp and Coated Papers Group, produced four distinctly different kinds of paper: (1) forms bond, envelope, tablet, and offset paper for office or computer use; (2) publication gloss for magazine printing; (3) coated printing papers; and (4) specialty papers such as microwave popcorn and fast-food french fry grease-proof papers.

Androscoggin was a fully integrated mill; that is, it produced all the wood pulp it needed to make its paper. The mill was laid out to receive logs or chips of wood at one end and, about a mile farther down, to ship packaged "logs" of paper from the other end. (See Figure A1 for a layout of the mill; the production flow is from left to right.)

PART ONE: PROCESS DESCRIPTION

A Brief and Simplified Description of Papermaking

The paper we use today is created from individual wood fibers that are first suspended in water and then pressed and dried into sheets. The process of converting the wood to a suspension of wood fibers in water is known as pulpmaking, while the manufacture of the dried and pressed sheets of paper is formally termed papermaking. The process of making paper has undergone a steady evolution, and larger and more sophisticated equipment and better technology continue to improve it.

The Woodyard and Woodrooms

The process at Androscoggin began with receiving wood in the form of chips or of logs 4 or 8 feet in length. From 6 A.M. to 10 P.M. a steady stream of trucks and railroad cars were weighed and unloaded. About 40 percent of the deliveries were of wood cut from International Paper's own land (over 1 million acres in Maine), while the other 60 percent were supplied by independents who were paid by weight for their logs. The mill also received wood chips from lumber mills in the area. The chips and logs were stored in mammoth piles with separate piles for wood of different species (such as pine, spruce, hemlock).

When needed, logs were floated in flumes from the woodyard into one of the mill's three woodrooms. There, a ring debarker scraped bark off of the logs. The

FIGURE A1 Layout of International Paper's Androscoggin Mill.

In the woodyard, wood being unloaded. (Courtesy of International Paper)

A chip unloading station. (Courtesy of International Paper)

A groundwood log conveyor. (Courtesy of International Paper)

logs then fell into a chipper; within seconds a large log was reduced to a pile of chips approximately 1 inch by 1 inch by 1/4 inch.

The chips were stored in silos. There were separate silos for softwoods (spruce, fir, hemlock, and pine) and hardwoods (maple, oak, beech, and birch). This separate and temporary storage of chips permitted the controlled mixing of chips into the precise recipe for the grade of paper being produced.

The wood chips were then sorted through large, flat vibrating screens. Oversized chips were rechipped, and ones that were too small were collected for burning in the power house. (The mill provided approximately 50 percent of all its own steam and electricity needs from burning waste. An additional 50 percent of total electricity needs was produced by harnessing the river for hydroelectric power.)

Once drawn from the silo into the digesters, there was no stopping the flow of chips into paper.

Pulpmaking

The pulp made at Androscoggin was of two types: Kraft pulp (produced chemically) and groundwood pulp (produced mechanically). Kraft pulp was far more important to the high-quality white papers produced at Androscoggin, accounting for 80 percent of all the pulp used. Kraft pulp makes strong paper. (Kraft is German for strength. A German invented the Kraft pulp process in 1884.) A paper's strength generally comes from the overlap and binding of long fibers of softwood; only chemically was it initially possible to separate long wood fibers for suspension in water. Hardwood fibers are generally smaller and thinner and help smooth the paper and make it less porous.

The groundwood pulping process was simpler and less expensive than the Kraft process. It took high-quality spruce and fir logs and pressed them continuously against a revolving stone that broke apart the wood's fibers. The fibers, however, were smaller than those produced by the Kraft process and, although used to make newsprint, were useful at Androscoggin in providing "fill" for the coated publication gloss papers of machines 2 and 3, as will be described later.

The chemical Kraft process worked by dissolving the lignin that bonds wood fibers together. It did this in a tall pressure cooker, called a digester, by "cooking" the chips in a solution of caustic soda (NaOH) and sodium sulfide (Na_2S), which was termed the "white liquor." The temperature in this cooking process reached as high as 340°F, and the pressure was as great as 11 atmospheres. Recently, the process had been altered to introduce "oxygen delignification," which used liquid oxygen to remove lignin. This eliminated the need for elemental chlorine (Cl_2) in the subsequent bleaching process and was better for the environment than the traditional technology.

The two digesters at Androscoggin were continuous digesters; chips and liquor went into the top, were cooked together as they slowly settled down to the bottom, and were drawn off the bottom after about three hours. By this time, the white liquor had changed chemically to "black liquor"; the digested chips were then separated from this black liquor.

In what was known as the "cold blow" process, the hot, pressurized chips were gradually cooled and depressurized. A "cold liquor" (170°F) was introduced to the bottom of the digester and served both to cool and to transport the digested chips to a diffusion washer that washed and depressurized the chips. Because so much of the lignin bonding the fibers together had been removed, the wood fiber in the chips literally fell apart at this stage.

The black liquor from the digester entered a separate four-step recovery process. Over 95 percent of the black liquor could be reconstituted as white liquor, thereby saving on chemical costs and significantly lowering pollution. The four-step process involved (1) washing the black liquor from the cooked fiber to produce weak black liquor; (2) evaporating the weak black liquor to a thicker consistency; (3) combusting this heavy black liquor with sodium sulfate (Na_2SO_4), and redissolving the smelt, yielding a "green liquor" (sodium carbonate + sodium sulfide); and (4) adding lime, which reacted with the green liquor to produce white liquor. The last step was known as causticization.

Meanwhile, the wood-fiber pulp was purged of impurities like bark and dirt by mechanical screening and by spinning the mixture in centrifugal cleaners. The pulp was then concentrated by removing water from it so that it could be stored and bleached more economically.

By this time, depending on the type of pulp being made, it had been between $3\frac{1}{2}$ and 5 hours since the chips had entered the pulp mill. All the Kraft pulp was then bleached. Bleaching took between 5 and 6 hours. It consisted of a three-step process in which (1) chlorine dioxide (ClO_2) was introduced to the pulp and the pulp was washed; (2) a patented mix of sodium hydroxide (NaOH), liquid oxygen, and hydrogen peroxide (H_2O_2) was then added to the pulp and the pulp was again washed; and (3) chlorine dioxide (ClO_2) was introduced and the pulp washed a final time. The result was like fluffy Cream of Wheat. By this time the pulp was nearly ready to be made into paper.

From the bleachery, the stock of pulp was held for a short time in storage (a maximum of 16 hours) and then proceeded through a series of blending operations that permitted a string of additives (for example, filler clay, resins, brighteners, alum, dyes) to be mixed into the pulp according to the recipe for the paper

A pulp washer. (Courtesy of International Paper)

Continuous digesters at the pulp mill. These work like pressure cookers, dissolving the lignin bonds between wood fibers. (Courtesy of International Paper)

grade being produced. Here, too, "broke" (paper wastes from the mill itself) was recycled into the pulp.[1] The pulp was then once again cleaned and blended into an even consistency before moving to the papermaking machine itself.

Papermaking

The paper machine was a simply awesome engineering creation, stretching hundreds of feet. At Androscoggin, there were five of varying size. The paper machine had a wet end and a dry end. The pulp entered the machine at the headbox, which released the heavily diluted pulp through a slit onto a moving belt of synthetic fabric. This belt was called the "wire" because originally it was made of bronze mesh.

As the wire with its deposit of pulp stock moved away from the headbox, water drained through it. Suction was also applied. Within 60 feet after the headbox slit, so much water had been removed that it could be said the wire carried paper, rather than a suspension of pulp in water. From the wire, huge woolen felts picked up the paper "web" and started it through a series of rollers and steam-heated drying drums, which pressed and evaporated even more water out of the web. If the paper was to be coated, the coating would be applied first to one side of the paper and then to the other and more drying done. If the paper was to be shiny, it would be pressed on smooth, shiny rollers called calenders. Drying and pressing having been done, the paper was essentially finished and was picked up from the machine on winders.

The speeds at which all this happened were incredible. The fastest machines (machines 2 and 3, devoted to publication gloss) produced over a mile of paper every two minutes. This great speed was made possible by continual improvements made by the machine's builders and by computerized process controls, that constantly adjusted the machine's settings based on the values registered by numerous electronic sensors scattered along the length of the machine.

Once on the winders, the "logs" of paper could be slit directly into widths the customers had ordered, or they could be slit into two logs of equal width and stored until needed. These stored logs, called "parent logs," were then placed on rewinders for successive slitting to customer order. Once cut to order, rolls were packaged, labeled, and then shipped.

Maintaining the Environment

Being a relatively new mill, Androscoggin had environmental control equipment designed into it. Pulp and paper mills were large users of water. Androscoggin took water from the river, filtered it, and then used it in the process. Before being released back to the river, the water was treated in three stages to remove the effluent it had picked up.

1. A primary clarifier (two large cone-shaped basins) allowed particles to settle to the bottom. A slow-moving rake forced the settled sludge to the middle, where it was removed to be burned.

2. In a 37-acre lagoon the clarified effluent was aerated by a collection of churning fountains, and a special collection of microorganisms broke down the effluent over the course of $1\frac{1}{2}$ to 2 days.

---

[1]It made a difference whether the broke was of coated or uncoated paper, and whether it was white or colored. White, uncoated paper could be recycled immediately. Colored, uncoated paper had to be re-bleached. Coated papers, because of the clays in them, could not be reclaimed.

Paper machine 5, built in 1977. (Courtesy of International Paper)

3. A secondary clarifier (two more large basins) settled more solids (including dead bacteria from the lagoon) from the water.

The entire treatment process took 2 to 3 days.

Air pollution control was another area where great strides had been made since the early 1960s. Gas collection systems to collect and burn noncondensible gases from the digester and evaporators had largely eliminated the rotten egg smell that had been characteristic of paper mills. Scrubbers and precipitators on the stacks at Androscoggin had gone even further in removing sulphur and other particulates from the smoke and air at the mill.

The Design of the Androscoggin Mill

Vertical Integration

The Androscoggin Mill was vertically integrated; that is, it combined pulp-making and papermaking at the same site. Not all mills, especially not the older ones, were designed to combine both activities. Several advantages argued strongly in favor of vertical integration:

1. Integration removed the transportation costs of transporting pulp between a pulp mill and a paper mill. Vertical integration eliminated the double handling of pulp, a cost saving in any event. In addition, because the mill shipped all over the country and because it specialized in lightweight grades of paper, transportation costs for finished paper were not

Paper machine 4, recently reconfigured for new grades. (Courtesy of International Paper)

affected significantly by the mill's location; and so a location near the supply of pulp was highly desirable. Pulp drying and reslushing costs were also eliminated.

2. Integration provided for better quality control. Since the quality of the paper produced depended heavily on the quality of the pulp, vertical integration permitted hour-by-hour control over the quality of pulp entering each paper machine. Such control greatly reduced the chances for paper breaks on the machine and eliminated any quality problems caused by old pulp or other deficiencies.

3. The wood preparation and pulpmaking operations generated sawdust, bark, chemicals, and wood chips that could be burned as fuel for the whole plant, thus cutting down on plant-wide energy costs.

Although the Androscoggin Mill integrated pulpmaking and papermaking, the extent of the mill's vertical integration could have been even broader. For example, only about 40 percent of the wood used at the mill was cut from land owned by International Paper. The company could have integrated backward even more by raising that 40 percent figure. It chose not to do so, however, because the 40 percent figure, and modest variations around it, (1) permitted good forest management of International Paper's own land and (2) meant that the company could add directly to the area's economy by purchasing from independents. There were no substantial cost differences between independent and company tree harvesting. Only if independent loggers could not supply the mill's needs would the company have harvested more from its own land.

By the same token, the operations at Androscoggin could have been extended by forward integration, so that the plant converted more of its paper into end uses (for example, sheets of bond paper rather than rolls of it). The company chose not to do this as well. For one thing, adding converting facilities would have greatly increased Androscoggin's already large size and would have diluted management's attention from the mission of producing quality paper efficiently. Converting operations (and International Paper operated many of them) were also best located closer to markets, since the nature of conversion often placed the paper in bulkier and more awkward packages that were harder to ship and were often shipped in smaller quantities than Androscoggin's full truck and rail carloads. Splitting conversion from papermaking, at least for white papers, meant lower overall transport costs, whereas there were no real economies in the linking of the two operations.

Capacity

Over time, the size and capacity of individual paper machines had grown enormously. There were distinct advantages to this large scale of operation, because the largest and latest machines could produce more tons of paper per worker, thus reducing costs. The increases in machine size and speed enabled the newer mills to house fewer paper machines and to employ fewer workers than older mills and yet produce more paper.

At its current size, the Androscoggin Mill was about as large as it was likely to grow. However, there were always new efficiency projects underway. A recent project converted the #4 machine from uncoated business paper to coated printing paper. In addition, the #5 machine had also recently been upgraded to increase the average daily production from 108 tons to 125 tons per day, at a cost of $1.5 M. The machine ran gummed paper, cigarette and gum wrappers, popcorn bags, and similar specialty papers.

The output rates of its five paper machines, its two continuous digesters, its groundwood mill, and its three woodrooms were all reasonably well balanced. As it was, the pulp mill had been deliberately built larger so that another mill down the river and other International Paper mills could be supplied with pulp.

Location

The Androscoggin Mill's general location in central Maine was attributable largely to three factors:

1. The production of strong, good-quality white office papers demanded long wood fibers. This demand favored a Maine location because cold winter weather favors the production of longer fibers in both the softwood and hardwood trees that Maine and neighboring Quebec grow in abundance.

2. A paper mill uses so much water that it has to be located on either a lake or a river, and preferably a river because of environmental factors.

3. This part of central Maine enjoyed the availability of a good supply of labor.

Technology

In pulpmaking and papermaking, keeping abreast of the latest changes in process equipment and technology is critical to a company's continued success. At International Paper the main responsibility for keeping up with technology rested with the corporate staff. The staff was also instrumental in the selection of major new equipment or process changes. The plant, however, did play an important role by providing managers (such as the plant engineer or the manager of finished products) who joined the corporate staff in studying any new capacity addition or process technology change. This team was responsible for developing the project's capital appropriation request and its supporting documents.

Loading the Factory

Production Planning

Orders for any of the white papers produced at Androscoggin would be taken by the company's central order department in Memphis, Tennessee. Orders, as they were received, were placed in the next available open time in the planned weekly production cycles. One week before the start of the next weekly cycle, the manager of operations control planned the production schedule for that cycle. This production schedule allocated the types and weights of paper to be produced at each mill by each machine for every day of the weekly cycle. These machine assignments and the orders they represented were then transmitted to each of the company's plants.

Each quarter, a linear program was run to develop the optimum schedule. Marketing and customer constraints were factored into the quarterly plan by operations control. This plan was reviewed with product line managers and was used to establish weekly cycles.

The assignment of types and weights of paper to each paper machine was a sophisticated enterprise. Because the company's machines were all slightly different from one another, due primarily to their different vintages, their capabilities differed. That is, they were often relatively more successful and/or more cost efficient at making certain types and weights of paper than others. In assigning products to machines, therefore, the corporation took care to make the assignments in such a way that the company's total contribution to profits and overhead was maximized. This assigning required not only information on the mix of papers demanded for the period and on machine capabilities, but on distribution and transportation costs as well. Thus for some grades, colors, or weights of paper, depending on the situation, Androscoggin might have filled an order that might otherwise have been filled by a mill much closer to the customer.

At present, Androscoggin's five paper machines were assigned the following "paper machine products":

Machine 1—various types of bond or offset paper in white or colors

Machine 2—coated publication gloss

Machine 3—coated publication gloss

Machine 4—coated printing papers

Machine 5—specialty grades

Demand for paper products was cyclical in nature. Volume requirements tracked the general economy very closely, although lagging it slightly both upward and downward. In good economic times, Androscoggin and other mills could be running flat out, with sales so strong that customers had to be put on allocation and orders monitored very closely. This situation was far different from some recessionary times when mills took any order and still had to cut back production.

While the company's central order department (operations control) decided what would be produced on what machine on which days, the mill still had its own considerable production planning problems. Customer orders not only specified the type of paper but also the size (width) to be cut, the quantity (the diameter of the roll), and some other features. In planning for any specific run on a paper ma-

A paper machine coater. (Courtesy of International Paper)

chine, the mill wanted to group together all those orders calling for the same diameter and in such a way that the entire width of the paper machine's output was accounted for. The mill did not like to leave any waste, since even an inch of paper unaccounted for could cost the company foregone revenue of several thousand dollars. The mill used a computer program to optimize paper machine trim.

The mill also wanted to schedule slitting the rolls to minimize additional handling. This goal meant slitting as much off the machine winder as possible but with small widths cut from the center portion to reduce the risk of distortion in slitting.

Two production planners scheduled orders on the mill's five machines. They had to remain flexible enough to allow at least some changes in customer orders as late as the Wednesday before the start of the next week's production. The mill also had to schedule trucks and railcars for order shipments.

Inventories and Purchasing

Most of the wood that Androscoggin Mill used was provided by contract for 10,000 to 100,000 cords per year. International Paper did not cut its own wood, but contracted that task out as well. The company's woodlands division was responsible for purchasing the mill's wood and managing the woodyard at economical inventory levels. In addition, the mill stood ready to purchase, by weight, the wood of small, independent loggers without prior commitments being made. The mill did, however, deliberately seek the building up of wood in inventory in the fall and winter so that the spring thaw and the mud it brought did not disrupt the mill as it disrupted logging. It was not uncommon to have 30 days of production in pulp wood inventory. All the work-in-process inventories were small and temporary, used mainly to permit the mixing of different types of wood chips or pulp

Paper machine heated dryer "cans." (Courtesy of International Paper)

and to permit production to continue in case some portion of the process went down temporarily.

The extent of finished goods inventory varied. Comparatively few finished goods were held for the products of machines 2 through 5. Some were kept to permit stray order fulfillment or order amendments, but most paper production was soon headed out the door, waiting only long enough for all items in the order to be gathered together. The parent log and finished goods inventories for machine 1 (bond and offset papers) were very much larger, typically about 15 days of production. Such a large inventory was required to meet customer needs on any of the 48 paper machine products that machine 1 was qualified to manufacture, while keeping to a minimum the number of machine setups over the course of a year.

At Androscoggin, all responsibilities for production planning, loading machines, product distribution to customers, and finished goods inventories rested with the planning, scheduling, and distribution department because it was felt that all of these items affected one another at the plant and should be controlled by the same authority.

The Workforce

The Androscoggin Mill employed about 1300 people, about 175 of whom were salaried, with the remainder paid according to the hours worked. Following a lengthy strike in the late 1980s, there were no longer any manufacturing employee unions at the plant. In 1992, the United Paperworkers International Union and the International Brotherhood of Firemen and Oilers were decertified, and in

1995, the decertifications were reaffirmed overwhelmingly, despite the fact that over 1000 of the 1100 formerly striking workers had been called back by then.[2] This was dramatic confirmation of the improvement in workforce relations that had occurred since the resolution of the strike in 1989.

Work at the mill was defined as either day work or tour (shift) work. Most work was in fact tour work. At the suggestion of the workforce, most of the mill operated a modified 12-hour shift.[3] Workers worked 16 out of every 28 days for an average of 42 hours a week. Every day, except Thursdays and Fridays, workers worked either 7 A.M. to 7 P.M. or 7 P.M. to 7 A.M. On Thursdays and Fridays, they worked more traditional 8-hour shifts. Workers worked no more than 5 days in a row and no more than three 12-hour shifts in a row. This implied that workers worked 2 out of every 4 weekends, but got 3 days off for one weekend and 6 days off for another weekend in every four.

Even though one crew or another was at the mill 24 hours a day, there were still some occasions that warranted overtime pay. Overtime was paid on a daily basis past either 8 or 12 hours of the regular shift and after 40 hours a week of regular time.

All of the jobs in the mill were classified and assigned different rates of pay according to the hierarchy of knowledge and responsibilities required. When job openings came up, usually precipitated by a worker's transferring or terminating for one reason or another, workers in the next lower position were advanced according to some selected job criteria, and not simply seniority, as had been the practice before. Increasingly, peer review among the workers themselves governed this process. When a high-level job became vacant, a cascading of open positions was triggered, as workers moved up in the hierarchy. Transfers within the mill were permitted, in addition to promotions within the same department. For most hourly workers, the typical career path would entail transfers and promotions up to the highest paying jobs.

A paper machine take-up reel. (Courtesy of International Paper)

---

[2]The only union present at the site was the Office and Professional Employees International Union that represented 40 people.

[3]One department had reverted to an older "Southern swing" schedule that worked rotating 8-hour shifts of 7 days on, 4 days off, 7 days on, 2 days off, 7 days on, and 1 day off. Most maintenance workers worked a 4-day 10-hours-per-day schedule.

Because there were no manufacturing unions anymore, there was not a typical union grievance procedure for complaints. Rather, there was a peer review procedure that involved mixed panels of salaried and hourly personnel. This was among the many changes that had been instituted in recent years. In general, the workforce had been given more freedom to address the clearly expressed goals of the plant. There had been more training given for both technical skills and personal development. A new gym had been constructed and free physical exams were given. An employee handbook replaced the old union contract.

More teams, especially self-managed teams, had been organized. The hydro maintenance team was an example. (Along the Androscoggin River, there were 4 small hydroelectric generating stations, with 22 hydro generation units, that supplied power to the mill.) This 9-person team had its own mission statement: "We, as a high-performance team, will provide our customer with cost-effective power. We will operate and maintain in a safe and environmentally responsible manner." The team decided for itself what to work on and set its own priorities, handling issues with a majority vote. The team established its own operating rules and mechanisms. The team prepared its own budget, developed its own work schedule, determined criteria for overtime, trained members, hired new members, evaluated each other on 46 separate points, selected and monitored contractors for special work, and worked with the Federal Energy Regulatory Commission on relicensing the hydro plants. Such changes were somewhat stressful on the team members, and they sometimes meant longer hours, but the teams' results were exemplary. In 1995, during a summer with the lowest flow along the river, the hydro maintenance team had produced record quantities of power for the mill's use.

Changes such as these created new roles for the supervisors at the plant. Supervisors were no longer involved so much in day-to-day operations, but instead served as coaches, counselors, facilitators, and providers of resources to the workforce. This required that they learn new skills.

Over the years, as papermaking equipment grew in size, speed, and sophistication (particularly with the advent of computerized process controls), papermaking became less and less an art and more and more a science. This change also had left its imprint on the workforce. Not only could a new paper mill be operated with fewer workers than an old one, but the requisite worker skills were less manual and more cerebral. The latest breed of papermakers had to be more highly ed-

The hydro maintenance team, in their self-constructed team room, during lunch. (Courtesy of International Paper)

ucated, in general, and more analytical. With this in mind, considerable resources were expended on training.

The mill had adopted a quality improvement process (QIP) that used teams of workers and managers to solve particular problems, many necessitating considerable data-gathering and mathematical and statistical analysis, and this had required substantial training. Happily, the QIP had been a great and continuing success that had helped the plant to enjoy significant productivity gains that had stood it in good stead even when the economy turned downward. The mill's quality and competitiveness had assured it of constant operation, and a number of customers from all over the world, including Japan.

Controlling the Operation

The entire papermaking process at Androscoggin was designed to manufacture paper with as little downtime as possible. Equipment maintenance could generally be scheduled during the periodic changing of the paper machine's "clothing" (i.e., changing the worn wire and felt, accomplished every 3 to 4 months). Process control equipment and workforce skills were geared to react instantly to production disruptions, such as paper breaks, or to product changes in weight or color. The time it took to correct a disruption such as a paper break varied enormously (from, say, 3 minutes to an hour). But the average break time was in the 5- to 10-minute range. A color change normally took about 10 minutes, and a careful weight change could be done without any downtime.

Paper was continually being tested for quality, and the feedback to the workforce was swift so that any needed adjustments could be made. The workforce also kept their own process control charts that statistically tracked the process's ability to make quality paper and that signaled when changes to the process were called for.

In general, operations at the mill could be described as quiet and watchful. Because the elements of the process were so interdependent, skilled managers and workers were required in every phase of the mill's operations. Indeed, many of the mill's supervisors had been promoted out of the ranks and were thus intimately familiar with the mill's operations.

Changes in the process, routine capital acquisition, and maintenance were the province of plant engineering. Plant engineering was constantly engaged in projects, about half of which involved repair and half new capital investments, many of which were driven by environmental considerations. Here is a sampling:

Converting bleaching to be free of elemental chlorine

Oxygen delignification for the pulp mill

Annual inspections, repairs, and rebuilds for the digesters

Bleach tower tile repair

Modernizing the rotating screens for groundwood pulping

Repair of an acid sewer

Evaluating Mill Performance

The mill was evaluated as a cost center; it had no control or authority over prices, markets, or revenues. The mill operated to a budget. Given a sales forecast from marketing function at headquarters, prices, and a product mix, the mill developed standard costs for producing the quantity of each paper product forecasted. The budget reflected these standard costs and the mill was held to the budget. However, if the product mix changed, the resulting cost changes were charged to marketing, not the mill. The mill was accountable only for those costs over which it had control.

While the efficient production of paper was an important goal, it was by no means the only aspect of mill operations that was evaluated. Others played an important role: employee safety; management and worker training; commitment to environmental controls (not only meeting present standards but also keeping the environmental control equipment balanced in capacity with the rest of mill operations and advancing in technology); expenditures for new capital appropriations and for maintenance; and workforce relations.

PART TWO: DISCUSSION

International Paper is in no way responsible for the following views and presentation. They remain solely the responsibility of the author.

The Process Flow

The process of making paper, while a frightfully complicated endeavor, follows a clear-cut and rigid pattern. All of the paper that the Androscoggin Mill produces—however different in appearance, weight, and feel—proceeds through essentially the same production steps, from logs of wood in the woodyard to "logs" of paper at the shipping dock. This kind of production process can be readily portrayed in a diagram like Figure A2, which is commonly called a process flow diagram.

The process flow diagram of Figure A2 is a fairly general one and could be made considerably more detailed. Whether more detail is desirable depends, naturally, on the use to which a process portrait like Figure A2 is put. Several points about the diagram ought to be noted:

FIGURE A2 Process flow diagram for International Paper Androscoggin Mill

1. Actual processing operations are usually distinguished from storage points in the process. In the diagram, processing operations are indicated by rectangles and inventories by triangles. (Rectangles are used here because it is easier to fit the descriptions in them. However, typically in industrial engineering, circles are used to indicate processing operations and rectangles are used to indicate tests and inspections.)

2. Several operations could be bypassed and are indicated by two arrows emanating from one operation and pointing to others. For example, all of the woodroom's output need not have gone directly to the silos but could have been placed in the woodyard for storage. The rewinders were superfluous for those orders that could be slit directly from the main winders.

3. The continuous nature of the process is evident by the very low level of inventories and by the designation of the silo chip and pulp additive inventories as temporary.

Information in the Process

A production process is more than a series of operations performed on a collection of materials. What a process flow diagram can depict—the sequencing of process steps, the choice of equipment and technology, the capacity of process steps, the tasks required of the workforce—while critical, is only part of the story. Another part of the story involves the procedures that have been put in place to direct the process flow. We can usefully think of a companion to the process flow diagram—namely, an information flow diagram. Figure A3 provides an example of what might be placed in such a diagram. Note how the actions of different layers of managers and workers are distinguished in the diagram and how information is fed back up the channels of communication.

Most of the information flow in this continuous flow process is directed from the top down. Feedback is needed only to acknowledge receipt of information and to signal significant problems in the actual workings of the process. The process is designed with such care and the workforce so carefully trained that workers do

FIGURE A3 Information flow diagram for International Paper's Androscoggin Mill.

not have to be in repeated touch with management to do their jobs well. The information needs of the process simply are not great, although the thought and effort standing behind that information (such as scheduling tasks of both the corporate office and the mill itself) are considerable and sophisticated.

Capacity

Capacity in this continuous flow process is fairly well defined and can be spoken of in physical terms—namely, tons of pulp and paper manufactured and cords of wood consumed. Likewise, there is a straightforward meaning to the term *capacity utilization.* In fact, all one needs to do is check to see whether the paper machines are running. If they are, capacity (all of it) is being used. Simply compiling the time the paper machines have run over some period of time and dividing that sum by the total available machine-hours gives a splendid indication of capacity utilization. Indeed, only when sales are insufficient or when the machine is broken or down temporarily for a setup or a change of "clothing" would we expect capacity utilization that was less than 100 percent.

Despite the relative ease with which we can talk of capacity and capacity utilization in this continuous flow process, on closer inspection of the concept a number of disquieting ambiguities surface. The ambiguities surface largely because the capacity of the mill is dependent on a number of factors. Among them:

1. *Product mix.* Some grades and weights of paper are more difficult to produce than others. Newer machines, of course, are apt to run at faster speeds than older machines, given the same kind of paper. But, given similar vintage paper machines, thin papers and high-quality finish papers have to run at slower speeds than others. Thus comparing the capacity of the Androscoggin Mill with that of other paper mills or with its own in other years can only be done with some understanding of the product mixes involved.

2. *Run lengths.* Every time a paper machine must be set up for a different grade, weight, or color of paper, capacity is lost. Although some changes are inherently more time-consuming than others, every change implies at least a small reduction in theoretical capacity. The capacity of machine 1 was somewhat lower than that of machine 4 at least in part because machine 1 was scheduled to produce 48 different paper machine products in white and in colors, whereas machine 4 was devoted primarily to white.

3. *Maintenance.* A paper machine might also lose capacity because it was being repaired or because its "clothing" was being changed. The machines that could be kept running until only regularly scheduled maintenance interrupted production were those that lost the least capacity.

4. *Slitting schedule.* Slitting paper "logs" from the winders and rewinders was purposely scheduled so that as little waste as possible resulted. The more successful the schedule, the less waste there was.

For these reasons, the terms capacity and capacity utilization were not as unambiguous as might have been anticipated. Nevertheless, the process was extraordinarily well balanced and smooth running, and this made discussion of capacity and capacity utilization easy.

Demands of the Process on the Workers

Over the years, papermaking, like other continuous flow processes, has become a process where increasingly machinery "does it all." Pulpmakers and papermakers have been systematically removed from playing their traditional direct "hands-on" roles in the process. Instead, papermakers are more and more "indirect" labor-setters, monitors, and repairers of equipment that makes paper much faster and more reliably than any crew of traditional papermakers could using the older technology and their own skills. Where papermaking was "art," it is now "science." The former lengthy apprenticeships from sixth hand on a paper machine to machine tender are no longer justified by the need to learn the art. Despite the change to science, the level of skill required in the process remains high. The workforce may have been removed to gazing at control panels, adjusting knobs, and throwing switches, but the technical demands of the process are even higher in a modern, as compared to traditional, paper mill. Training is therefore an important consideration and an apprenticeship, while different from before, is still required. The lines of worker progression in the mill are clear (in fact, they were diagrammed for each department in the labor agreement), and workers are paid accordingly.

What comprises any job in the mill, while somewhat restricted, has been increasing steadily, however. The team concept, job rotations, and the collapsing of the traditional classifications into many fewer, had helped to broaden the definition of jobs at the mill. The new labor contract permitted these changes that encourage productivity and kept everyone well occupied.

Skilled workers are needed everywhere in the process, largely because the process is so interdependent. If one aspect of the process falls down (e.g., quality of the pulp), another aspect is likely to suffer (increased risk of a paper break).

Demands of the Process on Management

The interdependence and capital intensity (a high ratio of plant and equipment value to labor payroll) of a continuous flow process like papermaking place tremendous demands on management, especially in the realms of coordination and of the choice and care of equipment. Furthermore, these demands are made not only of the mill's own management but of the corporation as a whole. Profitability in such processes largely rests on (1) assuring that the proper technology is selected, (2) balancing the capacities of all segments of the process so that as little capacity goes to waste as possible, (3) scheduling the use of that capacity as completely as possible, (4) keeping the equipment running up to speed and up to quality standards (let us review these points in turn), and (5) an ever-continuing effort to improve in all areas of the operation.

Choice of Technology

The march of technological change is inexorable. While the output of continuous flow processes seldom changes by much, there can be upheavals in how that output is manufactured. The introduction of process control equipment to papermaking is a case in point. Management must be constantly aware of equipment advances across the industry, and savvy manufacturers engage in regular dialogues with equipment makers so that their own ideas and needs can be tried out in new equipment designs. The impact of technology is so fundamental that the corporate staffs of continuous flow process industries are usually charged with monitoring and selecting major new technology for all the plants of the company. Individual plants may have representatives on any plant and equipment choice studies, but corporate-level managers are apt to take the lead in the study and decision-making process. Many of the latest technological advances had involved changes spurred by pollution control issues or energy savings.

What is true for technology decisions is also true for decisions on how vertically integrated the process should be. This is generally also a corporate decision and one that is the province of corporate staff.

Balancing Capacities

The papermaking process, as we have seen, can be broken down into distinct segments (as in the process flow diagram); associated with each of these segments are machines and other equipment, often very large. Frequently, these machines and equipment are manufactured by different companies and do not come in just any size. It is management's responsibility to select the equipment for each process segment that represents both the suitable technology and size for the contemplated plant or plant expansion. One segment's capacity should be balanced, as well as possible, against that of other segments, so that as little extra capacity as possible has to be financed. After all, in an integrated, continuous flow process the capacity of the entire process is determined by the lowest capacity segment.

In reality, balancing process segment capacities is a difficult chore, and choices have to be made as to which process segments are to be assigned whatever excess capacity may exist. Often such a choice entails an investigation of equipment costs, with the relatively cheaper equipment being assigned any excess capacity. In papermaking, for example, the big bucks get chewed up in financing paper machines and bleacheries. Woodrooms, digesters, and rewinders are relatively less expensive. Thus, frequently, the spare capacity is to be found at the ends of the process (woodrooms, rewinders) rather than in the middle (bleacheries, paper machines). Having spare capacity at the rewinders increases the flexibility of the process as well to modifications of the product mix or order specifications. With excess capacity in place, unusual orders can be serviced without undue strain or delay.

The need for, and the expense of, maintaining a balance of capacities in a continuous flow process like the Androscoggin Mill are dramatically highlighted by the 1980 rebuilding of paper machine 2 and its conversion from carbonizing tissue to publication gloss. That conversion speeded up the flow of paper from about 20 miles per hour to nearly 35 miles per hour and raised the mill's net yearly tonnage by about 100,000 tons. To accommodate a change of that magnitude meant altering the pulpmaking capabilities of the mill as well as its papermaking capabilities. When process segments are tightly coupled, capacity changes echo throughout the entire process.

Scheduling

Large, high-speed continuous flow processes are geared to high-volume production of standard items. Typically, they are low-cost processes, but they often sacrifice the ability to respond quickly to changing customer specifications without introducing a lot of waste and thus destroying their low-cost character. In order then to satisfy customer orders at low cost, continuous flow processes must schedule their capacity well in advance, offering their customers longer lead times than may be common in other types of processes or else filling orders out of in-process or finished goods inventories.

At International Paper, as we saw, the broad "paper machine products" scheduling proceeded one week in advance for production and the schedule devised was of a one-week period. The customer orders that were produced in each run, however, were set at the plant level only two days in advance of the production cycle. As many customer orders as could be slit right off the machine winder were scheduled, to eliminate rehandling and converting of paper logs. More exotic orders for special colors, grades, or weights from machine 1 were often filled out of finished goods inventory to avoid having to schedule special production runs.

Scheduling at International Paper, as these observations indicate, was a sophisticated enterprise.

The idea, of course, behind such sophisticated scheduling is to keep the process flowing as continuously as possible. Generally, the process could be more responsive to customer orders, but to do so would necessarily mean interrupting production to set up equipment. Capacity would be reduced and costs increased. By stretching out deliveries or by keeping finished goods inventories, the continuous flow process can keep its costs down.

Equipment Maintenance

Most continuous flow process plants are evaluated as cost centers. As with the Androscoggin Mill, such plants are not given authority over revenues (no sales forces are tied to them), and so the plant is judged by how well it can adhere to a budget. The plant has an incentive then to keep its equipment well maintained; if it does not, it risks assuming costs that can be very high (equipment breakdowns force high repair costs and expensive makeup work.) Given such an evaluation scheme, most managers would opt to spend all of their budget for maintenance to avoid the chance, however slim, of suffering a huge cost increase and an instantly bad reputation for plant management.

Questions

1. The changeover of machine 2 from carbonizing tissue to publication gloss involved changes in other parts of the process. Why was this so? Speculate in as much detail as possible about the kinds of changes that would have had to occur as a consequence of such a paper machine changeover.
2. Much of the "higher-level" production planning for Androscoggin Mill occurs in International Paper's Memphis and New York headquarters, whereas "lower-level" production planning occurs at the mill itself. Why is there this division of responsibilities? What would happen if Memphis or New York handled all the production planning or if Androscoggin did it all?
3. If you were a production planner at the Androscoggin Mill, what might you be most likely to consider important? Why? How would these priorities affect your production plans?
4. Why did the Androscoggin Mill choose vertical integration for its design? What would be some of the advantages and disadvantages of increased forward integration for the mill?
5. How is the workforce organized at the mill? What are some of the operational implications of this workforce composition?
6. As a manager, which aspects of a continuous flow process appeal to you? Which aspects might not?

Situation for Study A-1
Beacon Glass Works

Beacon Glass Works, located in Marysville, West Virginia, manufactures hollow glass tubing for use in catalytic converters. Beacon is a large division of one of the leading glass manufacturers, and was founded when the Environmental Protection Agency strongly urged the development of antipollution devices for trucks and automobiles. The hollow glass tubing manufactured at Beacon comes in around 30 different size combinations. The lengths are from 6 to 12 inches, and the inside diameter ranges from $\frac{1}{32}$ to $\frac{1}{16}$ inch.

These tubes are produced by extrusion. The molten glass is first forced through a die that determines the inside diameter of the tube. The tube then is cooled and cut to the proper length. After the cut edges have been finished so that they are smooth, the product is sent to a holding area where it waits to be packaged. Once the tubing is packaged, it is again stored, this time awaiting shipment to Beacon's customers, the four major domestic motor vehicle manufacturers.

The extrusion process is basically a make-to-stock operation driven by production scheduling. Based upon anticipated stock shortages, Jose Torrez, the production manager, schedules the next week's production, and the necessary dies are readied. Each die is used until about one month's demand has been produced. Then, the dies are changed and another product with a different inside diameter is run. Actually, since several lengths have the same inside diameter, several products can be extruded with one extrusion run.

Once the product cools to the proper cutting temperature, the cutting area cuts the proper lengths, again based upon the stock needs determined by the production manager. The product is then stored in a holding area waiting to be packaged. Packaging is usually done to customer order, as different customers want different quantities and want them packaged differently.

Sometimes, however, Jose will schedule the packaging department based on what he believes will be the customer orders, so that he can use the packaging machinery efficiently. This scheduling sometimes results in excess inventory for one customer while another customer's order is backordered because of a stockout.

Jose is concerned that his process scheduling is not as good as it could be and thinks that possibly the first step he should take is to diagram the production flow and the information flow for the process.

1. Diagram the production flow.
2. Diagram the information flow.
3. Discuss possible problem areas for Beacon's production process.

Situation for Study A-2
Sunmeadow Dairy

Sunmeadow Dairy produced and distributed a variety of products including whole milk, skim milk, 2 percent milk, ice milk, fruit drinks, buttermilk, eggnog, chocolate milk, and many different mixes used to produce ice cream. The production of milk, however, was 90 percent of the operation.

From 8 A.M. until 5 P.M., raw milk (unpasteurized milk direct from the farm) arrived by refrigerated tanker truck at or below 42°F. The raw milk was pumped from the tanker (capacity 5500 gallons) to one of three refrigerated storage silos (capacity 70,000 gallons total) adjacent to the receiving area. During this transfer, the milk flowed through a plate heat exchanger to lower its temperature to 37°F. From these silos, the milk was pumped to the second floor as needed for production and was stored in four of six storage tanks. The empty tanks were used for mixing and diluting the raw milk, which was 3.5 to 4.0 percent butterfat.

Because whole milk contains 3 to 5 percent butterfat (depending on its source) and some skim milk products contain as little as 0.5 percent butterfat, a certain percentage of butterfat had to be removed from the raw milk. A separator was employed to remove the excess butterfat. (A separator is a centrifuge in which raw milk is spun at high speed, forcing the separation of the butterfat from the heavier milk and allowing the isolation of the two fractions.) One by-product of this process contained 40 percent butterfat and was pumped off (at a rate of 1000 to 1500 gallons per day) into nearby holding tanks and shipped to a butter factory once a week. The other by-product was 0.5 percent milk; it was pumped into an empty tank and mixed with 3.5 percent raw milk to obtain the desired butterfat level for the product being packaged next in the plant. This mixing was called "standardizing" the product. From an information chart on obtaining the percentage of butterfat needed for each product, the separator operator determined the exact quantity of each input (3.5 percent milk and 0.5 percent milk) to be mixed in the empty tank.

From the holding tanks the standardized product was pumped into one of two pasteurizers (capacity 1500 and 4000 gallons per hour). (Pasteurization is the process of heating raw milk to 161°F for 16 seconds to kill harmful bacteria.) The pasteurized milk was pumped into one of two homogenizers, which blew the milk through a very small opening to break up the fat globules and create a uniform, or homogenous, mixture. The pasteurized, homogenized milk was directed into any one of seven pasteurizing holding tanks to await packaging on the first floor. Because packaging might start as early as 5:30 A.M., pasteurization usually began at midnight—to build a buffer inventory in the holding tanks for the first and second products to be run that day.

Milk could be pumped into one of five packaging processes:

1. The filler filled plastic gallons and half-gallons at a rate of 70 per minute. The plastic containers were made in the blow-molding department and arrived at this machine by overhead conveyor. This conveyor continued through the completely automated processes of filling, capping, and storing the filled containers in metal cases for shipment. These metal cases were stacked six high and sent to the cooler for order filling.

2. The H-75 machine produced paper half-gallons (capacity 75 units per minute) and automatically filled, sealed, and stacked them. Manual attention was needed only to take the wax cardboard containers from the adjacent stockroom and load them into the feed mechanism. Each carton was automatically unfolded, heat-sealed at the bottom, and filled with the product being produced in this run; the excess foam and overfill were drawn off the top, and the carton was heat-sealed. The cartons were then automatically stacked into metal cases and put on the conveyor for the short trip to the cooler.

3. The Q80–110 machine operated the same way as the H-75 but was for half-pints, pints, and quarts (capacity 80 quarts, 110 pints, and 110 half-pints per minute).

4. The NEP 210 machine (capacity 210 half-pints per minute) also operated the same way as the H-75. The unique feature of this process was that it produced only for schools.

5. Using the bag and box filler was a totally manual process for filling 5-gallon plastic bags inside boxes. These were shipped to local schools and hospitals for use in self-service milk dispensers.

While each process was running, there was at least one operator with each machine at all times. The high volume of production demanded constant attention and minor adjustments, especially to keep the product from becoming caught in the moving parts. Once packaged, the product was carried by conveyor from the packaging areas to the 38°F cooler, where it was stored according to how soon it would be used to fill orders on the daily trucks. The cooler operated on a first-in, first-out (FIFO) basis; rotating the product this way kept the buffer stock as fresh as possible. The product was moved to the loading areas on the same conveyor that circulated through the packaging and cooler.

Orders to the dairy were called in by the branches and other customers, usually two or three days in advance. The salesclerks wrote the orders on computer-generated, preaddressed order sheets for each account. Special phone orders and adjustments could be made until shipment, because of the buffer inventory in the cooler.

Local orders were written by the drivers of the route trucks while visiting each customer on their daily schedule. The day before shipment, the cooler supervisor scheduled and consolidated all orders for filling based on the usual arrival times of the incoming trucks. Two order copies stayed in the sales office, two copies were sent with the order, and one stayed with the cooler supervisor. After delivery, the signed order copy was compared with the original order and all necessary information was entered into the computer. This update triggered the daily report on actual production, cooler inventory, actual units loaded on all trucks by product line, and total amount needed for the next day's production. The plant manager received this printout early the following morning. Two 10-hour shifts were needed to accommodate each day's scheduled production. The same order of production was run each day (such as 2 percent milk first and chocolate last.) To accommodate the trucks that started arriving at 4 A.M., the buffer inventory in the cooler at the start of the day for the last two products run might be as high as 60 percent of total production.

The quality control supervisor was responsible for product quality throughout the plant. Quality control was a major factor in the production of milk. As the tankers arrived from the farms, three quality checks were done to make certain the raw milk was within the acceptable range of temperature, bacteria count, and acidity. Except during pasteurization, milk was maintained at 38°F throughout the plant. In addition to the standardization checks for butterfat content, two tests were done after pasteurization to check the bacteria count and type of bacteria still in the milk. Raw milk arrived with a bacteria count of 10,000 to 20,000 per milliliter and was shipped out at about 500 per milliliter. Each worker was acutely aware of the importance of quality control, and all machinery and equipment were thoroughly washed at least once a day to ensure cleanliness. Most of the equipment—including tankers, silos, and storage tanks—was stainless steel to facilitate cleaning and reduce the chances of contamination.

1. Diagram the process and information flows.

2. What do you see as the challenges that the management of the dairy faced?

3. Recently the dairy lost a large contract for supplying milk to a chain of grocery stores. How do you think the loss of sales will affect the operations of the dairy? Be as specific as you can.

TOUR B

A Job Shop

Norcen Industries
Jersey Shore, Pennsylvania

(Courtesy of Noreen Industries)

It had been years since Joe Gehret finally gave in to his desire to control his own company and resigned his position as general foreman in the machine shop of the Litton Industries plant in Williamsport, Pennsylvania. In July 1967, Joe and a partner (who has since left the firm) began Norcen Industries by selling stock and taking over an old garage in Jersey Shore, about 15 miles west of Williamsport. They initially intended for Norcen to be a plastics distributor and fabricator, but it soon became apparent that both their experience and the demands of industry in north central Pennsylvania dictated a change of course. Norcen quickly became mainly a metalworking machine shop, and the machine shop accounted for almost 90 percent of gross revenues.

Joe Gehret beside a lathe. *(Courtesy of Norcen Industries)*

The company had experienced reasonably steady growth. In 1981, Norcen moved into a new 21,000-square-foot building on the outskirts of town. Sales in 1996 had grown to over $2 million and employment to 39, and Norcen was currently planning an expansion of 13,750 square feet to accommodate laser cutting equipment for even thick metal plates and to permit the expansion of currently inadequate space in the factory, such as the inspection area.

PART ONE: PROCESS DESCRIPTION

Products, Sales, and Order Handling

As a general machine shop, Norcen was capable of producing a seemingly endless succession of metal and plastic parts that a host of companies typically assembled into machines and other products. Norcen specialized in close tolerance work for the electronics and aerospace industries. Almost all of Norcen's customers were manufacturers, but 95 percent of this business Norcen had to win by submitting low bids. The purchasing departments of Norcen's customer firms generally requested Norcen and at least two other machine shops to "quote" the work they wanted done. The request always specified (1) the number of pieces desired, which varied enormously, from 5 pieces to over 1000, although most lots were less than 250; (2) the nature of the material required and whether it was supplied by the customer; (3) the design of the piece (a blueprint would be sent); and (4) the date by which the order had to be received. During peak years, Norcen bid on as many as 250 such requests each week, knowing that on a long-run average its quote would be accepted about 15 percent of the time. (In the past this figure had sometimes been as high as 40 percent.)

Joe Gehret was responsible for deciding all metalworking quotes. Naturally, it was easier for him to quote jobs that Norcen had done before. Not only did he know the hourly charge-out rate (currently, $34.50 per hour for general machining and $45 per hour for electronic discharge machining [EDM]), which would cover both direct labor and overhead expenses, but he had a past record of what the piece had actually cost Norcen to make on all previous occasions. (See Figure B1

FIGURE B1 A sample record card for a particular item manufactured at Norcen Industries.

Notes:

1. This record card is for a so-called "transformer" (not what we would ordinarily term a transformer) for a company whose name has been withheld. This part is distinguished at Norcen by its part number, 53147, which also corresponds to a blueprint and a process sheet (see Figure B2).

2. The material to work on is furnished by the customer company.

3. This is a part that Norcen has machined for years. This record card is sheet #3. On this sheet, we can see at the top of the columns that the first order was placed on January 4, 1984, under purchase order (P.O.) number 53368. That job was assigned job number 17503 and consisted of 6 separate shipments of varying shipment dates (such as 2/14, 1/16) and corresponding and separate invoices to the customer (such as 121074, 11813). The shipment quantities varied as well (for example, 66 units, 77 units, 63 units). The total for the entire order is 441 pieces.

   The latest order (#65630), dated 9/10 and shipped 10/2, involved just 59 pieces. It carried job number 20414 and was billed on invoice 18004.

4. The quoted price for the first order on the card (job number 17503) was $9.20 per piece. The total billing for the first invoice (#12107) was $607.20. The total billing for the entire order was the sum of the six relevant invoices, $4,057.20.

5. A total of 136.9 hours of labor were spent fulfilling the first order. The total labor cost of the job was $1,175.44 (the sum of the cost total column).

   For the latest job, a total of 26 hours of labor was expended at a cost of $259.89. The total billing was $722.16 for the 59 pieces shipped, quoted at a price of $12.24 each.

6. Norcen Industries made its charge-out rate in the latest completed job. The labor hours of 26 times the prevailing charge-out rate of $24 per hour equals $624, which is below the actual revenue for the job of $722.16.

7. Two special notations are worth explaining: (1) The latest entry for P.O. number 55590 is a charge of $182.40 for an extra setup. The customer company had not provided the material on time, requiring Norcen Industries to incur an additional, unscheduled setup. Norcen charged the customer for that setup.

   (2) P.O. numbers 60938 and 61673, involving job numbers 18980 and 19206, were able to be run with a single setup. This was advantageous to the shop (denoted by the notation "made on 18980") and resulted in a lower quote for P.O. number 61673.

MATERIAL DESCRIPTION						COMPANY	PART NAME	PART No			
OFHC Cu						Some company	Transformer	512864			
LINEAL INCHES	AREA (SQ IN)	DIMENSIONS				COMPUTATION-MTL REQD	PREPARED BY	PG OF	REV		

EQUIPMENT					OPERATION		ESTIMATED			
FIXTURES & TOOLS	MACH	SPEED	FEED	No	DESCRIPTION		No OF PIECES PER HR	TIME		
								PER PC	SET UP	
Arbor collet				10	Rough face to turn O D to size (972 974) on Arbor					
				20	Face waterfall drag down off of open end					
				30	Face off other end to 400 long					
				40	Deburr					
Collet template				50	Dress radius & grind radius in part holding length to size (381)					
				60	Deburr					
				70	Inspect					

Notes:

1. A collet holds the workpiece. An arbor is another device to hold the workpiece.
2. A template was used to help guide the grinding.
3. The waterfall was excess metal, a humpline bulge, that had to be machined off the part.
4. Various dimensions were given in steps 10, 30, and 50. They were also available on the blueprint of the part.
5. In the material description, OFHC Cu means oxygen-free copper, which is a very pure copper.

FIGURE B2 A sample process sheet used at Norcen Industries.

and the discussion on record keeping below.) In addition, Norcen would already have a blueprint of the piece and a "process sheet" (Figure B2), which would outline the steps the shop had previously taken to manufacture it and the time standards for each of those steps. Deciding quotes for pieces Norcen had not previously made was more difficult. In such cases, Joe had to ponder the blueprint and develop, at least in his mind, a rough-cut process sheet.

Sometimes the request for the quote included a process sheet developed by the company itself, and this was a great aid. Other factors such as delivery dates (rush orders, being more trouble, commanded higher margins) and the prevailing load in the shop (the more slack in the shop, the lower the margin) also influenced the quote.

The acceptance of a Norcen quote typically came by phone and was confirmed later by letter. Upon notification of acceptance, Joe's wife, Lillian, who was responsible for all bookkeeping, wrote up two copies of a job sheet (Figures B3 and B4). One copy was kept in a record book, and the other was attached to a blueprint and placed in a special tray. The production manager and the shop foreman were then responsible for looking over each job sheet to see whether any materials not provided by the customer needed to be ordered and whether any tooling needed to be done. Job sheets that awaited materials or tooling were kept in a separate tray. When enough materials were on hand to complete the order, the job sheet and blueprint were placed in a special drawer. This action released the order to the shop.

Plant and Personnel

The machine shop operated on two shifts: 6:50 A.M. to 3:20 P.M. and 3:30 P.M. to midnight, with a half-hour break for lunch or dinner and two 10-minute break periods. The day shift consisted of 24 hourly workers, and the evening shift currently

ORDER No. ___60938_____ JOB __18980___

PART No. __53147_____ LOT SIZE _____

MATERIAL _Furnished_____ 245

DELIVERY __2/10_____

Checked By	Date	Name	Operation	Qty.	Hrs.	Acc. Hrs.
	1/14	RP.G	255			
DM	1-16	J.C.	Lathe		8.0	8.0
	1-17	JL	LATHE		8.0	16.0
	1-18	JL	"		8.0	24.0
	1-19	JL	"		5.0	29.0
	1-21	JL	"		2.5	31.5
	1-21	Doyle	Deburr		3.9	35.4
	1-22	Doyle	Deburr-Buff		4.2	39.6
DM	1-22	DM.	Set up & Gr.		2.0	41.6
	1-22	O.R.	Gr.		0.7	42.3
JJ	1-23	OR.	Gr.		8.0	50.3
DM	1-24	O.R.	Gr.		8.0	58.3
JJ	1-25	JJ.	Deburr		2.0	60.3
	1-25	Doyle	wipe-Buff		1.5	61.8
	1/25	JJ	DeBuff, insp		1.5	63.3
	135	Pcs	To Ship	1/25	JJ	
	1-25	OR	Gr.		8.0	71.3
JJ	1-26	OR	Gr.		2.5	73.8
DM	1-28	OR	Gr.		4.0	77.8
	1-29	OR	Gr.		4.5	82.3
	2-7	Doyle	CLEAN Deburr-Buff		5.2	87.5
	2-8	JJ	INSP		1.0	88.5
	118	Pcs	To Ship	2/8	JJ	

FIGURE B3 A sample of the job sheet used at Norcen Industries.

Notes:

1. This job sheet accompanied job number 18980 around the shop from the initial receipt of materials from the customer (255 pieces on 1/14) until shipments on 1/25 and 2/8 of 135 and 118 pieces, respectively.

2. The lot size on this job changed. It was increased to 245 (253 were actually shipped) when P.O. number 61673 came along, and the shop was able to do both jobs with a single setup.

3. Dates worked, worker initials, operation done, time spent, and total time to date on the order are filled in by each worker after he or she completes working on the job. Periodically, others have checked the order's work (DM and JJ).

4. The accumulated labor hours are 88.5. This figure is also displayed on the record card.

ran with only 6 workers. (This shift operated primarily the company's direct numerical control [DNC] lathes and mills and was also used to expedite rush jobs.) Norcen's hourly wages (the highest paid by any of the machine shops in the area) started at $9 per hour for unskilled workers and went to $13.75 per hour for the most demanding work. This pay was augmented in two ways:

1. Overtime pay at time and a half
2. A bonus plan, payable at Christmas and in the summer

The size of each bonus depended on the fortunes of the company over the previous six months. Currently, bonuses averaged about $1500 per employee, greater by far than the dividends paid to the company's shareholders. In leaner years, of course, this bonus was much lower. The size of the bonus for each worker, like the number of vacation days, depended on seniority. The workers recognized this sys-

ORDER No. _____60938_____   JOB _18980_

PART No. ___53147___   LOT SIZE _245_

MATERIAL _____

_____

DELIVERY ___2/10___   _10.24_

Checked By	Date	Name	Operation	Qty.	Hrs.	Acc. Hrs.
	1/13	OL.	246	50		29
	1/20	GJ.	33	25	3.5	32.5
		OL.	21	25	2.5	35
		OR	231	20	27.2	62.2
		DM	19	00	2	64.2
		DD	71	52	9.6	73.8
			622	72		
		chgd	155.29			
	1/27	OR	72.25		8.5	82.3
	2/3	DD	40.04		5.2	87.5
		GJ	9.50		1	88.5
			121.79			
		chgd.	156.68			

FIGURE B4 A sample showing Lillian Gehret's office copy of a job sheet.

Notes:

1. This job sheet was compiled by Lillian Gehret after job 18980 was completed. The information for the job sheet was derived from (a) the job sheet (Figure B3) that follows the job around the shop, (b) worker time cards (Figure B6), and (c) information on worker hourly rates.

2. The top portion of this job sheet contains the same information as Figure B3 and includes as well the quoted price on the job ($10.24 per piece).

3. Worker times are gathered by the week, with the weeks being dated from their start on a Sunday (1/13, 1/20). Workers' hours spent on this job in each week are listed in the Hrs. column. The cumulative hours for the job as a whole are totaled in the Acc. Hrs. column. In the center columns are listed the worker pay for the week due to the job. By dividing this pay by the hours, one can see that workers have different hourly wages. GJ has an hourly wage of $9.50 ($33.25/3.5).

4. The total wage bills for the job are $622.72, charged to invoice 15529, and $121.79, charged to invoice 15668. Recall that job 18980 combined two purchase orders and ran them on the same setup.

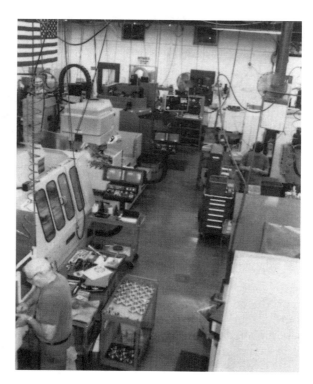

The shop as seen from a balcony. *(Courtesy of Norcen Industries)*

The shop as seen from a balcony. *(Courtesy of Norcen Industries)*

tem as an incentive for continued good work. In the words of a lathe and drill press operator: "The better we are to the company, the better the company is to us."

A rough layout of the plant, showing the general groupings of machines, is included as Figure B5. An inventory of the most important machines in the shop, along with their weekly average hours in use, is provided in Table B1.

The Workings of the Shop

Although Joe Gehret spent a good deal of time on the shop floor, responsibility for shop operations rested with Rob Thomas, the production manager, and Dan Steinbacher, the shop foreman. Their duties were varied, but the first concern for the smooth running of the shop was to see that all workers were assigned tasks and that they understood these tasks well, both their nature and their time standards. Moreover, Rob and Dan knew that it was important to the success of the company that tasks be assigned in a way that saved Norcen money. Cost reductions from such scheduling and advance planning could come about in several ways:

1. Before an operator could machine any of the myriad jobs Norcen was capable of performing, the necessary machine had to be set up. The setup varied from about a half-hour for simple jobs to 4 hours for the most complex. An average setup was about 1.5 hours. Since, once set up, the machine could produce any number of pieces with only minor adjustments, it made sense to run full lots whenever possible. In this way, setup costs were spread over all the units in the order.

2. Frequently, especially with automatic equipment, the running time of the machine per piece produced was long enough so that, by staggering operations, a single operator could attend two different machines at the same time. That is, while one piece was being machined, the operator could be working at another machine, typically inserting new material or removing a finished piece. To exploit

(Total plant area = 21,000 square feet)

Workforce (39 total)

1 general manager
1 production manager
1 QC manager/project engineer
2 foremen
1 bookkeeper
1 computer programmer

25 machine operators
1 full-time inspector
1 inspector/operator
1 maintenance man
1 shipper/receiver
2 utility people (cleanup, etc.)
1 manager of the plastics business

FIGURE B5 Plant layout and workforce at Norcen Industries.

TABLE B1 Inventory of Major Machines at Norcen Industries

Machine and Number Owned		Percent of Scheduled Time Machine Is Run
1	Hardinge HXL	100
1	Hardinge Conquest superprecision lathe	100
1	Hardinge Conquest GT Gang Tooler lathe	100
1	Hardinge Conquest T42 lathe	100
1	Hardinge Conquest ST 25 Swiss turn lathe	50
5	Hardinge CHNC II lathes	100
2	Large slant bed lathes	100
3	Hurco machining centers	100
2	Matsuura machining centers	100
1	Fadal machining center	100
1	Kitamura Mycenter machining center	100
2	Mitsubishi traveling wire EDM machines	75
1	Sodick die-sinker EDM machine	30
1	Current EDM drill CT 300 hole driller	30
1	Blanchard-type grinder	40
1	Do-All automatic cut-off saw	40
1	OGP Smart Scope computerized video measuring microscope system	30
1	Sheffield coordinate measuring machine	50
2	J&L 20″ optical comparators with power feed and digital readout	75
2	O.D., I.D. universal grinders	50
1	Super-precision universal tool and cutter grinder	30
1	Heat treat facility (size limitations, muffled main furnace, nitrogen induction)	75
1	Special roll grinding unit	50
1	110 ton Cincinnati hydraulic punch press	30
	+ surface grinders, manual mills, old lathes used for very small runs or for tool and die work or in support of the highly used machines (i.e., for creating fixtures, tooling)	25

these possibilities, Rob and Dan had grouped similar kinds of machines together on the shop floor. It was to Norcen's advantage for Dan to identify and to match together those jobs that permitted this kind of labor savings.

3. As might be expected, some operators could perform certain machining tasks relatively better than others and thus held a comparative advantage over other workers in the shop for some jobs. It was worth it for the foremen to keep these special capabilities in mind in his assignment of jobs.

4. Cost reductions could also occur through improvements in the process sheets that were kept in special binders. Often, changes in the sequence of drilling, cutting, milling, grinding, tapping, threading, deburring, and so on, could have profound effects on the total time Norcen had to allocate to a particular job. Rob and Dan had to be alert for possible improvements they could make in the process.

5. The probability of successfully reducing costs was naturally greater for more complex operations and for repeat business. Furthermore, cost reductions could lie in more than process sequence changes. To cite an example, Norcen machined a part composed of a thin molybdenum strip bonded to steel. The customer's initial process specifications called for cutting two semicircles into the part using a lathe, but Joe Gehret recognized this technique as a high-risk, low-yield way to machine this part. By changing the process to use a specially adapted grinder, Norcen was able to machine the part successfully with much higher yields than would otherwise have been the case. Such dramatic success was not to be found often, but its significance was great enough to demand a good deal of the foremen's thoughts.

Even more important to the foremen than assigning tasks in money-saving ways was seeing to it that the delivery schedule was met. Norcen could not miss deliveries and still expect to receive repeat orders. The foremen were constantly aware of the promised delivery dates, and they attached high priorities to imminent deliveries due. Their scheduling of jobs was further influenced by Norcen's cash flow needs. Other things being equal, and particularly at the end of the month, small jobs were given preference so that billing could proceed at once.

The foremen dealt also with worker morale, training, and development, with materials handling, and with quality control. But job scheduling was the most demanding on the foremen's energies. They tried to stay one day ahead of the work-

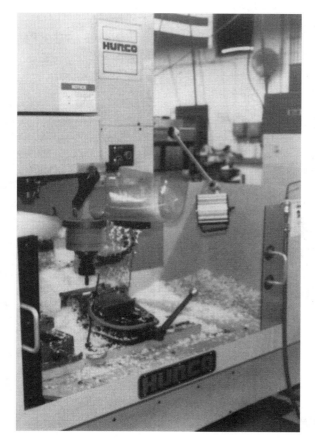

A Hurco machining center down for a changeover after machining some white plastic parts. (Courtesy of Norcen Industries)

ers, so that they knew precisely which job would go next to every machine, who would work that job, and when they would start on it. As Joe Gehret put it: "Scheduling is the most difficult function we have around here. It's the easiest thing in the world to say no to a customer, that we can't fit his job into the shop. But after a few noes, you may not have a customer."

During recessions, scheduling was even more difficult than usual. The drop in orders then meant that the foremen had fewer chances to group compatible orders together to avoid bottlenecks or to create labor-saving opportunities. In busier times, the foremen could choose among the many orders in the shop, spreading out demand for particular pieces of equipment and taking advantage of the economies possible.

Frequently, planned schedules had to be interrupted because of customer desires for expedited delivery, because materials were received late from the customer, or because of the breakdown of the machine or its tooling. In these cases quick, remedial action had to be taken. Often, this remedial action took the form of adding a new job or rerouting an existing job through the shop. Norcen had enough equipment on hand, typically, to permit a new or rerouted job to be set up on an unused machine. Joe Gehret purchased new machines for the shop with this kind of compatibility in mind. Not all jobs, of course, could be rerouted through the shop if things went awry, but it was possible with a sizable number, especially those that were not too complex. Some jobs could even be machined in an alternative sequence (e.g., milling could be done first rather than third), and this helped when remedial action was necessary. In general, the foremen preferred to have lathe work performed first, then milling, and only then grinding; but they were willing to abandon this sequence if necessary.

Some aspects of just-in-time manufacturing had repercussions for machine shops such as Norcen. Customers were now placing orders that required multiple,

A Hurco machining center. *(Courtesy of Norcen Industries)*

time-phased deliveries of smaller-than-usual lots. Even though many of Norcen's new machines were capable of running small lots economically, this trend did serve to complicate scheduling.

Technological Advances and Other Trends

Over the years, technological advances, especially in computers, have been revolutionizing the machine tool industry. The old fully manual lathes, mills, grinders, and other tools had been supplanted by a succession of newer tools:

1. The first set of newer tools were NC (numerically controlled) machines that could repeat operations exactly by reading punched paper tapes. The paper tapes had to be specially prepared and thus were typically suitable for only high-volume, repetitive jobs. Naturally, in job shops like Norcen with many low-volume, one-of-a-kind jobs, NC machines could find only limited use.

2. The next generation of equipment, the computer numerically controlled (CNC) machines, found more of a home in job shops like Norcen Industries. Much of this machinery was programmable, enabling operators to enter, at the computer console, the depths, speeds, and feed rates of cuts to be made along X-, Y-, or Z-axes. In addition, they could operate from tapes (paper or magnetic). These newer machine tools were more versatile, more accurate, and faster than previous ones. Their automatic features easily permitted an operator to run more than one machine at a time, although this doubling up was often less feasible for machine shops running small parts (Norcen) than for shops machining large parts.

3. The latest generation of equipment, the direct numerical control (DNC) machines, could be run directly by a computer, eliminating the need for the preparation of tapes or the case-by-case programming of the CNC machine. All of Norcen

The Hardinge Conquest superprecision lathe. *(Courtesy of Norcen Industries)*

Industries' 25 machines were now DNC controlled. These machines made use of Norcen's CAD/CAM equipment and a fiber-optic cable network that linked the computer to the machines it controlled. Parts could now be designed using CAD computer software (Norcen used CADKey). The design could then be translated by CAM software (Norcen used IGES translation and the Anvil 1000 MD CAM program) into the precise settings for each machine's operation, and then downloaded to that machine via the cable network. Norcen kept a library of its past jobs, so that any repeat job could be pulled from the library and the machine set in exactly the way it was done before, without any extra work. All of Norcen's lathe operators programmed their own jobs as well as some of the machining center operators. The computer programmer and the foremen helped to troubleshoot particularly difficult jobs.

Norcen Industries was continually buying new, trading in old, and upgrading existing equipment. Joe Gehret remarked that the introduction of new technology meant that Norcen could produce some parts for costs that were less now, in current dollars, than those same parts cost in 1967, when the company was started.

Doing more and more machining were some of the latest machines to be added to the shop: three electrical discharge (EDM) machines. These machines used wire electrodes of various, and often small, diameters to machine parts of any conductive material, such as metal. The conductive material would be charged positively and the wire electrodes negatively and the material would be "burned off" by the travelling wire. EDM machines produced no burrs (thus, no need for grinding) as they machined parts, and they were capable of very precise machining, even in previously hard-to-work corners of the material. This equipment was kept in its own air-conditioned "clean room."

The Sheffield coordinate measuring machine. *(Courtesy of Norcen Industries)*

Norcen did not have any flexible machining centers (FMS) that one could sometimes find in larger fabrication areas nor did it operate any machining cells. FMSs link several machines together and use sophisticated conveyors to move pieces from one machine to another. FMSs did not make sense for a job shop like Norcen because the tooling needed was too great and expensive, and jobs could be moved around more efficiently by the existing workforce. Similarly, machining cells were not employed because the continually changing nature of the product mix in the shop precluded the creation of product families with similar routings for those machining cells.

Nevertheless, the advent of the new technology permitted the shop's management to devise a number of cost-saving procedures. For example,

1. With carbide cutting tools and with EDM machining, Norcen could now harden metals by heat treating first and then machining them afterward. Previously, parts were machined, heat treated, and then re-machined (e.g., ground).

2. The new machines had multiple tool holders so that more facets of the job could be done while the part was held in position.

3. Parts could now be held in programmable indexers, which could automatically rotate the part so that different sides could be machined without operator intervention.

4. Some machines had multiple vices on them so that two or three pieces could be set up at once.

5. Some of the lathes had automatic bar-feeds.

The movement for just-in-time (JIT) manufacturing and concern for quality and inventory levels were affecting operations at Norcen Industries. Customers were less lenient about scrap, no longer providing an extra 10 percent of material

The Mitsubishi traveling wire EDM machines. *(Courtesy of Norcen Industries)*

The control box for the fiber optic cables of Norcen's CAD/CAM network. *(Courtesy of Norcen Industries)*

as a matter of course to cover potential scrap. Customers were also requiring multiple deliveries of their orders, forcing Norcen either to hold the inventory or to set up the job more than once. Concern for rapid delivery had also recently led the company to purchase a 110-ton punch press so that it could make its own blanks quickly for many of its parts. The press had also permitted the development of some press work for outside customers.

Quality Control

Quality at Norcen was pursued by following what the quality control manager termed "the Norcen way." Typically, these steps were followed in working on a job:

1. The foreman wrote the process sheet.
2. The foreman would then discuss the process sheet with the assigned operator and make any changes.
3. Each operator was responsible for his own setup.
4. The first piece would be checked, first by the operator, usually with the shop's coordinate measuring machine, and then by an inspector.
5. The job would be run in lots of 5 (usually) and each fifth piece would be inspected. If it did not pass inspection, all the previous 4 pieces would be checked 100 percent, and the next 5 pieces would be inspected 100 percent as well.
6. Quality was the joint responsibility of the operator and of quality control.
7. All finished jobs would be sampled by QC for final inspection.

The QC manager noted that the keys to quality were following the proper steps for the job and performing some steps with such tight tolerances that subsequent work, which relied on the previous machining, all fell within acceptable limits.

Record Keeping

When an operator completed his assigned task on any job, he completed the job sheet (Figure B3) attached to the blueprint. On this sheet he filled in his name, the date, the operation he performed, the quantity he completed, and the length of time it took him to complete the task, including setup time. In addition, at the end of the day, each operator completed a time card (Figure B6), listing the time spent on each job during the day.

FIGURE B6 A sample of an operator's time card used at Norcen Industries.

CHARGE NO	SUN	MON	TUE	WED	THUR	FRI	SAT	Total Hours
18980	✓	4 –	4 5					8 5
18593	✓	4 –	2 –			– 3		6 3
18976	✓		3 5	1 5				5 –
19363	✓			1 2		1 –		2 2
19191	✓			3 6	1 5			5 1
19192	✓			3 7	1 5			5 2
19363	✓				2 5			2 5
19116	✓				4 5	2 5		7 –
19215	✓					6 2	5 –	11 2
TOTAL		8 –	10 –	10 –	10 –	10 –	5 –	53 –

EMP. # 828 — EMPLOYEE SIGNATURE: Reading Orie Reading / Orie — WORK PERIOD 1-24-

START: 7:00 7:00 7:00 7:00 7:00 7:00
STOP: 3:30 5:30 5:30 5:30 5:30 12:00

Notes:

1. This is Orie Reading's time card for the week beginning January 24. This was a busy time at Norcen, and Orie worked 53 total hours during the week, including two hours of overtime from Tuesday through Friday and five hours on Saturday.

2. During the week, Reading worked on nine different jobs. He worked on the job we are most interested in, #18980, on Monday and Tuesday, for 4 and 4.5 hours, respectively. On Monday he also worked 4 hours on job 18593, and on Tuesday, he worked on job 18976 as well.

3. By totaling the hours by each worker on each job as recorded on these time cards, Lillian Gehret has another, independent estimate of the hours worked on any job. These estimates can be compared with the hours totaled on the job sheets.

In this way, Lillian Gehret had two records of the time each operator spent on each of the jobs done in the shop. Knowing the times and the wages of each operator involved in any job permitted Lillian to calculate the labor cost of that job. She made this calculation weekly and took care to see that any discrepancies in the two time records were resolved. Usually, the daily time cards were more accurate than the job sheets.

Knowing this information, at the close of every job Lillian would complete the record card (Figure B1), which Joe relied on for making quotes on repeat business. As a rule of thumb for calculating the profitability of a job, Lillian multiplied total labor-hours by the relevant charge-out rate and compared that total with the total price Norcen had quoted. She alerted Joe to any major deviations in that comparison, either positive or negative. Subsequent bids could be based accordingly.

Norcen Industries had recently purchased an IBM A/S 400 minicomputer so that it could run some job shop–specific job control software. This software, called "Classic" by DCD Corporation of Minneapolis, began to automate much of the bookkeeping work that had been done by hand; for example, estimating, quoting, order entry, job scheduling, material planning and purchasing, labor reporting, job costing, job histories, and other features. It was giving Norcen another tool to help it control its operations and to determine those jobs that best added to its profitability. Job histories were now being kept on the computer, by customer and by part number, so that quoting was becoming easier. It handled the order entry of jobs; inventories; and job tracking in the shop itself. It was planned for the foremen to issue special computer-generated job cards to the workers so that workers could use these cards on the shop floor to start the paperwork for a job and again use them to clock a job out. Billing and financial tasks such as payables, receivables, and the general ledger were being moved to the computer.

PART TWO: DISCUSSION

Norcen Industries is in no way responsible for the following views and presentation. They remain solely the responsibility of the author.

The Process Flow

Compared with the continuous flow process at International Paper's Androscoggin Mill, the job shop process at Norcen Industries is strikingly loose and ill-defined. A process flow diagram becomes difficult to draw in any precise or meaningful way. For example, we might sketch a process flow diagram such as in Figure B7. Although many of the parts made at Norcen Industries would have passed through exactly this sequence of operations, many more would have required a different set of operations and a different order. Some of the differences might be minor, but there are a host of parts for which the differences are major. At best, Figure B7's flow diagram can be termed a dominant flow or, perhaps, a preferred, simplified flow. For the most part, the job shop process exhibits great product flux and flexibility. Work-in-process can be routed anywhere within the shop so that even extraordinary machining requirements can be met.

The Information Flow

What is not flexible but is almost totally rigid in the job shop is the flow of information through it. In stark contrast to the diversity of paths a machined part can take through the shop, information flows in a prescribed way (see Figure B8). Record

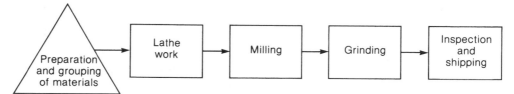

FIGURE B7 A dominant, or preferred, process flow diagram for Norcen Industries.

keeping is done in the same manner for every order; the responsibilities of the workers, bookkeeper, and managers toward information in the process never vary. Everyone has fixed information tasks to perform: quoting, job sheet and blueprint preparation, release to the shop, filling out of job sheets and time cards, labor cost calculations, updating of quote record cards, and signaling of any variances.

The reason for all this rigidity, of course, is that the job shop lives and dies by its ability to process information. Significantly, too, the information flows in the job shop are as much from worker to management (job sheets, time cards, process suggestions, machine breakdowns) as from management to worker (job and machine assignments, schedules, quality control checks, troubleshooting, training). Without suitable records, there would be no clear or readily available means of routing an order through the shop or of specifying exactly what should be done to satisfy it. Without suitable records, the job shop's managers would have little idea how to bid for various jobs. Without suitable records, advances in productivity would be more sporadic and less well retained for future use. Without suitable records, managers would not be able to load the shop effectively. Information and the responsibility of everyone in a job shop to maintain its accuracy and smooth flow constitute the glue by which this type of process is held together.

Capacity in the Job Shop

In the job shop at Norcen Industries, capacity is as ambiguous as the process flow's pattern. No single measure of capacity makes complete sense. While a paper mill can measure its capacity rather straightforwardly in tons per day or some

FIGURE B8 An information flow diagram for Norcen Industries.

similar measure, a machine shop like Norcen Industries cannot readily do the same thing. The large and constantly changing mix of products in the typical job shop ensures that a simple count of units produced is a meaningless way to gauge what the shop's effective capacity really is. We must avoid that simple measure in favor of one that transcends the product mix problem. The easiest remedy is to measure capacity in dollar terms, but that still leaves us with a variety of options. Dollars of typical output per unit of time? Dollars of output per worker? Dollars of output per machine? Dollars of output per dollar of machine value (at cost? at replacement cost?)? All of these measures grab a piece of what we mean intuitively when we say capacity, and yet no one of them fully describes the concept. Only over the long term, when we can feel comfortable that the mix of products has been representative, can we point at differences in shop output over time or output per worker or output per machine as valid measures of high or low capacity. In the short run, no capacity measure is clearly appropriate. Any measure of the shop's capacity is dependent on a host of factors, such as:

1. *Lot sizes.* The larger the lots ordered, the fewer setups in any one day and the greater the number of pieces produced, other things being equal.

2. *Complexity of the pieces worked on.* The more complex the piece, the more likely it will require a large succession of operations and thus the more likely its manufacture will demand a succession of time-consuming setups and difficult scheduling decisions. Of course, this factor is relatively more important in accounting for differences in the number of units manufactured than it is in accounting for differences in dollar value measures of capacity.

3. *Mix of jobs already on the shop floor.* The number and nature of orders already released to the shop floor affect the capacity of the shop in at least two ways: shifting bottlenecks and worker-machine interference.

Many of the orders in the shop may require the services of particular machines. We can expect, then, that some orders may back up while awaiting a particular machine or operation. Further, we can expect to see such bottlenecks occurring from time to time all over the shop. That is, we can expect to see work-in-process inventories building up in different places and at different times in the shop. A smooth-running, well-scheduled job shop will have a low number of such "shifting bottlenecks," but given the diversity of output and run lengths within a job shop process, they are absolutely unavoidable.

In a typical job shop, there will be many machines that require the constant attention of a worker when they are in operation. Increasingly, however, automatic equipment is entering the shop with its ability to perform without the constant "hands-on" attention of the workforce. This advance is not without a challenge of its own. While automatic equipment frees up worker time, only the (sometimes fortuitous) scheduling of two or more jobs to the same worker actually leads to greater worker productivity apart from any speed advances built into the automatic equipment itself. If the scheduling cannot mesh two or more jobs together, the machine can be said to "interfere" with the worker, and capacity in the shop drops relative to the situation where the worker can easily operate two or more pieces of equipment at once. For this reason, Joe Gehret and his managers positioned machinery within the shop to maximize the possibilities for reducing worker-machine interference.

4. *Ability to schedule work well.* As Joe Gehret himself put it, "Scheduling is the most difficult function we have around here." The matching of workers to machines and of workers and machines to jobs often separates a profitable job shop from an unprofitable one. Good scheduling lessens shifting bottlenecks and worker-machine interference. Poor scheduling introduces more work-in-process inventory to the shop than is necessary. In particular, if too many rush orders are permitted in the shop, their scheduling will become difficult, often necessitating the interruption of runs on machines already set up.

As was noted in the process description, in recessionary times management has many fewer jobs from which to choose to keep all the shop's machining centers busy and to avoid bottlenecks. In better economic times, management can search through the released orders for jobs that can help smooth the flow of work through the shop.

5. *Process improvements.* Any advances in the methods employed in producing a part at Norcen Industries permitted the shop to increase its capacity and thus its profitability. With so many orders passing through the shop, there are many opportunities for improving the process: resequencing of operations, different use of machines, quicker setups, special jigs or fixtures for increasing speed and/or accuracy, possible redesign of the piece ordered. Because any of these improvements takes time to work through, it is likely that only the higher volume, repeat business will benefit from such attention.

6. *Number of machines and their condition.* It is obvious that, even without expanding the workforce, the addition of equipment to the shop is likely to increase capacity detectably. For one thing, rush orders will be less likely to necessitate the dismantling of existing machine setups before completion of the run. Having more machines also increases the probability of finding favorable combinations of orders to lessen worker-machine interference. Fewer bottlenecks, too, are likely to occur with the addition of more equipment. It is evident as well that machines in good condition are less likely to break down and thus demand attention both for themselves and for the rescheduling of operations through the shop.

Technological advances, notably the evolution from manual to NC machines to CNC machines and then to DNC machines, have greatly influenced the shop's capacity. Setups are often easier with the more advanced machine tools; more time can be spent actually cutting metal. Moreover, the newer tools permit fancier machining (such as curved shapes) to be done with greater accuracy, higher speed, and less scrap. And given that the machining was accomplished via tape or computer instruction, the new equipment does not tie up workers as long as the older equipment did.

7. *Quantity and quality of labor input.* Another obvious set of factors affecting the capacity of a job shop is drawn from the labor force itself. Overtime and second shift work is a standard way to augment capacity with the same stock of plant and equipment. Employing inexperienced workers and having to train them is a drain on capacity, however.

Obvious in identification but subtle in design and application is an incentive system for the workers. At Norcen Industries, the bonus plan that was dependent on company profits was viewed by the workers as a fair and reasonable spur for continued good work. But it is not the only payment system that could be installed; different systems might have different effects on worker effort and thus on capacity.

Increasing the capacity of a job shop in the way outlined here, at little or no cost, is important to the shop because that is how it makes its money. Of course, the shop must be flexible enough to bid on a tremendous variety of jobs, but the shop's ability to earn any profit, once granted the business, is linked fundamentally to its capacity and its knowledge of that capacity. As we have discussed, these two items are influenced by a number of factors, many of which require the accurate processing of information around the shop.

The Role of Standards and Incentives

Time standards for all of the operations to be performed at Norcen Industries are an integral feature of its cost estimation and bidding responsibilities. Some of the standards are developed internally, mostly through past experience doing the same thing; but others are supplied by the customer when bids are solicited, having been worked out for or by the customer.

The standards are a useful guide for both workers and managers. For the workers, the standards (written on the job sheet) provide continual feedback on how well they are doing the job. For managers, the standards provide information on how long certain jobs should take and thus how they might be scheduled. The standards also provide management with a yardstick for worker performance that is useful not only for making advancement/layoff decisions but also for determining which tasks each worker does relatively better.

Other than by furnishing feedback for each worker, the time standards are not tied formally to any incentive system. Incentives for good work and/or for speedy work are provided either through knowledge that such work often contributes to better company profits (although such work is not the only determinant of profits, by far) or by the prodding and cajoling of the foreman. In job shops like Norcen Industries, the foreman carries much of the responsibility for pacing work through the shop and for ensuring that the quality is satisfactory.

Questions

1. Write up a hypothetical job sheet for an order and briefly explain each column entry. How do the functions of the job sheet and the record card differ?
2. Can you make any generalizations about cost reductions from the example of Norcen Industries? Do these generalizations apply to any other process with which you are already familiar?
3. Why might scheduling be "the most difficult function" in a job shop?
4. "The job shop lives and dies by its ability to process information." Discuss this comment and compare the information flow in the job shop with that in another type of process.
5. Discuss three of the factors that influence a job shop's capacity. What might be "the perfect set of circumstances" in a shop foreman's eyes?
6. As a worker, which would you prefer: the calm predictability of the continuous flow process or the frequently frantic unpredictability of the job shop? As a manager, which would you prefer? How might your attitude affect the setting of standards and incentives in each process?
7. Norcen's foreman places particular emphasis on meeting customer due dates. Due dates thus significantly affect the scheduling that is done. Suppose, however, that due

dates were not as important to you as to the foreman. What other factors could take precedence? How could they serve as the basis for scheduling jobs through the shop? Under what circumstances might different factors take precedence in establishing scheduling rules?

8. Suppose that you were forced to justify to upper management the purchase of new technology, such as a CNC machine, for an existing job shop. Where would you look for the benefits of such an addition to the shop. How would you measure the extent of those benefits?

9. What advantages do you see to a layout such as that used at Norcen Industries? What disadvantages?

Situation for Study B-1
Owens, Inc.

Fred and Ralph own and operate a small machine and metal fabrication shop. Most of their business involves small orders from local industry. These orders are usually ones that the larger customer firms farm out because they do not have the excess capacity. In other words, Fred and Ralph provide "slack" capacity to the larger firms. Figure B9 shows the plant layout.

Fred and Ralph feel that if they can once get an order in their shop, they can learn how to make the part and then underbid on future orders. Moreover, they think they can make most parts more cheaply than the customer can in-house.

They are currently considering bidding on part 273. Figure B10 is an engineering sketch of this part. For the first order the customer will supply a coil of $1\frac{5}{8}$ cold-rolled steel (CRS), but Fred and Ralph are investigating to see whether

FIGURE B9 Plant layout for Owens, Inc.

FIGURE B10 Engineering sketch for part 273, a bracket.

other processes might use other sizes of raw material more efficiently. The proposed order is for 500 pieces, with possible future orders of 500 per month. The proposed bid must be submitted in 2 weeks, the bid award determined within 1 week, and the 500 units delivered 1 month after that.

Fred has generated the estimates shown in Table B2. The cost estimates used for bids are $10.55 per hour for labor and $18.50 per hour for machines—or $29.05 per hour for one worker/one machine operations. Any time "sold" at this rate makes Owens a margin of 25 percent with which to cover indirect costs such as administrative costs.

1. If you were Fred and Ralph, what other aspects of the shop, the market, and the future would you consider regarding the bid for part 273?

2. Analyze the current proposal and generate a bid to the customer and a rough shop schedule.

TABLE B2 Process sheet for part 273 (Owens, Inc.)

Operation Sequence	Machine	Operation	Setup Time (Minutes)	Operation Time Per Unit (Minutes)
1	Shear 3	Shear to length	5	0.030
2	Shear 3	Shear 45° corners	8	0.050
3	Multispindle drill press 1	Drill both holes and deburr	15	3.000
4	Brake press	Bend 90°	10	0.025
5	Tumbler	Deburr	5	a
6		Pack in boxes		30.000

[a]The deburr operation can be left unattended, so the only labor required is to load and unload.

Situation for Study B-2
Streeter Die & Stamping Company

Streeter Tool & Die Company was founded in 1956 by entrepreneur Jack Streeter. For 20 years the small firm flourished, furnishing tools, dies, jigs, and fixtures to metal stamping firms. In 1976 the firm became Streeter Die & Stamping Company (SDS) and began a move toward a new business. Today SDS has two plants in Toledo, Ohio, furnishing metal stampings and assemblies primarily to the major U.S. automakers. In the most recent year, General Motors (GM) accounted for 85 percent of SDS's sales.

The main plant (plant 1) had 14 presses, ranging in power from 20 to 1000 tons, that stamped out metal parts from raw steel. Production was usually based on firm customer orders, but occasionally some forecasting of future orders was done in an attempt to get longer, more efficient production runs.

The secondary plant (plant 2), representing a type of forward vertical integration for SDS, was more labor intensive than plant 1. Plant 2 specialized in the assembly and welding of parts stamped at plant 1. Extra space at plant 2 was used as a finished goods warehouse for any parts made at plant 1 or 2 that would not be shipped within 1 week.

The orders that SDS normally produced to were contracts that SDS had won by submitting quotes to the customer. In the case of GM contracts, it was known at SDS that price was not always the deciding factor; SDS's record for quality and timeliness played an important role in winning many of these contracts.

Raw materials arriving at SDS, almost all of them coils weighing 1 to 5 tons, were stored in a warehouse adjacent to plant 1. When the steel was needed in the shop, a forklift picked it up and brought it to the press where it was to be used. From this point, the steel could go through many different combinations of presses and operations, depending on the specific part being made.

In general, the first operation involved running the steel through an automatic press. Steel coils were hoisted onto a reel and fed into the press automatically. The stamped parts fell off the press into bins, which the press operators occasionally checked to see whether the parts were being stamped properly. When the order had been completed, the remaining part of the steel coil was removed from the reel and stored against the shop wall. For several parts this operation was the only one necessary; a random sample of these parts was inspected by quality control and, if the parts were good, they were taken to the loading dock and prepared for shipping.

After passing a quality inspection, bins of more complex parts were moved to nonautomatic presses for the rest of their stamping operations, such as piercing, drawing, and forming. These operations were much slower, because the parts had to be placed manually into the dies by the press operators. These operations completed some parts. Other parts were sent to a vendor for sandblasting, painting, heat treating, and/or deburring before being shipped to the customer; still others were sent to plant 2, where several component parts were welded and/or assembled into the finished product.

The finished goods inventory at SDS was relatively small. Parts that were to be shipped within one week were stacked along the walls of the loading docks at both plants so that forklift drivers could easily spot which parts must be loaded onto a certain truck.

Smooth operations at SDS were extremely dependent on a coordinated, accurate information flow. The information flow followed a cycle that began and ended with engineering submitting a quote for a contract. If information was not accurate at one point in the cycle, the results could have a domino effect on the various departments at SDS. To help improve information flow, all departments at SDS used an IBM System 34 computer extensively.

After analyzing customers' blueprints and past SDS results on similar parts, engineering quoted prices per piece for lot sizes ranging from 100 to 600,000 pieces per year. Reflecting the fixed costs of initial tooling, the price per piece decreased as the lot size increased. After winning a contract, SDS had 6 to 8 months before its first shipment was due on a new part and 3 to 4 months on a carryover part.

During the 6 to 8 months before the first due date, engineering was responsible for getting the shop ready for production. This included ordering the tooling from a vendor, drawing up process sheets for each subassembly, determining what presses could or should be used to stamp each part, assigning part numbers to new parts, and entering all pertinent data about each part into the computer. Engineering also sent a copy of the contract and process sheets to production planning so that they had a record or parts that had to be scheduled in the near future.

Production planning needed no further information until 13 weeks before the first shipment due date. The data systems manager had designed a computer program that received information directly from GM's computer each Monday morning and printed out a list of SDS's week-by-week requirements over the next 13 weeks; the first 2 weeks were required by contract to be firm. When new parts showed up on the list, production planning had to (1) check with engineering to see how the tooling was progressing, (2) order materials, and (3) schedule a sample run. No full production runs could be shipped to GM or other top customers until samples had been approved.

The Monday morning printout listed other important information for each part, such as the number of pieces on hand, the week in which the number on hand would be insufficient to cover cumulative requirements, and the amount of components and raw materials on hand for each part. The production scheduler used this report to determine which parts would have to be made two weeks into the future. The scheduler filled out a small card for each operation that must be performed and posted the card on a schedule board that enabled him to schedule work on each press for the present week and the next two weeks.

While the scheduler was busy loading the presses, a production planning assistant used another copy of this report to determine raw material requirements over the entire 13 weeks. Any materials that SDS would not have enough of to meet these requirements were written on a material requisition, which was delivered to the purchasing agent for further action.

Each morning, after surveying the progress on the shop floor, analyzing the previous day's production summary, and updating the schedule board, the scheduler brought to the shop foreman (1) a schedule of parts to be stamped in each press, (2) routing cards for each part, and (3) process sheets with pictures of each operation. Press operators used counters on the presses to count the number of pieces stamped each shift, each day, and each production run. When the total count for the run reached the number on the routing card, the operator signed the routing card, wrote on his activity card his shift count and his hours spent on the part, and signaled the foreman for a new job. At the end of each shift, the foreman gathered all the activity cards and summarized the data into the daily production summary. In addition to the scheduler's use of this summary, the inventory control specialist combined this information with shipping and receiving data to update inventories on the computer files daily. Keying in this inventory data and some additional cost data also updated financial and job cost data, thus completing the information flow cycle and ensuring that accounting and engineering had access to the information necessary for preparing monthly financial statements and accurate quotes on parts contracts.

A somewhat separate line of information flowed between the shipping department and the billing clerks. Each day shipping filled out a list of the parts, with quantities, that it had shipped. This list was delivered to the billing clerks who, at the end of each day, wired these shipments into the customers' computers. With this method, the customers' procurement agents knew exactly from day to day which parts were in transit, and both SDS and its customers had a common reference date if questions arose about a particular shipment.

Often, the information flow was less formal when customers' procurement agents called and asked for early delivery or when SDS was behind schedule on a part. Information flow became a matter of someone from production planning personally expediting these orders through the shop and arranging special rush transportation.

1. To the extent that you can, diagram the process and information flows.

2. Sales at Streeter Die & Stamping recently increased and bottlenecks emerged in the operation, although the exact cause of the bottlenecks was not immediately obvious. How would you determine where any bottlenecks were? Be specific.

3. How would you control the levels of inventory? How would you monitor and, perhaps, change the status of jobs in the company? What kinds of things would you have the computer do?

TOUR C

A Batch Flow Process

Jos. A. Bank Clothiers
Baltimore Manufacturing Operations
Baltimore, Maryland

(Courtesy of Jos. A. Bank Mfg. Co.)

Jos. A. Bank Clothiers was a maker of high-quality, traditionally styled men's clothes—primarily suits, sport coats, and slacks. It sold these clothes along with shirts, ties, and other accessories through approximately 80 stores across the nation and an extensive mail-order business. Compared with retailers of similar clothes, the company used lower price markups and had a lower overhead. These features, combined with manufacturing efficiencies, permitted Jos. A. Bank to market its high-quality clothes at prices significantly lower than those of its competitors. Begun in 1902, the formerly family-owned business had been sold to Quaker Oats in 1981, resold to a group of investors in a leveraged buy-out in 1986, and most recently, in 1994, taken public, with its stock sold on the NASDAQ.

The company employed 478 people in manufacturing, 23 of whom were salaried managers. There were two manufacturing plants in Baltimore: Brookhill Road and North Avenue. The Brookhill Road plant housed the cutting room, piece goods storage, marker making, production planning, design, and piece goods and trim testing. The North Avenue plant assembled, finished, and pressed the company's coats and pants. All warehousing and distribution were accomplished in Hampstead, Maryland, at the company's headquarters. The North Avenue facility had opened in 1988 and the Brookhill Road facility in 1994. Prior manufacturing operations in Hampstead had been closed. The Baltimore plants were well located to attract a suitable, skilled workforce.

PART ONE: PROCESS DESCRIPTION

The Process Flow

The making of a high-quality sport coat or suit coat was a complex endeavor, encompassing 140 to 150 distinct operations (see Figure C1). The coat was an assembly of various parts, including sleeves, backs, fronts, facings, collars, and pockets. Each of these parts, in turn, combined the basic fabric for the coat itself (known as piece goods) with 40 to 50 trim items. These trim items included linings, fusings (the firm material fused by heat to various parts of the piece goods to help them retain their shape and resist wear), pocketing, stays, tape, thread, and buttons. The assembly of pants was less complex.

The Cutting Room

The assembly of a suit or coat began when a bolt of fabric (the piece goods) was received, examined, and then placed into raw materials inventory. Any flaws were marked so that they could be trimmed out during the cutting process. Once it was decided to use a particular bolt of fabric, the goods were pulled out of inventory and then carefully laid on long cutting room tables. This task was known as "spreading" the cloth; depending on the particular order, the number of layers spread ranged from 1 to 110. It was easier to spread a plain cloth than to spread a cloth woven into a pattern. Plaids were traditionally the most difficult to spread so that the cutout pieces would match up well together once assembled. Jos. A. Bank had developed a technique of spreading plaids over special pins that assured the matching of cutout pieces, and saved considerable time, and thus cost, in the assembly of a coat or pair of pants.

Once spread, a paper pattern known as a marker was placed over the layers of fabric. The coat and pants pattern pieces were carefully arranged on it so that as little fabric as possible was wasted. This arrangement was generated by one of two computer-based marker-making instruments (AM-5s, made by Gerber Garment Technologies) and was printed out, ready to be used. The AM-5 could easily adjust sizes and arrange the pieces in the most efficient pattern. For example, certain suit sizes (such as 40 regulars and 41 regulars or 39 regulars and 43 regulars) might be combined efficiently on the marker pattern. Once spread, with the paper marker in place, the material was cut by one of two Gerber cutting machines. These cutting machines utilized a vacuum to keep the material in place and, with high-speed, computer-programmed movements, cut the various pieces of the coat or pants to be assembled.

```
RPT-PAY032              MODEL MASTER LISTING              1/04/96
```

MODEL-C236ZCS5NC PLN

OPER	DESCRIPTION	WRKCTR	PRICE	S-A-M	SINGLE	SUB-FLAG
SUB ASSEMBLY 00030-SLEEV						
28	JN 1ST SLEEVE	00701	.1161	.0000	.1277	
132	UP 1ST SLV SM	00701	.0700	.0000	.0736	
32	MK SLV VT CRN	00701	.1309	.0000	.1441	
130	CRS SLVBT FUS	00701	.0754	.0000	.0831	
82	JN LBWSM PNST	00701	.2433	.0000	.2676	
133	U/PR 2ND SLSM	00701	.0906	.0000	.0952	
SUB ASSUMBLY TOTAL			.7263	.0000	.7913	
SUB ASSEMBLY 01045-SLVLG						
227	MK SLVLG HRMY	00702	.1174	.0000	.1291	
270	MK SLBTN 2&3	00702	.0344	.0000	.0360	N
287	FELCF TRN SVL	00702	.1345	.0000	.1483	
289	SW 3BT SL TRN	00702	.1038	.0000	.1142	Y
377	TCK SL LG TRN	00702	.1372	.0000	.1440	
400	PR OUT/SD LBW	00702	.0725	.0000	.0762	
415	MT/ATJKTKLTSL	00702	.0297	.0000	.0000	
428	MATCH SLEEVE	00702	.0867	.0000	.0889	
SUB ASSEMBLY TOTAL			.7162	.0000	.7367	
SUB ASSEMBLY 04155-BACK						
753	MKBKF/LNOVTPN	00705	.1445	.0000	.1590	
835	PRBKF/L NO/VT	00705	.1366	.0000	.1433	
843	BSTCNSMFLNOVT	00705	.0843	.0000	.0885	
841	FIT BACK F/L	00705	.1033	.0000	.1085	
903	MATCH BACKS	00705	.0389	.0000	.0408	
SUB ASSEMBLY TOTAL			.5076	.0000	.5401	
SUB ASSEMBLY 06161-FACLG						
1037	JOIN LINING	00707	.1744	.0000	.1918	
1058	COMPO IBP	00707	.1151	.0000	.1264	
1082	FIN2PKT/UNLBL	00707	.0000	.0000	.0000	
1087	SW BNK/CRE LB	00707	.1076	.0000	.1129	Y
1103	SEW EXTRA LBL	00707	.0574	.0000	.0602	N
1164	U/P LGFC 2PKT	00707	.0900	.0000	.0945	
1203	PR IN FACING	00707	.0422	.0000	.0444	
SUB ASSEMBLY TOTAL			.5867	.0000	.6302	
SUB ASSEMBLY 08066-FLAP						
1523	DIECUT FLP PN	00709	.0162	.0000	.0170	
1531	MAKE2FLPPL/ST	00709	.0712	.0000	.0783	

FIGURE C1 Model master listing for a coat.

Notes:

1. This portion of a Model Master Listing details the specific operations to perform, in sequence, for various subassemblies for the coat of suit model 236, a plain fabric model. These subassemblies include the sleeve, sleeve lining, back, facing-lining, flap, and so on. The entire listing contains 10 different subassemblies.

2. Each line consists of an operation number, a description of the operation, the work center number where it is performed, the piece rate price for a standard bundle, the standard allowed minutes (not applicable to the coat shop), and the piece rate price for a single unit. The sub-flag column denotes exceptions to the standard that are made for selected coats.

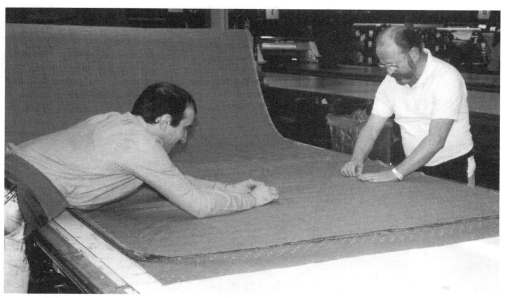

Spreading plaid cloth. *(Courtesy of Jos. A. Bank Mfg. Co.)*

Many of the cut pieces needed to be combined with "fusings," which in essence were special, lightweight backings that added stiffness to the fabric and helped the garment to keep its shape. After this process, the piece goods were then ready to be taken to the North Avenue plant for assembly.

The Coat Shop

The pieces that composed the same coat and/or pants were cut from the same layer in the spread fabric. After being cut, they were matched together and assembled (this assembly was termed "fitting") into various groups of materials—one group, for example, for the pants, one group for the coat. These matched and assembled cutouts of fabric were then either stapled with special identifying numbers by the Soabar marking and ticketing machine (see Figure C2), or, increas-

Inspecting newly received cloth. *(Courtesy of Jos. A. Bank Mfg. Co.)*

The Gerber cutter in action. *(Courtesy of Jos. A. Bank Mfg. Co.)*

ingly, they were tagged with paper labels by a Meto "gun." The Meto gun was easier to use and the small paper labels often did not need to be removed by hand from the garment as they were sometimes cut out of the garment during the course of assembly or else attached in a spot that was entirely hidden once the garment was assembled. These numbers were critical in ensuring that material cut

FIGURE C2 Sample Meto and Soabar tickets used by Jos. A. Bank to identify cut fabric.

Meto label for a pair of pants (regular)

The new Meto "gun" with an older Soabar machine in the background. (*Courtesy of Jos. A. Bank Mfg. Co.*)

for the same suit would stay together throughout the process. After being tagged, the pieces destined for a coat or pants were subdivided and assembled, or "fitted," into special bundles usually of 12 units for coats and 20 units for pants in each bundle. Bundles were fitted for various subassemblies of the coat, such as sleeves, fronts, backs, collars, facing, and linings.

Each bundle (batch) of materials to be processed in the coat shop would have the same operations performed on each of the pieces in the bundle. For the most part, workers in the shop did the same things to successive bundles of materials. A record of what was to be done to each bundle and how many items were in each traveled with the bundle.

Most operations in the coat shop consisted of sewing pieces of the fabric together and/or attaching various trim items to the fabric. The bundles representing parts of the coat were worked on separately in various areas of the coat shop. Periodically, some were brought together to make larger subassemblies before these were joined in the assembly that was the coat itself. At two key places in the shop and at several minor locations, these parts were matched before being sewn into a major subassembly. These matching stations served to control the process, ensuring that all pieces in each bundle were accounted for and that only those pieces of fabric that had been cut together would be assembled into a coat. Once the coat was fully assembled—linings in, welts and flaps sewn, facings fabricated and assembled to fronts, and sleeves assembled to the rest of the coat—it was ready for finishing. In finishing, any basting (temporary stitches) was removed, various parts of the coat were pressed, and the coat was thoroughly inspected. Once inspected, the coat was transported to the matching warehouse in Hampstead. At the matching warehouse, pants and coats for the same suit were placed together and taken to the adjacent distribution center. Orders were filled from the distribution center.

Pants underwent similar, although simpler, processing (see Figure C3).

```
RPT-PAY032              MODEL MASTER LISTING              1/19/96
```

MODEL-P95XAPS5NP PLN

OPER	DESCRIPTION	WRKCTR	PRICE	S-A-M	SINGLE	SUB-FLAG

SUB ASSEMBLY 21043-- W/B

OPER	DESCRIPTION	WRKCTR	PRICE	S-A-M	SINGLE	SUB-FLAG
6050	FUSE W/B	00801	.0215	.0000	.0226	
6051	CUT W/B FUS	00801	.0225	.0000	.0225	
6052	LOOP MAKE PRS	00801	.0246	.0000	.0259	
6078	ROCAP WB	00801	.0339	.0000	.0356	
6103	LABEL SEW 1	00801	.0193	.0000	.0203	
6126	CT WB PR BNDL	00801	.0214	.0000	.0224	
SUB ASSEMBLY TOTAL			.1432	.0000	.1493	

SUB ASSEMBLY 22598-ASEMB

OPER	DESCRIPTION	WRKCTR	PRICE	S-A-M	SINGLE	SUB-FLAG
6219	ATT METO TKTS	00802	.0561	.0000	.0000	N
6220	ATT JOKER TKT	00802	.0221	.0000	.0000	N
6227	FIT&LOAD PNTS	00802	.0729	.0000	.0765	
6237	FT&BKSRB/STND	00802	.1166	.0000	.1282	
6277	SET RGT FY LG	00802	.0264	.0000	.0278	
6301	SET LEFT ZIP	00802	.0359	.0000	.0395	
6317	SW 6 PLT TOP	00802	.0790	.0000	.0869	
6320	PRSFRTPLTTPST	00802	.0559	.0000	.0587	
6327	JN SERGE HIP	00802	.0525	.0000	.0656	
6354	FAC ODD LABEL	00802	.0496	.0000	.0544	
6378	FRT PKT FAC	00802	.1113	.0000	.1225	
6402	RGT&LFT FLY	00802	.1146	.0000	.1261	
6415	SERG CROTCHPC	00802	.0293	.0000	.0324	
6430	HANG POCKET 1/8 TOP	00802	.0698	.0000	.0770	
6453	FRTPKT CRD&TK	00802	.1082	.0000	.1192	
6503	SEW 2 DARTS	00802	.0357	.0000	.0393	
6526	COMPO SET HIP	00802	.0674	.0000	.0741	
6552	PR2HP&TRNBLCK	00802	.0650	.0000	.0683	
6604	HIP PKT CLSE2	00802	.0799	.0000	.0879	
6605	STITCH HIP PKT	00802	.1009	.0000	.1060	
6637	2TKS EAPKT OP	00802	.0818	.0000	.0900	
6680	PRJNSSPNST1/8	00802	.1393	.0000	.1534	
6703	PRS SIDESEAM	00802	.0468	.0000	.0493	
6727	CLS SIDEPKT	00802	.0762	.0000	.0762	
6739	TACK FRNT PKT	00802	.0409	.0000	.0431	
6756	CUT/SETLPS6-8	00802	.1763	.0000	.1938	
6776	WB PRESS-VIET	00802	.0669	.0000	.0703	
6827	SET 2HOOK&EYE	00802	.0278	.0000	.0293	
6856	MKFRTCRNRGW/B	00802	.0774	.0000	.0852	
6906	PRSRT&LFT FLY	00802	.0986	.0000	.1035	
6926	ST RTFLY RGEX	00802	.0336	.0000	.0369	
6927	JSTLTFLY RGEX	00802	.0309	.0000	.0341	
6952	MS/JNPN/STMET	00802	.0973	.0000	.1069	
6977	WAISTBAND FEL	00802	.0546	.0000	.0575	
7005	LOOP TK 10	00802	.1445	.0000	.1589	
7032	FLY/PKT/EXBH3	00802	.0839	.0000	.0922	
7054	INSM SW PN/ST	00802	.0943	.0000	.1037	
7079	ZIPLOCK PN/ST	00802	.0701	.0000	.0737	
7102	CROTCH SEW	00802	.0678	.0000	.0744	
7126	TAIL SEW	00802	.0569	.0000	.0597	

FIGURE C3 Model master listing for a pair of pants.

Notes:

1. This portion of a Model Master Listing details the specific operations to perform, in sequence, for a pair of pants, a plain fabric model.
2. Like the Model Master Listing for the coat, each line indicates the operation number, operation description, work center number, standard bundle piece-rate price, standard allowed minutes, single unit piece-rate price, and the sub-flag (exceptions) indication.

The Workforce and the Piece-Rate System

Except for some nonunion clerical workers, all the workers in the manufacturing facilities were members of UNITE, the Union of Needle Trades Industrial and Textile Employees. These workers were paid an incentive wage, although the type of incentive differed across departments. Workers in the coat and pants shops were paid piece rates. These piece rates were the prices in dollars per piece that the company paid for each piece of sewing, pressing, matching, or inspection.

When workers finished their assigned tasks, they detached the appropriate cardboard coupon from the perforated sheet of coupons (Figure C4) that traveled with the job. On the coupon was an operation number that was uniquely

FIGURE C4 Coupons.

Notes:

1. This is a portion of a page of coupons for the assembly of a pair of pants. Workers, as they completed a bundle, detached the relevant coupon and put it on a sheet for the day's work. The payroll department then wanded the top row with a laser scanning wand.

2. The top row of each coupon is used for payroll purposes only and indicates the shop number, bundle number, and operator number.

3. The middle row of each coupon provides a description of the operation (e.g., press sideseam, close sidepocket) and, where appropriate, indicates what trim items are to be used.

4. The bottom indicates the bundle number, the cut number (same as shop number), the operation number, and the quantity in the bundle.

identified with the piece rate for performing the indicated job. By accumulating these coupons and turning them in at the end of the day, workers were paid for exactly what they had done. There was no minimum payment and no maximum payment. In actuality, the wage payment averages in the coat and pants shops ran about 110 percent of the established standard, with a range for experienced workers from 80 percent of the standard to 160 percent. The coupons that workers turned in were read by a laser wand so that payroll and work-in-process were tracked automatically.

This piece-rate system was modified somewhat for the cutting room workers. Time standards were set for all operations in the cutting room—spreading the fabric, cutting the patterns, and other tasks. The standards were called "standard allowed minutes" (S-A-M) and workers in the cutting room were paid for the standard allowed minutes that they acquired rather than for the pieces of work that they were able to finish. However, a pay floor was established; workers who did not accumulate 8 hours of standard allowed minutes during the day earned a set base rate. Workers who accumulated more than 8 hours of standard allowed minutes were paid for those minutes. In fact, the average in the cutting room ran between 120 and 125 percent of the established standards, with the range being between 100 and 160 percent for experienced workers. Workers were paid by filing incentive declarations that documented start and stop times for various operations. There were no coupons to detach as in the coat or pants shop.

There were times when workers were not paid piece rates but were paid the average of their work. This occurred whenever a worker was taken off his or her standard job to do something else. For example, if a worker was asked to fill in for an absent colleague, that worker was taken off the piece-rate system. Similarly, if a worker was asked to work on something new or something special, piece rates were removed.

Applying fusings to cut out material. *(Courtesy of Jos. A. Bank Mfg. Co.)*

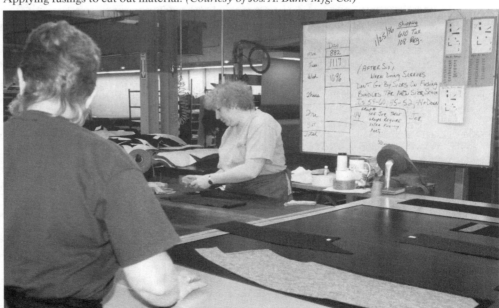

Once a piece rate had been established, it could not be changed without some change in model, materials, methods, or machinery. There were literally thousands of piece rates that could apply in the shop, and typically less than 10 percent of them were changed each year. Some had remained unchanged for years. Many changes were, in fact, triggered by a worker's retirement. (Turnover was only 2 to 3 percent a year.)

Management recognized that the piece-rate system caused some wage inequities in the factory, but there seemed to be no clear solutions. It was known, for example, that some piece rates were tight whereas others were loose; but if no changes were contemplated to those jobs, management could not remedy those inequities easily without union consent. Spotting such inequities was not always simple. Variations in performance across operators doing the same job could range from 90 percent of the standard to 150 percent. Given such variations, it was often hard to say that a particular piece rate was loose when for at least some workers it might be considered tight.

Setting New Piece Rates

Establishing new piece rates was the responsibility of the factory's industrial engineer, who spent about 60 percent of his time determining piece rates and the rest of his time calculating the factory's unit costs and following up on special projects (such as studying new equipment purchases). The first step the industrial engineer took in setting a new piece rate in the coat or pants shop was to meet with the foreman in charge to discuss the procedure that the foreman thought was required to do a good-quality job. An operator was then brought in and informed of the new task. He or she was given some time to become familiar with the work. After that time the industrial engineer observed the operator for about an hour and a half, informing the operator that this study would result in the establishment of the piece rate.

During this observation period, the industrial engineer used an electronic time study board—a clipboard to which was attached a special digital readout stopwatch that kept track of various times. By pressing a lever the engineer could indicate the beginning of one element of the job (jobs were composed of 2 to 30 elements) or the end of another. The time study board would then freeze the duration measured so that the engineer could write it down while at the same time accumulating the time of the next element of the job. In this way the industrial engineer isolated particular movements and tasks. The engineer could also evaluate whether the operator was working as efficiently as possible and just where improvements could be made.

Setting piece rates was complicated by an agreement the company had with the union. That agreement specified that workers would be given the opportunity to maintain the same average wage no matter where they worked in the shop. Abiding by this agreement meant that new piece rates for established workers in the company had to be constructed specifically for those workers. As could be expected, new jobs with new piece rates were generally assigned to new workers, since that was one means by which costs could be kept under control.

This company-union agreement made setting piece rates in the coat and pants shops somewhat more difficult than setting rates in the cutting room. To comply with the agreement in the cutting room, all that needed to be changed was the base pay of the operator. The standard allowed minutes for a task remained the same. However, for average wages in the coat and pants shops to be maintained, some juggling of the piece rates normally assigned to a worker had to be

Piece goods storage. *(Courtesy of Jos. A. Bank Mfg. Co.)*

done. The old piece-rate system was not as "clean" as the newer standard allowed minutes system, but it did work well for the coat and pants shops.

Once the piece rate was established, the industrial engineer informed the worker of it. The union was also notified. Often this was all that was needed, although many times some negotiation with the union ensued. Sometimes a restudy of the job was done to dispel any disagreements. Some restudies lasted as long as 8 hours. When a piece rate was first changed, it was deemed "unapproved," but usually after a month the union and management would agree that the piece rate was fair. Then the rate was formally approved until it had to be changed because of changes in model, materials, methods, or machinery. The company wanted to set rates that could be beat if the workers worked hard—but not so tight that the workers felt they were not earning a fair incentive wage. In 9 out of 10 cases there was little problem in establishing a piece rate, although company and union both had to compromise their initial positions to some degree.

The Nature of the Workforce

Many in the workforce had had years of experience in the apparel industry. Others, notably immigrants from Russia and Asia, were new to the industry and required considerable training to meet Jos. A. Bank's high quality standards.

For the most part, once a new operator was assigned a job, it was likely that he or she stayed at that job until retirement. Almost all of the workers spent many years at the same level in the company; only about 10 percent attempted to elevate their grade. Advancement was possible, and workers could request transfers to higher-rate jobs through a formal job posting system for vacancies.

The company's relations with the union were good. It helped that the company was growing in an industry that, for the most part, had suffered severe employment declines. In the last 25 years there had been only one strike, and it was resolved very quickly. Worker complaints were few—only two or three informal complaints each week, and these were usually resolved quickly. In general, complaints related to earnings, such as one alleging that a piece rate was set too low.

As many as 90 percent of these complaints were resolved by the factory's first-line supervision. There was, however, a formal grievance procedure, which involved supervision at the first level, the plant manager at the second level, the vice-president of manufacturing at the third level, and then arbitration at the fourth level. There had been only two arbitration proceedings in the last 20 years. Most of the complaints taken to higher levels of the grievance procedure related to firings, which typically occurred for absenteeism or poor quality. For the most part, union involvement could save a worker from the first threat of firing; but if the worker did not improve, management could fire the worker without union intercession. The only instant and uncontested dismissals were for theft, gross insubordination, or fighting in the factory.

Dismissal, of course, was the most radical form of discipline that the company used. Other levels of discipline were usually used before a dismissal. The most minor form of discipline was a verbal warning, and in most cases two or three verbal warnings were given before a written warning was issued. This written warning would give the reason for the warning, suggest a way for the worker to correct matters, state what the next step would be if the worker did not improve, and indicate at what future time the worker would be reviewed again. If the worker did not improve, there might be another written warning, and after that would come suspension from work. Some suspensions carried definite starting and ending dates, while others were of indefinite duration. Only if these measures did not resolve matters would the worker be dismissed.

Worker pay depended on the task and the shop. Average hourly wages in the Baltimore coat and pants shops averaged $8.75 for direct labor and $8.70 for indirect labor; in the cutting room, $10.71 for direct labor and $7.95 for indirect labor; and in the Hampstead distribution center, $8.45.

In addition to these wages, Bank paid about 43 percent of base salary in benefits. These included medical and disability insurance, life insurance, a pension plan, an eye care plan, a prescription plan, and holiday and vacation pay. The pension plan was administered by the company, but the medical and insurance plans were administered through the union.

It was the responsibility of the factory's industrial engineer to monitor costs and piece rates once they were set. Foremen also helped monitor tasks, since they had to sign off on all worker summary sheets and were required to calculate the percentage efficiencies for each worker. Thus, the workers who were consistently making well above average on their piece rates were known. If their high pay was a surprise, their jobs and/or quality were sometimes studied to make sure that they were not taking shortcuts.

Production and Quality Control

Jos. A. Bank's quality standards were rigid. Not only did the company not tolerate sloppy work in the factory, but it also wanted to make sure that a 40 regular one year exactly matched a 40 regular in every other year.

Quality control started at the beginning of the process. Numerous areas of the factory had their quality checked by the appropriate foremen on every coat or pants processed. The chief final inspection area, however, was in pressing, after the coat or pair of pants was fully assembled.

The foremen, who supervised between 30 and 35 people each, were responsible chiefly for checking quality and for instilling in the workers an appreciation of what quality is and a desire to flag quality problems themselves. It was the foremen's task as well to approach workers with any rework. Workers were responsible for the quality of their own work, and any rework on their portion of a coat or pants was done without pay. It was to the worker's advantage to do things right

Trolleys of pants in the pants shop. *(Courtesy of Jos. A. Bank Mfg. Co.)*

the first time, every time. The chief role of first-level supervision at Bank was to check and maintain quality. Nothing else took so much time and care.

The control of production, as opposed to quality, was chiefly the responsibility of the plant managers to whom the first-level supervisors reported. These plant managers were as well known to the workforce as the foremen. It was as if factory supervision had been split in two, with the foreman responsible largely for quality and the plant manager responsible largely for materials and production control.

Fitting in the coat shop. *(Courtesy of Jos. A. Bank Mfg. Co.)*

The factory could produce 900 coats and 1000 pants per day. It generally took 5 weeks for a coat to travel through the process, from the laying out of fabric in the cutting room to the transport of the finished coat to the distribution center. The primary concern of production control was to make sure that all the parts for a coat moved smoothly through the factory and arrived at the various matching stations at about the same time so that they could be joined with specific other parts for further processing. Naturally, some parts took more labor than other parts to complete. For example, backs might be sewn in 5 minutes, while fronts might take an hour. To ensure a steady flow of goods through the factory, the workforce on fronts was 12 times larger than the one on backs. If parts were not ready, production had to shift to another lot, and operations were not as smooth as they could be.

Two critical matching stations helped control the flow of parts through the process and uncover any shortages. The first matching station, located about a quarter of the way through the process, was where backs were matched with fronts. The other key matching station was where sleeves were matched with the front and back subassembly; this occurred when the coat was about 75 percent complete. Matching was accomplished by looking at the tickets that had been attached to the materials near the start of the process. As we saw in Figure C2, the ticket numbers supplied various information, chiefly the size of the coat being fabricated, the cloth lot to which it belonged, and the shade (a number for the bolt of cloth, which was the same for all pieces belonging to the same coat). The matching stations collated pieces by using these numbers.

If there were quality problems or if particular parts could not be located, fabric sometimes had to be recut. Naturally, Jos. A. Bank wanted any recuts to be

A sewing operation in the pants shop. *(Courtesy of Jos. A. Bank Mfg. Co.)*

A sewing operation in the coat shop. *(Courtesy of Jos. A. Bank Mfg. Co.)*

from the same bolt of cloth that the original had come from; thus, lot numbers and shade numbers, as well as shop numbers, were recorded for any item that had to be recut. One day was allotted to do a recut and to rework the materials so that they could rejoin their bundle in the standard flow of work through the shop. Production control did not want to break apart any bundles of material except for super-rush jobs, which occurred about once a week. For all other jobs the bundles were kept the same.

Formal records were kept, showing which lots were started in the shop through the fitting operation and where the bundles were in the shop. Using the laser wand on the worker coupons provided the information needed to keep this tracking up to date.

Because of rework needed or production problems that might be encountered, the capacities of the upstream operations tended to be slightly higher than the capacities of the downstream operations. To avoid the accumulation of work-in-process inventory, the factory wanted to make sure that it could easily recoup any extra time spent in the early stages of the process. Some models were more difficult to make than others—for example, double-breasted tuxedos. When and how many of these coats to make at one time had to be carefully evaluated. This concern for extra capacity in the early stages of the process was particularly evident when plaids were done. As mentioned previously, plaids were the most difficult fabrics to work with because of pattern alignment for pockets, collars, back seams, and so on. This pattern alignment led to a 10 to 15 percent drop in production and a good bit more rework. (Rework in plain fabrics amounted to only 2 or 3 percent of any production lot, but in plaids the rework figure generally climbed to between 5 and 8 percent.)

As noted earlier, the first-level supervisor's prime responsibility was quality. Another of his or her tasks was to deal with absences. The first 15 minutes of the morning were spent determining whether everyone was there (absences averaged only 5 percent) and finding replacements for those absent. A number of the workers were cross-trained to fill in on other tasks; when such a switch occurred, they were paid their average earnings rather than the piece rates for these jobs. (There were also some specified utility workers who were paid their choice of a flat rate or a piece rate for the job.) The workers who were put on absentee work generally came from those who were ahead of the pace of the factory as a whole and could thus afford to take time off from their jobs.

The flow of information to the worker from the foreman generally concerned rework or methods. The flow of information from worker to foreman could be for a variety of problems: machine malfunctions, damaged goods, poor quality upstream. The plant managers handled all grievances about piece work and about change in the operation.

Loading the Factory

The specific planning for, say, the next year's spring fashions began in March. From March through June, the merchandising division reviewed planned sales for both retail stores and the catalog. As a result, manufacturing received a production "layout" for spring deliveries. From the layout, purchase orders for goods were sent on to manufacturing, authorizing production.

Orders for particular bolts of cloth (piece goods) were then placed with various mills. Jos. A. Bank had long had dealings with many mills and knew exactly which mills it wanted to produce particular fabrics, although, especially for fashion items, the company was doing more spot buying. For many piece goods, about 10 percent extra was purchased so as to give the company some flexibility if demand exceeded the forecast. Because Jos. A. Bank fashions changed in only subtle ways from year to year, any surplus material could probably be used the following year; being caught with more fabric than required was not nearly as much a problem as being caught with too little. On those rare occasions when there was not enough fabric for a particular model, the merchandising division sometimes was able to reorder fabric from the mills. The fabric ordered for the next year's spring fashions arrived during the summer. Any necessary examining or sponging (preshrinking) was done, although, increasingly, fabric arrived from the mills "needle-ready." Cutting began in August. Delivery to the distribution center started in October and delivery to the stores in December. From December to June or July the spring line was sold.

Manufacturing had no responsibility for the purchase of fabric, the factory's single most important raw material. All responsibility and authority for selection and purchasing rested with the merchandising division. However, manufacturing was charged with the purchase of the numerous trim items that were combined with the piece goods to make coats or pants. Manufacturing also kept track of the status of the piece goods inventory: quantities remaining and their locations. For trim items such as shoulder pads, fusings, and sleeve heads, there were always two sources of supply; the split between the vendors depended upon price. Commitments to vendors typically extended six months in advance, but the shipment of items was specified for much narrower, weekly, time periods.

Many of the vendors had been dealing with Jos. A. Bank for 30 years or more. New vendors were occasionally chosen, and, increasingly, spot buys were

Pressing seams open in the pants shop. *(Courtesy of Jos. A. Bank Mfg. Co.)*

done for highly fashion-sensitive items or when bargains were available. Vendor qualification was handled by design/quality control, which tested the item's physical characteristics (such as stretching and pulling) as well as the way it behaved when sewn or dry cleaned. If a vendor was deemed qualified, the trim purchasing manager negotiated the price. Typically, new vendors started with small orders as a further check on quality and delivery capabilities and on the stability of the pricing structure. Only if these tests were passed would the order be enlarged for subsequent years.

Production Planning

The production plans began with broad, large-scale decisions, which were subsequently refined and made more detailed. The broadest plans involved ranges—aggregate counts of fabric needs by type. Thus, there were ranges within plains, within stripes, within herringbones, and within plaids. These ranges were then broken down into particular quantities of specified fabrics required; they helped define what was cut and assembled during the entire season. A particular week's production plan was part of a monthly batch of work from the merchandising division. The merchandising division balanced finished goods de-

The major matching station in the coat shop where sleeves join up with the body of the coat. (Courtesy of Jos. A. Bank Mfg. Co.)

liveries to meet catalog and retail store sales. It was the merchandising division's responsibility to monitor sales and to adjust subsequent batch "purchase orders" accordingly.

The production schedule set was typically for an 8-week period. The first week was allocated to planning, the next 2 weeks to cutting, and the ensuing 5 weeks to the shop. What was cut in a particular week depended on the expected finished goods inventory and piece goods availability.

Once the merchandising division provided the initial batches (batches contained specific purchase orders for defined finished goods deliveries), the batches were matched to the available piece goods inventories. Paperwork was then initiated to direct and control the transformation of fabric into suits, coats, and pants. The production plan for any week triggered several actions in the cutting room office. The key document was the computer-generated group sheet (Figure C5), which detailed how many units of a particular model would be cut for each size. Given that information, a cloth pull sheet (Figure C6) was authorized to withdraw fabric from inventory. Authorization to cut the cloth was also provided by the computer. It created a cutting slip and the accompanying cutting chart (Figure C7), which indicated, for each lot number, the quantities and the size combinations for the markers or patterns that were actually used to cut the fabric. The cutting slip and the cutting chart traveled with the job. After the materials were cut and fitted, the Soabar report (Figure C8) was issued by the cutting room office. This report indicated not only the lot number but also the make, model, and size for all the bundles of fabric to be processed. The data entry for the Soabar report generated, via a special computer program, the fitter's report, which indicated the lot, bundle, and quantities, by size, that were to be run through each shop. The fitter's report in turn generated the coupons that traveled with the job and were critical to the operation of the piece-rate system.

The paperwork just described served to follow up on the production planning by initiating work in the cutting room and the shops of the factory. Other pa-

GROUP SHEET

| GROUP # 107 SHOP: | CMODEL C710H REG: 7435 | PMODEL# SHRT: 7437 | VMODEL# LONG: 7436 | YRSEA 5F XLONG 7438 | DUEDATE 960204 MAKE: 03 | OTM MONTH | ISSUE DATE: 01/25/96 PG PATTERN   STR |

COMMENTS:

| LOT # 26851 | PO # 48348 COLLECTION EXEC | DESCRIPTION : INSTRUCTION :2ND ORDER 86851 | CLASS/VENDOR/STYLE/COLOR   1170/05000/1203/141 CONTENT: 100% WOOL |

LOT #

REGULARS SHOP #: 7435														SHORTS SHOP #: 7437							
TOTAL	37	38	39	40	41	42	43	44	45	46	48	50	TOTAL	36	38	40	41	42	43	44	TOTAL
1398	1	23	41	85	85	157	99	118	36	85	43	7	780	2	5	32	11	29	6	7	92

LONGS SHOP #: 7436											X-LONGS SHOP #: 7438					
39	40	41	42	43	44	45	46	48	50	TOTAL	42	43	44	46	48	TOTAL
3	24	36	85	65	98	25	77	59	24	496	8	2	8	5	7	30

LINING: DK NAVY 3914.40	FUSING: H N CLR 3960 3960 T	BUTTON: U.S. BUTTON T1785	THREAD EDGE UC-03	THREAD BTNALE 574	SIL: ABEF 1398
UC 9431 166.43	CHEST 471 PIECE 1398	SHOULDER 34 PAD 1398	SLEEVE 41 HEAD	THREAD PNT-TS BLK	THREAD SERGE 10658	ZIPPER: YDDS ***** SLIDER
PANT POCKET: BLK	WB: ******	F/L 4613.40	PKT-SET1398	

FIGURE C5 Group sheet.

Note:

This is the group sheet for a sport coat, model C710H. The group number is 107 and the shop numbers are 7435 through 7438. The various components of this sport coat are noted on the group sheet. The group sheet tells how many of which sizes and variations are to be made. Note that the 42 Regular is the single most popular size.

perwork served to help control the movement of materials through the factory and to cope with irregularities (such as rework, recutting, and failed matchings).

Technological Innovation

Apparel manufacture, especially the manufacture of high-quality merchandise such as Jos. A. Bank's line, still required operator involvement and manual handling of suit parts. Innovations such as automatic thread trimmers and needle positioners, and work aids to improve operator efficiency and to reduce handling time had been implemented. There were some automatic machines for pocket cutting and other tasks, but most of the factory's sewing machines were strictly manual.

There had been other investments over the years in improved technologies, especially in the cutting room. The AM-5 machines for automatically generating markers for the cutting room were among the first of these. They eliminated waste in laying out the piece goods, and they automatically increased sizes, saving considerable time in the design of the markers themselves. New equipment for piece goods inspection, for fusings, and for steaming cloth had also been purchased and implemented. More recently came the introduction of the Gerber cutting ma-

MODEL: C710H SPORT COAT   **TYPE OF CLOTH:** STRIPE – WOOL   WK8

DELIVERED BY: **RECEIVED BY:**   **DATE:** 12-18

	Lot No.	Ydg. Rec'd	Shade	Ydg.	Loc.	Shade	Ydg.	Loc.	Shade	Ydg.	Loc.	Shade	Ydg.	Loc.
F95	26851	2.12					(745.5)							
61	7435R	332/704	(R165A)	25.6	4208	109	51.0	4209	122	63.2	4209			
60½	7436L	216/458	868	51–	S95	103	108.5	4179	107	106.0	4179			
59	7437S	40/85	81	73.2	4179	100	104.7	4178	109	107.2	4179			
⊥	7438 XL	14/30	74	106.1	4179	balback								
P.O.	48348	(1277)												
			L 121	105.5	FLR	105	26.4	4209	139	107.5	FLR			
			81	105.2	FLR	75	36.0	4074	(165)	80	4208			
							(460.6)							
			S138	126.5	4209									
			XL											

FIGURE C6 Cloth pull sheet.

Note:

This is the cloth pull sheet for group 107, sport coats of model C710H. The sheet indicates the yards of fabric cut for each lot, the shade (bolt of fabric), and where that bolt of fabric was located (the bin number). It shows how much of what to use and what to tell the spreaders.

chines and the development of the plaid spreading process. Productivity had improved each year in all product types.

PART TWO: DISCUSSION

CUTTING CHART   Page: 1

GROUP #	107	COAT MODEL C/710/H/		PG PTRN	STR	MAX PLY	35
PO #	48348	PANT MODEL				# SIZES	96
LOT #	26851	VEST MODEL		TABLE LENGTH			
PATTERN		MAKE	03	TOTAL UNITS	1398	DATE	01/25/96
WIDTH	.	FIBER 100% WOOL	1170	DUE DATE	96/02/04	OTB MONTH	

SPREAD INSTR:
SPECIAL INSTR: 2ND ORDER 86851

	1	2	3	4	5	6	7	8	9	10	11
MARKERS	Remnant	Remnant	Remnant	Remnant	DEV05	DEV02	DEV07	DEV04	DEV09	DEV10	DEV14
WIDTH											
LENGTH YD/INCH											
CUMM LENGTH											
SIZES	40R	41R	42R	46R	40R 41R 42R 46R	40R 41R 42R 46R	43R 44R 44R 48R	42R 42R 43R 44R	38R 39R 43R 45R	39R 40R 41R 46R	42R 44R 45R 48R
NUMBER OF SIZES	0	0	0	0	4	4	4	4	4	4	4
48348/26851 TOTAL STR DK NAVY					35	35	35	35	23	15	8

-ENDS- 40R, 41R, 42R, 46R

```
PO #: 48348
============
REG:    7435
SHRT:   7437
LONG:   7436
XLONG:  7438
```

FIGURE C7 Cutting sheet used by a spreader.

Note:

This is a portion of the cutting chart for an order for group 107, sport coat model C710H, a dark navy stripe. The cutting chart indicates which size combinations will be used for the markers on this order and how many of each lot and shade of fabric are to be cut.

The Process and Information Flows

In comparison with the job shop of Norcen Industries, the flow of production at Jos. A. Bank is better defined. While there are some understandable differences between the coat shop and the pants shop, we can compose a process flow diagram for each of those shops that adequately represents the process, at least in general terms (see Figure C9). A more detailed process flow diagram, one that encompasses the actual operations described on the coupons, would reveal that there are still substantial differences between various products (such as suit coat versus sport coat), models, and materials. Variations in any one of these lead to the inclusion of certain process steps and the exclusion of others. In general, however, the flow of materials through the process is fairly smooth and easily directed. Concern for materials routing is much less critical in this batch flow process than in a job shop.

Because of the wide variety of materials, models, and sizes, the factory must deal with a vast array of different batches. These variations underscore the still

SOABAR REPORT

| GROUP # 107 | VARIATION: REGULAR | | SEASON YEAR: 5F | | DUE DATE: 96/02/04 | | FACTORY: H | | Drop Table #: 1 |

	DROP SIZES	46	46	46	43	43	41	41	41	41	40	40	40	39	39	39	39	39	37	37	
		50R	50R	50R	48R	48R	46R	46R	46R	46R	45R	45R	45R	44R	44R	44R	44R	44R	43R	43R	TOT
REG: 7435 48348/26851 STR DK NAVY COLLECTION: EXEC SKU: 1170/05000/1203/141 CMODEL: C710H PMODEL: VMODEL:		2	2	3	8	35	15	35	35		5	8	23	5	8	35	35	35	1	5	
	TOTAL SIZE			7		43				85			36					118			
		50R	50R	50R	48R	48R	46R	46R	46R	46R	45R	45R	45R	44R	44R	44R	44R	44R	43R	43R	
GRAND TOTAL		2	2	3	8	35	15	35	35		5	8	23	5	8	35	35	35	1	5	
COMMENTS:																					

FIGURE C8 Fitter's or Soabar report.

Note:

This is a fitting or Soabar report for shop number 7485, the regular versions for group 107, sport coat model C710H, due out of the shop on February 4, 1996. The report indicates the exact sizes and how many of each should be made for the lot of fabric fitted.

very strong need of the batch flow process for information and control. In their own way, the information flows of the batch flow process are inflexible, although compared with the job shop, the flow of information between workers and management is somewhat reduced. While workers are responsible for notifying management of machine malfunctions and quality problems, the major information flows to and from workers revolve mainly around the coupons that move with each bundle, as shown in Figure C10. In essence, the coupons serve as both process sheet and job sheet, to borrow language from the Norcen Industries example. The coupons inform the worker of what must be done to the batch, and they also keep track of who did what to each batch of work.

FIGURE C9 A simplified process flow diagram for a Jos. A. Bank suit.

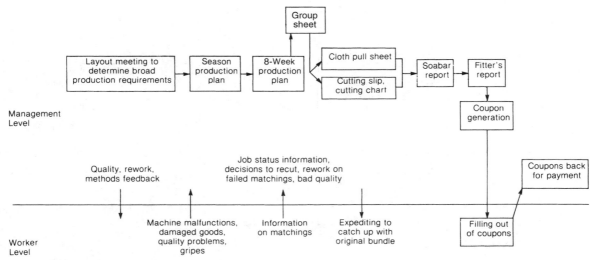

FIGURE C10 A simplified information flow diagram for Jos. A. Bank.

The increased stability of the batch flow process reduces the amount of information that must be communicated from management to workers. The foreman typically has less troubleshooting and expediting to do and fewer scheduling changes to make. Therefore, it is often possible to supervise more people in a batch flow operation than in a job shop. The foreman at Jos. A. Bank has time to track quality and improve methods rather than having to make schedules and troubleshoot.

The need for continuous flow of information is reduced in the batch flow process, primarily because its product selection, while large, is still limited and well known in advance. Furthermore, it seldom has to bid for contracts, and so precise, order-specific cost information is not required.

Capacity in the Batch Flow Process

The notion of capacity is only slightly less ambiguous in the batch flow operation than in the job shop. Nevertheless, the wide arrays of products that can be produced in any week make it difficult to specify a batch process's capacity in specific units of output without pegging it first to some standard mix of products.

The capacity of the batch flow process is influenced by many of the same factors that determine the capacity of the job shop.

1. *Batch (or lot) sizes.* Although the setup time for any bundle of materials is low at Jos. A. Bank relative to Norcen Industries, certain procedures are necessary (change of thread and needles) before a new batch can be processed. As mentioned in the process description, the larger the batch, the more satisfied is the worker; too many low-count batches spur complaints from workers.

2. *Complexity of the products run through the operation.* As noted, plaids and stripes are markedly more difficult to handle than plain fabrics; when the production schedule includes a higher-than-normal percentage of these materials, the capacity of the entire coat shop declines.

3. *Nature of the jobs already on the factory floor.* Batch flow operations, like job shops, are subject to shifting bottlenecks and worker-machine interference. However, the definite

limits to product diversity in batch flows generally mean that the severity and frequency of these two capacity thieves are reduced.

4. *Scheduling.* Scheduling is still an important consideration with the managers of the batch operation but the task is generally simpler than in the job shop. Again, the reduction of products and capabilities offered accounts for the bulk of this difference. With the batch operation, scheduling begins to shed some of its critical importance to the success of the operation as a whole. Given a reasonable composition of orders for the week, scheduling becomes much more routine.

5. *Process improvement.*

6. *Number of machines and their condition.*

7. *Quantity and quality of labor input.*

The last three major influences on capacity, like many of the other influences cited, take on less importance for the typical batch operation than for the typical job shop. This is because the batch flow process itself is better defined, with workers more apt to be assigned to particular machines and less free to float among machines. The transition from job shop to batch operation accounts already for considerable process improvement (such as specific methods, worker aids at the workstation, quicker setups). Considering its routing tickets (coupons), assigned machines, and specialized training, the batch operation is more likely to treat machines and workers as one producing unit. Thus, capacity can be enhanced significantly by increasing both in similar proportions. This is not to say that equipment improvement cannot be made in the typical batch flow operation. Jos. A. Bank, for example, had made substantial investments in new cutting tables and spreading technology.

The Role of Standards and Incentives

At Jos. A. Bank the role of standards takes on a different function than at Norcen Industries. At Norcen, you will recall, standards were used to estimate times and costs for bidding on jobs and also to provide information for scheduling jobs through the shop. Although the second function for standards is retained at Bank, standards are not used for job cost estimation because there is no bidding for new orders. Rather, standards in the form of piece rates and standard-hour (i.e., the standard-allowed minutes system) incentives are used explicitly to determine worker compensation and thus to spur worker effort and output. In a sense, the piece-rate and standard-hour incentives act to pace work through the factory.

As the process description made plain, the setting of incentives at Jos. A. Bank is serious business. Great care is taken to see that they are both accurate and fair. Considerable time and expense are spent setting new piece rates, observing workers trying out new piece rates, and testing modifications in methods. The procedures for setting and using incentives and for resolving disputes over them are well established and routine.

Demands of the Process on Workforce and Management

The demands made on the workforce center around the incentive system. The system, rather than foremen, acts to pace production; thus, the demands for worker output are mainly triggered by the incentive system itself. Demands for quality output, on the other hand, come from the foremen. The foremen's most important job is to check the work that has been done and make sure that the methods being followed are proper.

At Jos. A. Bank, the ambition of workers is not great, and so not a lot of effort is expended to provide career paths for the workforce. Some other batch flow operations are more concerned with such issues. Of course, there is cross-training in a batch flow operation like Jos. A. Bank. Not only does cross-training help cope with absenteeism, but it also helps break bottlenecks, particularly chronic ones.

Clearly, one of management's chief concerns in a process like Jos. A. Bank's is the incentive system. The incentive rates should be fair to the workers but not so loose that costs get out of control. Striking a suitable balance is an important endeavor.

Apart from the incentive system, management must also be concerned with keeping the flow of work smooth. This means grouping work well and staying within guidelines for the materials mix. Not only must management be wary of the policies by which it loads the factory, but it must also track jobs through the process and act immediately to remedy any difficulties. While the flow of information is not as rigid and sophisticated as in a job shop, management must still pay considerable attention to the information pertinent to the flow of materials and jobs.

Questions

1. Compare and contrast the characteristics of the information flow in the batch flow process used by Jos. A. Bank with the information flow characteristics of the two other processes discussed in Tours A and B. Which process requires the least in the way of information flow from its managers? From its workers? Does anything replace the flow of information to workers or managers?

2. The typical duties of first-line supervision at Jos. A. Bank are divided between two people. What are the strengths and/or weaknesses of such an arrangement, as you see them?

3. Discuss the difference between the piece-rate and standard-hour schemes at Jos. A. Bank. Could the cutting room have been put on a piece-rate system? Had that been done, what complications would you have anticipated?

4. Under what conditions do you have the most confidence in the factory's ability to produce 900 coats a day? Under what conditions do you have the least confidence? Why?

5. How would you describe the market for Jos. A. Bank? What relationship, if any, does this market have to the production process chosen by the company?

6. In what ways is the union a help to Jos. A. Bank? A hindrance?

7. Could the low rate of movement of workers among jobs in the factory be related to the activities of the industrial engineer? Elaborate.

Situation for Study C-1
Brown, Smith & Jones (Bs&J)

Paul Alvarez has just been hired by BS&J as superintendent of the fabricated tank division. Paul's previous experience had been with a leading manufacturer of home heating systems where the processes were highly automated. At the previous firm the goods were also processed in a continuous manner, with a product line being set up for a year or more of production.

The products manufactured by the fabricated tank division were typically oil storage tanks made from sheet steel, which were sent to the customer much like a kit and were erected in remote oil fields. Occasionally, the firm sold the tanks in various sizes to other customers for other uses, such as to the military for the storage of diverse liquids like water and jet airplane fuel. Figure C11 is an example of

FIGURE C11 Typical tank and parts.

Notes:

1. A typical tank stave (1) is trimmed (if needed), (2) has holes punched on all sides, (3) is rolled to the approximate shape (depending on the tank diameter) on the pyramid roll, and (4) is flanged on both ends in a large brake press. The press is set up with a flanging that also causes the stave to be formed to the final shape according to the tank diameter. There is a flanging tool for each diameter tank.

2. The roof and floor sections are made from material similar to the tank staves, ranging from 1/8 inch to 1/4 inch, per the engineering design. If necessary, these sections can be made from material 4 feet by 12 feet. BS&J uses standard mill sizes to avoid the extra costs involved in having special sizes available; also, pieces that are too big would create construction problems. Two sections are usually cut from a single sheet:

a tank and some of the parts that must be fabricated. Table C1 is a partial process sheet for these parts. Figure C12 is a layout of the relevant processes.

Many of the smaller parts are common to most tanks, and they are made on a continuous basis to inventory requirements. There are three parts that are unique to each tank size: the tank side parts called staves, the triangular roof, and the bottom sections. The smallest tank, 1500-gallon capacity, requires five staves, five roof sections, and five floor sections. A 55,000-gallon tank, five rows high, re-

TABLE C1 Partial outline of the process (Brown, Smith & Jones)

Stave		Roof and Floor Sections	
Operation	*Process*	*Operation*	*Process*
Shear edges true	Sheet shear	Shear edges and split each sheet on diagonal	Sheet shear
Punch bolt holes in both ends	Brake press setup with punches	Punch/shear small end*	Punch press
Punch bolt holes in both sides	Brake press setup with punches	Shear large end	Circle shear
Roll to tank diameter	Pyramid rolls	Clean and paint	Paint line
Flange both ends	Brake press setup with correct flange	Pack and ship	
Clean and paint	Paint line		
Pack and ship			

*For typical tank sizes there were punch press tools for this. Others had to be laid out, circle sheared, and single punched.

quires 13 roof sections, 13 floor sections, and 65 staves. The typical order is for three tanks of the same size, but an order can be as small as one tank and has been as large as 15 tanks. The tanks are made to order, but BS&J has a backlog estimated at 1 ½ months' production.

Paul was hired because the fabricated tank division has been unable to meet scheduled shipping dates, quality problems are cropping up, and the workers are unhappy about never being able to earn any incentive pay. Paul thought he would focus on the manufacture of the side staves, roof, and floor sections. What information does he need next? What information should be included on parts routing sheets?

1. Draw a process flow diagram for the two major tank parts.
2. What information would you need in order to set up a production schedule for this shop?
3. What approaches would you suggest to Paul to help him with both his quality problems and his incentive pay problems?

Situation for Study C-2
Welch's Ice Cream

Ice cream production took place every weekday at Welch's, a shop that sold ice cream to the public. The entire process of making the ice cream was performed by Brad Gentry, an hourly employee. In addition, Brad had sole responsibility for inventory maintenance, quality control, and production scheduling. He worked about four hours a day during slow periods and about twice that during the peak season. Because he knew more than anyone else at the shop about production needs at any given time, and because he was decoupled from the sales portion of the business by an inventory of finished ice cream, Brad set his own hours. He usually worked from about 10 A.M. to 2 P.M.

The shop owned one ice cream machine with a 40-quart batch capacity. (The capacity refers to the finished volume rather than the volume of ingredients.) The

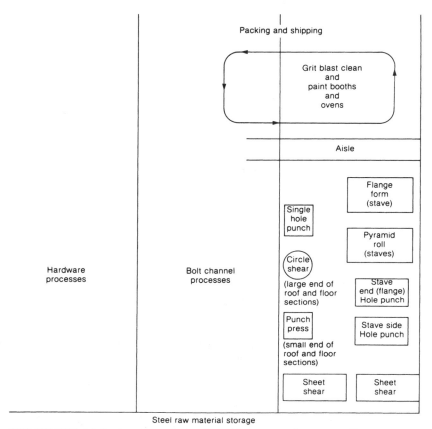

FIGURE C12 Fabricating process layout for a side stave, roof section, or floor section.

manufacturing process involved rapid agitation and aeration of the ingredients, which nearly doubled the batch's volume. Hence, a 40-quart batch required approximately 20 quarts of mix.

The machine itself resembled a stainless steel 20-gallon water heater, lying on its side on a waist-high stand. The cylinder had a refrigeration layer on the outside, through which refrigerants circulated when the machine was in use. At one end of the cylinder was the motor unit, which drove the refrigerant pump and the agitation blades inside the tank. At the other end was a lower spout, through which the finished ice cream was pushed by the rotation of the blades. A table was positioned here so that buckets on it could catch the ice cream. Above the spout were two built-in funnels, through which extracts and flavorings could be added. On top of the cylinder was a stainless steel tub, which held a little over 20 quarts of liquid.

The ice cream machine was located in a small room called the process room, which also contained a few shelves of supplies, reusable plastic buckets, scales, and a large sink. Three doors in the process room provided access to a walk-in refrigerator where the raw mix was kept, a walk-in freezer ($-30°$F) called the hardening box, and the rest of the premises.

The ingredients used in production were of three general types. The major type was the "mix," which was milk containing sweetener and a high cream content. An order of mix was delivered daily by a local dairy. This order consisted of five 50-pound cartons. Welch's placed an order with the dairy every day for delivery the next day, even though a different quantity was rarely ordered.

The second type of ingredient was the flavor bases: the various syrups and extracts that were added to the mix during agitation. The third type consisted of nuts, cookies, and some syrups that were "marbleized" into the ice cream. (Marbleization means that the ingredient is not beaten into the mix, but is poured into the stream of finished ice cream as it comes out the spout.)

The major vendor for the second and third types of ingredients was a company that usually delivered within 7 to 10 days after an order had been placed. This supplier paid freight costs but required a 15-case minimum. Brad took inventory on flavor bases once a month, and on marbleizing ingredients every 2 weeks. After taking inventory, Brad gave his boss a list of supplies needed and the boss did the ordering.

A production run began with sterilization of the ice cream machine and enough plastic buckets (a bucket equals 10 quarts) to hold the day's batches of ice cream. Each batch required 20 quarts of mix, and Brad usually made 6 batches a day, so Welch's received about 125 quarts of mix every day. Because the mix doubled during processing and the other ingredients also took up space, Brad used about 25 buckets per day.

While the machine and buckets dried, Brad checked the stock of ice cream in the tempering box, a walk-in freezer (adjacent to the hardening box) kept at 6°F. Ice cream in the hardening box was too cold to scoop, and so a sufficient inventory in the tempering box was necessary to ensure that Welch's did not run out of servable ice cream. After seeing which flavors were running low, Brad rotated those flavors from hardening to tempering box via a doorway connecting the two freezers. A map of ice cream locations was posted in the tempering box so that people who worked out front could easily find whatever flavor they needed. Maintaining this map was important because there were usually about 150 buckets ranging over 40 flavors stocked in this freezer. Welch's complete inventory comprised the contents of (1) the tempering box, (2) the hardening box (also an average of 150 buckets), and (3) the glass-topped refrigerators located in the service area (usually 32 buckets).

After rotating the stock, Brad took from the stock room the flavor bases and any other ingredients he needed that day. On Monday and Friday mornings, he took inventory of the hardening and tempering boxes and on the basis of this decided which flavors to make on a given day. Because he did not work weekends and Welch's sold 65 to 75 percent of its ice cream from Friday to Sunday, Brad had a target inventory for each flavor that he wanted to have on hand by Friday. The Monday inventory informed him how much of each flavor was sold over the weekend and therefore how much he needed to make above daily usage to reach Friday's target. The Friday inventory was a check that enough of each flavor was on hand for the weekend in the tempering box. By comparing usage figures from week to week, Brad could schedule flavor production to reflect demand. The target inventory was not a specific figure but rather a rough number that Brad carried in his head and altered according to his judgment. He did keep track of what he produced during the week, and he used this list to avoid duplicating batches or forgetting needed flavors. It was usually necessary to make two batches of vanilla a day, because about a third of all sales were vanilla.

Brad scheduled the batches from lightest taste and color to heaviest taste and darkest color. This way he avoided having to rinse the machine after every batch and saved 5 to 10 minutes, plus the ice cream that stuck to the blades. Vanilla was always first, because what little stayed in the machine blended well with the following batch. Brad could usually run three different flavors before having to rinse the machine.

Brad dumped 20 quarts of mix into the tub and allowed it to drain into the tank. He then closed the valve between the two and poured another 20 quarts into the tub, ready for the next batch. He turned on the agitator and added a measured amount of vanilla flavoring and cream tone. Welch's provided a complete index of recipes and instructions, but Brad had those for the most popular flavors memorized. He timed the batch—the first batch of the day for 10 minutes and the subsequent batches for 8 minutes. The first took longer because the machine was not yet cold.

When the time was almost up, he took a sample and weighed it. The batch was done if one cup weighed 90 to 95 grams, though chocolate flavors ran a bit denser. When ready, the ice cream was run out into buckets, covered with waxed paper, labeled with flavor and date, and placed in the hardening box, where it stayed for at least 12 hours before being rotated to the tempering box. Ice cream usually stayed in the hardening box for more than 12 hours; it would keep indefinitely at that temperature. When the end of the batch would not fill most of a bucket, Brad filled a few pint and quart cartons which, after freezing, were stored in a confection box at the front of the restaurant and sold. Although not a large business segment, this procedure avoided waste.

Brad repeated this batch process until he had either used up the five cartons of mix or made all he wanted to for the day. Normally he used all the mix, although it could be kept in the refrigerator for several days. When finished, he again sterilized the machine and washed the walls and floor of the process room before leaving. The cleanup took about 45 minutes.

1. Diagram the process and information flows for this process.
2. How would you plan production for such a process (i.e., how would you schedule which flavors would be produced and when, both during the day, the week, and the month)?
3. What controls on ice cream production would you use in this ice cream parlor? Why?

TOUR D

A Machine-Paced
Line Flow Process

Carrier Corporation[1]
Indianapolis, Indiana

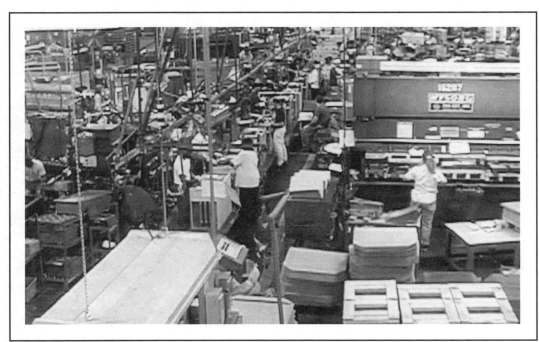

(Courtesy of Carrier Corporation)

Carrier Corporation was the world's largest manufacturer of air-conditioning, heating, and refrigeration equipment for commercial, residential, and transportation refrigeration applications. Carrier employed 35,000 people worldwide in 1996, had revenues of approximately $5.5 billion, and produced products in 12 countries. The Carrier Corporation produced a wide variety of products for home

---

[1]Used with the permission of Carrier Corporation.

comfort. These included gas furnaces, air conditioners, heat pumps, humidifiers, air cleaners, ventilators and fan coils. The Indianapolis plant of the Carrier Corporation was one of 10 plants that the company operated nationwide.

Carrier was the leading producer of gas furnaces and the Indianapolis plant was the world's largest gas furnace plant, and the only company plant producing gas furnaces and fan coils (the interior component of a heat pump system) for the United States. It was build in 1967 and had 550,000 square feet under roof. The Indianapolis site was also headquarters for the company's Residential Products division.

The corporation derived its name from Willis Carrier, who in 1902 designed the world's first scientific air-conditioning system. The Carrier Corporation was formed in 1915 and in 1955 acquired the Bryant Corporation whose founder, Charles Bryant, had designed the first tubular gas boiler in 1908. The Indianapolis plant's two leading name plates for furnaces were the Carrier brand and the Bryant brand.

Since 1979, the Carrier Corporation had been part of the United Technologies Corporation, whose other major business units included Pratt and Whitney (jet engines), Otis Elevators, Sikorsky Helicopters, Hamilton Standard (aerospace systems), and UT Automotive (components and systems). In 1996, United Technologies Corporation had revenues of $24 billion, and it ranked seventeenth in the Fortune 500 listing of major industrial companies.

The Indianapolis plant produced two major lines of gas furnaces, a non-condensing high-efficiency line and a condensing high-efficiency line. This tour will concentrate on the condensing high-efficiency line gas furnaces.

PART ONE: PROCESS DESCRIPTION

How a Gas Furnace Works

A residential gas furnace is made up of several key subassemblies. One is the burner box where the gas is ignited. The heat and the gases created by the combustion of the gas is carried through a series of heat exchangers and, in the condensing high-efficiency furnace, there are both primary and secondary heat exchangers. Air is heated around each of the heat exchangers and this heated air is then distributed throughout the house by the blower, another key subassembly for the furnace. (See Figure D1 for a cutaway drawing of a furnace.)

When a home thermostat calls for heat, the draft inducer, which is a fan that pulls air and combustion gases through the heat exchangers and out to the flue, clears out whatever air and gases may have been left in the heat exchangers and begins to pull fresh air in. The hot surface igniter, a ceramic head whose glowing surface ignites the gas, begins to heat up. Once this hot surface igniter is ready, the gas valve then releases gas to the burners and the burners are immediately ignited. Carrier's condensing high-efficiency gas furnaces have either two, three, four, five, or six burners, each of which is matched to a heat exchanger. Once the gas is ignited, the heat exchangers begin to heat up. The blower then kicks on and the warmed air around the outside of the heat exchangers is distributed throughout the house.

The Carrier condensing high-efficiency furnace was not only remarkably efficient in its use of fuel (as a maximum, it had a 96.6% annual fuel utilization efficiency measurement), but it was also multipoise. This meant that it could be in-

FIGURE D1   A gas furnace. *(Courtesy of Carrier Corporation)*

stalled either vertically or horizontally and laid on either its left or right side. This made installation easy and reduced the number of model variations that the factory had to produce. As it was, there were 93 different models of the condensing high-efficiency furnace (as compared to the more than 200 models of the older design non-condensing high-efficiency furnace).

Many of the components of a gas furnace consisted of sheet metal parts that had been stamped out and formed in various ways to create the housing for the furnace, the heat exchanger system, the blower unit, and many other components (a total of 85). The manufacture of these components was linked directly to the assembly line. Twenty-eight presses, all used to supply components to the condensing high-efficiency line, had, in recent years, been shifted from a separate press department into cells that manufactured parts to feed the assembly line. (See Figure D2 for a schematic diagram of the assembly line.)

A fabrication area. *(Courtesy of Carrier Corporation)*

The assembly line itself began with the construction of the housing (or "casing") for the furnace. A coil feeder fed a specially designed series of machines (the casing line) with coated sheet steel. These machines sheared the sheet steel, stamped it, punched out the various holes in the casing, and then formed the casing into a three-sided unit with various flanges to which other sheet metal pieces would be attached. A blower shelf and other supports were Tog-L-Lok™'d into place using specialized equipment. (Tog-L-Lok™ was a unique, extruded, mechanical fastening process.) At this point, the unit took on a rigid structure.

Insulation was glued into the casing and the unit took a sharp left turn down the main assembly line. Feeding into the first major station of the main assembly line was the subassembly line that fabricated the blower. The subassembly started with two presses: one press dedicated to forming two endplates for the blower and one dedicated to the "wrapper" portion of the blower. A machine then crimped the two end plates to the wrapper. Workers assembled a motor and other purchased parts to this to make up the blower subassembly. (There were a total of 123 purchased parts in a furnace.)

The second major station on the line installed a complex subassembly of primary and secondary heat exchangers into the casing. This subassembly group of employees used various processes to stamp out the various pieces of the subassembly, wash them, form them, and assemble them into heat exchanger cells. A special machine automatically screwed the heat exchangers into place. This primary was then married to a smaller, but very sophisticated, secondary heat exchanger to which was also assembled the draft inducer that pulled air through both units.

FIGURE D2 Schematic diagram of Carrier condensing high-efficiency gas furnace line.

Along the casing line. *(Courtesy of Carrier Corporation)*

The third major station of the main assembly line installed an electronic control box into the in-process furnace. This control box was itself fabricated by its own subassembly line. From this point on, other stations on the line installed wiring, plumbing, a safety pressure switch that checked whether the draft inducer was working before any burners were fired, and then the burner box itself. The burner box subassembly line was fed by presses that produced the burners themselves and the housings for them. On the main assembly, the burner box, a gas valve assembly, and the manifold to connect them were installed into the furnace. The top plate was then installed and the furnace received its rating plate, its instruction booklet, and a bag of special parts for installation.

At this stage of the assembly, the furnace was operable, and every furnace went through a run test of a minimum of 2.5 minutes where the furnace was fired up and all aspects of its operation were electronically tested. After testing, the blower door to the furnace was installed into the assembly. An outer door was

The head of the main line, after the casing is complete. *(Courtesy of Carrier Corporation)*

Assembly stations along the line. *(Courtesy of Carrier Corporation)*

also fabricated and installed on the unit. The unit was then packaged and stretch-wrapped. Finally, the unit's bar coding was scanned for entry into the warehouse, or increasingly (currently 25%) for direct shipment to distributors.

The manufacture of a furnace took about half an hour, from the time that the sheet steel was first sheared to start the casing until the unit was stretch-wrapped and scanned. The workers on either the main or the various subassembly lines were supported by other workers in fabrication and other support functions. The cycle time for each worker on the line was calculated to spread the work evenly and was termed the "takt" time. In a shift's run, up to 21 different models could be made, although typically the number of models run during a shift averaged between 8 and 12. There was enough leeway within the takt time to make any of the models produced on the line without putting any worker in an overcycle condition.

The schedule for any week always had the same character. Every different model could have been produced in a week, starting with the smallest sizes, those

Some test booths along the line, enclosed for sound control. *(Courtesy of Carrier Corporation)*

with only two burners, and increasing in size by one burner at a time until the six-burner models were all assembled. Varying quantities of any one model were produced during the week, but the order of models always remained the same.

Loading the Plant

Planning Production

Orders for furnaces came from any of about 200 distributor locations throughout the country. Some distributors ordered monthly; others ordered weekly. The orders requested delivery at varying times in the future. About 15 to 50 percent of the orders requested "at once" delivery, that is, within 30 days. For the others, the delivery requested was for greater than 30 days. The distributors placed their orders via Carrier's Order Distribution System (ODS). That system showed the distributors exactly how much production was scheduled and how many units of the models scheduled were available for sale in which weeks. Distributors then placed their orders, and the orders were confirmed by the company.

The gas furnace business was a seasonal business. Demand was greater in the second half of the year. During this period, Carrier typically ran two shifts. The two-shift operation created the capacity to carry the company through the peak season.

Exactly what was to be produced was determined by the plant's master scheduler. He used the marketing department's running six-month forecast, the actual orders on hand, and the level of inventory in finished goods to determine, first, an "aggregate plan." The aggregate plan specified how much labor would be required, including overtime or a second shift, to produce all that the marketing department's forecast implied.

The aggregate plan was a higher level, medium-range plan. More detailed plans were needed to specify exactly how many of each model were to be produced each week. The detailed production schedule was frozen for a three-week period of time. Only beyond that three-week period of time could there be any change to the numbers of the different models that would be assembled in sequence for each week. The plant had plans to reduce the three-week frozen production schedule to just two weeks, making available changes to the schedule in the third week. (This was termed "slushy.") However, the company was busy working with its suppliers to reduce their lead times even more in order for this to occur.

The master schedule was linked to an MRP (Material Requirement Planning) system called Chess™. The MRP system took the master schedule and used it to determine the needs of the plant for its supplier-provided parts and materials. The MRP system was not used to schedule any activity within the factory. The MRP system was run daily and there was a "backflush" the following morning that netted out materials used for the finished goods produced during the previous day from the quantities in the computer system from the day before.

Carrier operated its second shift with exactly the same cycle time on the line as prevailed with its first shift. Indeed, the cycle time did not change during the year for either shift. Previously, the company had tried to match the increase and decrease of sales during the year by rebalancing the assembly line. Although periodic line balance resulted in less inventory to carry, it imposed costs on the company that were avoided by maintaining a constant line balance. It had been discovered that rebalancing caused more shifting of labor from job to job and, thus, more manpower training than under the current situation. Quality and waste were also adversely affected. In Carrier's current just-in-time manufacturing system (described below), rebalance meant changes to the quantities of parts produced at any one time and making such a change was costly as well. It had been estimated that by maintaining a constant balance over the year, the learning brought on by experience meant increases in productivity of a hundred or more units per shift per line over what had been the case when lines had been periodically rebalanced.

In 1996, the company turned its work-in-process inventory in excess of 50 times during the year, up significantly in the last 5 years. Its finished goods inventory turned less frequently. The lower finished goods turns reflected the seasonality of sales and the occasional holding of inventory for distributors as they awaited later production of other ordered models.

The plant shut down production one day a year to take a physical inventory of all that was in the plant. In recent years, this physical inventory was accomplished quickly because the plant operated with less inventory and had better inventory controls than ever before.

Purchasing

The plant used 105 suppliers to supply 1500 different materials or parts. This figure was down considerably from previous years where as many as 300 suppliers had been used. Almost all of the parts used by the plant were single sourced with supplier contracts of between one and five years. The plant itself negotiated contracts for some specific parts, but the high-volume, high-value materials and parts, such as steel, copper, aluminum, and motors were negotiated cooperatively with corporate purchasing.

Every two weeks, all of the high-volume suppliers received a copy of the plant's MRP system records for their particular products. For a select number of high-volume and high dollar value suppliers there was also a so-called mini-MRP

Completed furnaces ready for shipment. *(Courtesy of Carrier Corporation)*

report that gave the next three weeks' order-by-order schedule. This order-by-order schedule could be used by the suppliers to synchronize their own build schedules to Carrier's needs. The mini-MRP report took account of all the information available, including the inventory in the building and the inventory in transit. This report essentially acted as a release to the suppliers to go ahead and produce what Carrier needed. The company was moving toward even more autonomy for suppliers with "supplier direct releases" so that it was the supplier that determined exactly what to produce, and when, so as to meet the schedule that they had been provided by Carrier.

Increasingly, too, supply trucks were loaded in such a way that the first products off the trucks were the ones that were needed first by the line. There was no incoming inspection for these suppliers, although there were occasional audits made. The goal was for all suppliers to move into certified status.

Certification was increasingly difficult. At present only 7 suppliers were certified, down from 30 in previous years when certification was less stringent. Certification was granted to those suppliers that had fewer than 500 parts per million defects, as a 12-month rolling average, and had passed a rigorous and quantitative plant inspection. As it was, each supplier was rated every month on its performance: delivery, quality, supplier cost improvement, and its relationship with the purchasing department (e.g., communication).

During the peak season, the plant received about 50 truck trailers of parts a day, 15 of which were for steel. Ten loading dock doors were devoted to unloading product that went straight to the line. There were daily deliveries of items such as steel, motors, gas valves, and insulation. Less high-volume, less valuable parts, such as door switches, were received weekly. Less frequent deliveries were only for specialized, low use parts.

Quality

The plant had dramatically improved its commitment to and its sophistication in quality. The focus of the quality program had shifted from product inspection to process improvement. With this shift had come both dramatic decreases in the number of defects and impressive improvements in the performance of the products in the field. For example, since 1989, both supplier-related defects and factory-related defects had declined by more than 30 percent per year, every year. The first pass yields through the run tests on the line currently yielded factory-responsible failures that were much less than 1 percent. In 1994, the plant earned ISO 9001 registration. Indeed, the plant was tri-registered with the American Gas Association, the British Standards Institute, and Underwriters Laboratory.

The shift toward more process improvement resulted in a number of changes in how quality was assured:

1. Statistical process control was in evidence on the condensing high-efficiency line. Seven key aspects of production there were charted including such things as the torque on the blower wheel. In addition, there were other tools used such as log sheets on leaks from the gas manifold.

2. There was a roving inspector for each line who among other things followed each product changeover to make sure that all of the models were produced exactly as specified and who also performed inspections of the process to verify that the process was effective.

3. Visual standards had been established for the operators and posted along the line.

4. Error-proofing systems had been developed, such as one that made sure that the draft inducer assembly was watertight.

A kanban storage area. *(Courtesy of Carrier Corporation)*

Steel, with its supplier kanban. *(Courtesy of Carrier Corporation)*

5. A number of process capability studies had been done to make sure that the assembly processes and testing processes were as specified by engineering. These included studies of secondary heat exchanger leaks and of the electric current draw and the electrical resistance, when cold, of the igniter.

A unit an hour was audited for each line. This audit reverified the run tests. One or two units a day went through a master audit that checked all the engineering data for each furnace. Some destructive tests were also done, mainly for things such as the Tog-L-Lok™ used for structural integrity of the casing and the primary heat exchanger.

The quality organization reported through channels separate from production. Under the quality assurance manager were both salaried and hourly people. The salaried people included engineers, each devoted to major lines in the factory. Engineers worked with suppliers for both value analysis and for supplier audits, corrective actions, and supplier certification. Supervisors, one per shift, worked on things such as new material sources, equipment qualification, or capital purchases.

The hourly employees of the quality assurance department were mainly technicians or line roving inspectors. There were technicians to help deal with supplier quality, precision inspection and calibration, and metallurgical testing.

Changes Toward Just-In-Time Manufacturing

The Indianapolis plant had undergone tremendous change in the past five years. In the early 1990s the plant employed only 400 direct labor workers and was not nearly as productive as it could have been. It could have been a short journey to plant closing. Starting in the 1990s, however, the plant was completely reorganized, and it quickly made tremendous improvements by following the precepts of the just-in-time manufacturing philosophy. (At Carrier, just-in-time manufacturing was known as "demand flow" manufacturing.) A number of initiatives had been taken in recent years:

1. The plant had been cleaned up and workstations rearranged.
2. "Point of use manufacturing" was adopted. All the locations of the presses were shifted from a distinct press department to positions close to the line.
3. Quality systems were upgraded.
4. A program of preventive maintenance was begun to increase equipment reliability.
5. Supplier relationships were restructured and improved to facilitate frequent deliveries of high-quality materials and parts.
6. The company began staging kaizen events. In 1996, for example, there were 26 such events of three and half days each. A half day was spent training and three days were spent attacking a problem. Each kaizen event usually involved 6 to 8 employees who worked in a particular cell of the plant, such as the blower subassembly cell or the heat exchanger cell. Kaizen events resulted in improvements in safety, ergonomics, quality, productivity, workstation layouts, and materials handling.
7. During this period of time, the organization of manufacturing changed as well. Each of the lines became more autonomous. Supervisory, materials, and manufacturing and quality engineering resources were assigned to each manufacturing line. These people had offices near the line and were fully committed to the line's operations. Engineers who had specified the equipment now helped to make it run.
8. The scheduling of fabricated parts was dramatically different with just-in-time manufacturing. Before, the press department filled a massive inventory that separated the press operations from the line. This was no longer true. There was no inventory storage area between the presses and the line. Typically, presses were either tied directly to the line or

they operated within a "pull" system, using kanbans. To each side of every kanbaned press there were small areas that held raw materials (the inbound stockpoint) and finished parts (the outbound stockpoint) in set quantities. Each worker chose exactly what to produce based on the quantities of parts that were left in his outbound stockpoint. Each part had a plasticized card (kanban) that indicated how many totes of parts triggered production. Fewer totes than that shown triggered the production of a set quantity of parts. Moreover, cumulative production could not exceed a specifically determined total number of totes.

9. Press operators were also responsible for changing the dies for their presses and for doing routine preventive maintenance on their equipment. They checked their own quality, usually with the first piece produced after a changeover. Each press operator was typically charged with the production of 10 to 15 different parts. These parts were thus "owned" by that operator who was responsible for keeping them flowing to the line. Typically there was just one or two days of inventory of sheet-metal parts ahead of the line.

10. Purchased parts were received into a purchased parts storeroom. From that storeroom, parts were delivered to the line. The quantities staged near the assembly lines averaged only hours' worth of production. Generally speaking, the press operators worked in the same sequence as the line did, making products for the smaller furnaces first and then shifting to the parts for the larger furnaces.

11. The move toward just-in-time also brought significant investments such as new equipment for the casing line, for the blower assembly, for assembling the heat exchangers, for the Tog-L-Lok™ equipment, and for the one-piece door that was the last thing to be assembled.

The success of the line was monitored on the andon board that tracked each major section of the line. Green indicated that all was well; yellow indicated that

A supplier kanban. *(Courtesy of Carrier Corporation)*

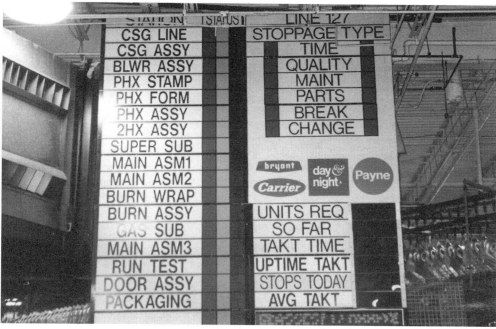

The andon board at Carrier Corporation. *(Courtesy of Carrier Corporation)*

an area of the line needed parts, and red indicated a quality problem. Any worker on the line had the ability to shut down the line for quality problems.

During the period of time from 1992 through 1996, production of condensing high-efficiency gas furnaces increased by 19 percent and productivity (total units per person) increased by 54 percent. Scrap was cut to a third of its former value and losses due to downtime were slashed to a quarter.

Workforce

There were presently about 1000 hourly employees at the plant. During the peak season, the number expanded by 15 to 35 percent. The hourly workers were represented by the United Steelworkers of America. By contract, only a percentage of the workforce at any time could be temporary. Thus, when the peak season began, the second shift was brought in as a mix of temporary and probationary workers. A probationary worker could become a full-time worker after 90 days.

The highest paid workers were the group leaders who led each of the "cells" in production or who led groups such as maintenance or receiving. For example, in the condensing high-efficiency furnace line, there were two group leaders in the press area and seven group leaders in assembly. Group leaders were paid a premium over the highest paid worker in their area. Group leader was thus a sought-after position, but it required significant training and only qualified people were chosen, not necessarily the most senior person. The group leaders reported to supervisors, who in turn reported to the unit manager for a line such as the condensing high-efficiency line. (See Figure D3.)

Training was important at Carrier. During the year all salaried workers received a minimum of 32 hours of training and all the hourly workers received a minimum of 24 to 30 hours of training. A new apprenticeship program had been

FIGURE D3 Selected aspects of the organization chart for the condensing high-efficiency furnace.

instituted and supervisors were being given intensified training on supervisory skills.

The company's relationship with the Steelworkers had generally improved over the years.[2] Grievances had been reduced over time to where in 1996 there were only eight grievances to reach the fourth step in the grievance procedure.[3] In recent years, there had only been one grievance that had gone to arbitration. In addition, over time, the number of labor classifications had been reduced; there were now nine groups with only four or five classifications in each group. Work rules had been simplified and there was a closer working relationship with the union.

Management

The plant's organization is depicted in Figure D3. Reporting to the plant manager were the managers of the fan coil and furnaces areas and various support func-

---

[2]Unfortunately, after more than 20 years of labor harmony, in 1996 there was a short one-week strike on the difficult issue of managed care. The cost of medical benefits for Carrier, much as with many other companies, had escalated and the company had moved to a managed care system, which, unfortunately, sparked the strike.

[3]The grievance procedure was in five ascending steps: (1) the front-line supervisor, (2) the department manager, (3) the area manager and a labor representative in the industrial relations department, (4) the area manager and the manager of industrial relations, and (5) binding arbitration.

tions such as engineering, quality assurance, industrial relations, safety/environmental, and finance. Under the area manager for both furnace lines were unit managers for each of the separate lines—condensing high-efficiency and noncondensing high-efficiency. Also reporting to the area manager was engineering support. The unit manager for the condensing high-efficiency furnaces had responsibility for supervision. Reporting in turn to the unit's supervisors were the group leaders. There were thus only three levels of management between the hourly workforce and the plant manager.

PART TWO: DISCUSSION

Carrier Corporation is in no way responsible for the following views and presentation. They remain solely the responsibility of the author.

The Flow of the Process and of Information

The process flow in a factory such as Carrier is complex. A blizzard of different tasks, equipment, and skills are required to assemble a furnace. Yet the process flow can be diagrammed in a very straightforward way. Figure D2 represents a rough-cut process flow diagram. A more detailed version would consist of recounting all of the workstations along the production line; it is these workstations through which every furnace passes. Thus, compared with a job shop or a batch flow process, the classic assembly line has a very well-defined process flow.

    With a process as complex and as closely scheduled as this one, it is not surprising that the information flow is complex as well. Figure D4 portrays an information flow diagram for Carrier. While the information flow is essentially one way, from the top down, the need to track materials both inside and outside the plant implies a great deal of communication between workers and management in the plant and between the plant, corporate level managers, and outside suppliers.

Capacity

The notion of what capacity is in a machine-paced line flow process like Carrier's is as clear as it ever gets. At Carrier, one furnace rolls off the end of the production line every so many seconds. Everything in the process is geared to making that happen. It is as though the process were a huge on-off switch: When it is on, one furnace every so many seconds is produced; otherwise, nothing is produced.

    Similarly, the notion of capacity utilization is relatively unambiguous. When the plant is up and running, capacity utilization is 100 percent. Otherwise, it is zero. Simply by tallying the hours the plant actually runs and dividing it by a count of hours the plant could be open gives an idea of what capacity utilization is. How many hours the plant could be open is subject to some debate, however. For example, it may be contrary to corporate policy to schedule a third shift of production, and so a capacity utilization measure for such an operation should be based on two shifts only. Another problem may lie in the determination of how much overtime is the maximum the plant could schedule without antagonizing workers. Is it an hour a day? Two hours a day? Every Saturday? Questions like these make a capacity utilization calculation fuzzy, but it is clear how much the process is capable of producing when it is up and running.

    In a machine-paced line flow process, capacity in the short run is severely constrained; it can be modified only by scheduling more or fewer hours. In the

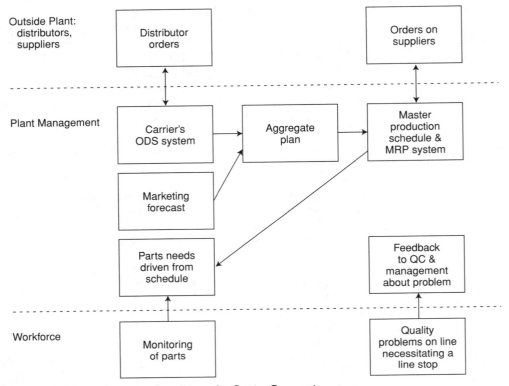

FIGURE D4 An information flow diagram for Carrier Corporation.

medium run, however, capacity can be substantially modified (without huge, new additions of plant and equipment) by adjusting the balance of the production line. Thus while the machine-paced line flow process cannot modulate its capacity smoothly, as can occur in job shops and batch flow processes, capacity can be adjusted in abrupt steps and by varying amounts. At the Carrier plant, however, rebalance was not done because it had been discovered that the shifting of jobs and the disruption that is inevitable with rebalance cost the plant more in output forgone than the extra cost of carrying the inventory. Thus, the plant does not rebalance, but works instead on learning better and better how to produce furnaces efficiently. The tour of the Burger King, on the other hand, demonstrates rebalance of a line that is quickly done, and is not so disruptive.

Demands of the Process on the Workforce

A machine-paced assembly line places special demands on a worker. In a sense, the worker is a slave to the moving assembly line. He cannot simply decide to take a break from his work and wander about chatting with co-workers. (But then neither can the second-grade teacher.) Moreover, the assembly line worker must perform the same, fairly routine task repeatedly throughout the workday. Many people view this as monotonous or degrading or worse.

But not all people hold to that view, and therein lies a fundamental point about assembly lines and assembly line workers. Happily, people are very different from one another in tolerances for certain activities and in expectations about their jobs. One class of personality savors proximity to power and influence and will forgo higher salaries to do so (consider many staff workers on Capitol Hill), while another will sacrifice salary for considerable freedom of schedule and the chance to be "my own boss" (such as many college professors). If the assembly line worker can be typed in this way at all, it is that he or she has forgone diversity in the job for relatively high wages and freedom from the anxiety many people suffer when they are confronted with decision making. For many people, that is not a bad trade to make.

Nevertheless, despite the matching of personalities to job types that goes on continuously in our economy, progressive companies like Carrier are constantly searching for ways to improve the quality of work life for their workers. Suffice it here to observe that in many plants such as Carrier (1) the personnel or industrial relations department is regarded as critical because of what it does for worker training, safety, and the promotion of worker involvement; (2) effective supervisors are consistently recognizing worker achievement and integrity and assisting workers in solving problems both on and off the job; and (3) the industrial and plant engineers study the tasks that make up the assembly and devise ways to eliminate or simplify more difficult or disagreeable aspects of the job. Within most machine-paced line flow processes, the career path of the worker is much less well defined than it is in many continuous flow processes or in the batch flow process. Lines of progression are not spelled out as directly, and most workers earn about the same pay. Most job changes involve transfers from evening or night work to day work, or from one department to another with what may be perceived as easier or more exciting work. Some promotions in job categories are frequently possible as well.

Carrier's adoption of just-in-time manufacturing principles and philosophy has thrust more responsibility on the workforce. The workforce has the authority to stop the line at any time for quality problems, and is responsible for monitoring parts and for essentially controlling the pace of production in the fabrication and subassembly areas of the operation. Workers are repeatedly engaged in kaizen events that lead to real change on the factory floor. More than ever before, the workforce is regarded as a key cog in the design, and redesign, of manufacturing, and not simply as the means by which the product is made.

Demands of the Process on Management

The machine-paced line flow process places a number of taxing demands on management. The products it produces are typically consumed in high volumes; therefore, they are likely to compete on price as well as product performance, workmanship, and perhaps even the reliability of delivery. This is a broad front on which to compete, and it means that line flow managers must devote their attention to cost reduction measures (items 1 through 4 in the following list) and to product performance and workmanship measures (items 5 and 6):

1. *Balance.* The definition and balance of the line, as discussed previously, is a critical aspect in ensuring that as little labor as necessary is placed on the line.

2. *Materials management.* Like the continuous flow process, the line flow process places very regular and steady demands on its suppliers. Because of this regularity, the line flow process can often avoid drawing on large raw materials inventories and paying the necessary finance charges, but only by carefully managing the purchase and logistics of supplies. Such materials management involves the establishment of superb information and control systems so that (1) parts in imminent danger of falling short are identified and noted and (2) parts from suppliers are tracked thoroughly and delivered on time. The process description noted how recent changes toward just-in-time manufacturing principles have contributed to coordinating materials more tightly.

3. *Technological change.* In processes as complex as most line flow ones there are always ways to improve their workings. Most such changes are incremental in nature, but periodically more significant steps can be taken either to speed up the process or to eliminate some stations through the introduction of new equipment. Computers, more versatile machine tools, and increased automation have often made significant contributions to process improvement.

4. *Capacity planning.* The managers of a process as rigid in capacity as the machine-paced line flow process must be very careful to plan diligently for its future capacity needs. Line rebalance may be called for or more drastic modifications to the design of the line. Design changes must be thought through carefully from the beginning of any planning cycle.

5. *Product design.* The high-volume products of the typical line flow process must be designed to be manufactured; the more exotic the demands the product places on the design of the line and the tasks workers perform, the more likely the competition will bury the product on price. Yet some of the best assembly line products give the impression that they were custom-made, there being so many options for the customer to choose from. The trick, of course, is to design flexibility into the product so that the same general worker task results in a different appearance or performance in the product. At Carrier, the same line can effortlessly switch to any of 93 distinct models.

6. *Workforce management.* In so many line flow processes, quality is fundamentally dependent on the workforce. Fostering pride in workmanship and creativity in the identification and solution of problems, when the tasks performed are as repetitious as they are, is a challenge but essential.

Carrier's adoption of just-in-time (JIT) manufacturing principles and philosophy has had dramatic implications for management, too. Managers are now directly assigned to each line and they more closely support what is happening on the factory floor. Management has become more visual, especially with the use of kanbans. JIT has changed the nature of supervision at all levels of the factory; now managers are more likely to coach and lead team meetings than to engage in the traditional direction-giving that characterizes more "old school" management.

Questions

1. The production process at Carrier used to combine a fabrication-oriented press department, a storeroom for finished press parts, and an assembly line. What happened to that way of producing furnaces, and why? What are the advantages to the new way of operating?

2. It has been said that industrial engineering is the most important element of control in a machine-paced line flow process. Do you agree? Why or why not?

3. What are the connections between the workforce and its supervision and product quality at Carrier?

4. Discuss in detail the relationship between the notion of capacity in a machine-paced line flow and the technique of line balance.

5. Based on different operations you have so far studied, in which operation would you rather work? In which would you rather be a manager? In which would you like least to be a worker? A manager? Support your answers with specific references to the processes.

6. Various changes in materials management were mentioned in the process description for Carrier. Trace the changes in both process and information flows that you would expect to result from these changes.

7. Suppose that you had just been designated the plant manager for a new plant about to be completed. You are in charge of assembling your own staff (such as in quality control, plant engineering, supervision, production planning). Based on the process descriptions to date, how would the composition and relative strengths of your chosen staff differ from one type of process to another?

8. Suppose Carrier has been designated to produce a new furnace. What aspects of the plant's operations do you think will be most affected by this change?

TOUR E

A Hybrid (Batch/Continuous Flow) Process

Stroh Brewery Company
Winston-Salem, North Carolina

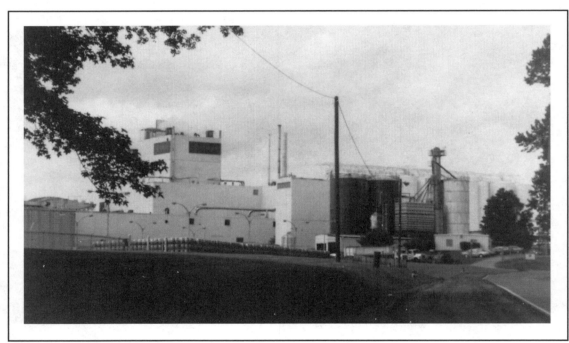

(Courtesy of Stroh Brewery Company)

In 1982, the Stroh Brewery Company of Detroit acquired the Jos. Schlitz Brewing Company of Milwaukee. In the process, Stroh acquired Schlitz's Winston-Salem brewery, which had begun production in June 1969. At the time, the Winston-Salem brewery was the largest brewery ever built at one time. It occupied 1.1 million square feet on 150 acres and cost $130 million. Originally constructed to produce about 5 million barrels of beer per year (a beer barrel is equal to 31 gallons), the brewery was now capable of producing about 6 million barrels of beer per year.

PART ONE: PROCESS DESCRIPTION

The Brewing and Packaging of Beer

Beer is a malt-and-hops-flavored drink that is fermented and carbonated. It has been popular for thousands of years and, in one form or another, exists in almost every society. Although known and enjoyed for so long, the chemistry of brewing is very complex and is still not understood in all its particulars. Brewing remains very much an art, as well as a science, with rapid innovation over the past 20 to 25 years; developments in brewing automation and control have reduced the need for manual labor by 75 percent and placed much of the control of the process on instrument panels.

The brewing process itself can be divided into two main stages: (1) the production of natural cereal sugars, called wort production, and (2) fermentation and finishing. (The process is depicted in Figure E1.) At Stroh, a batch of beer typically took about a month to brew and age.

Wort Production

Wort production starts with the weighing, cleaning, and milling of the malt, which gives beer its flavor. The malted barley and an adjunct (corn, rice, malt, and/or liquefied corn) are prepared separately. The adjunct is used because malted barley can convert more than its own weight of starch to fermentable sugars. To the milled or crushed barley, malt, and adjunct is added the brewing water, which is specially treated by filtering and pH adjustment to remove impurities.

This addition of water to ground malt is known as mashing. This occurs in large, stainless steel vessels in which the ground malt and brewing water can be stirred together and brought to a boil.

The Stroh's brand and its Stroh Light extension brand are famed for being "fire brewed." Instead of the wort being cooked by heat from steam coils, as was the common practice, the wort for Stroh's and Stroh Light is cooked using direct flame in the flammekessel. This step gives Stroh's and Stroh Light their distinctive taste.

After mashing, the mixture is transferred to a lauter tub, which separates the liquid (the wort) from the undissolved solids of the mash. The lauter tub is a large, circular tub with a false bottom and a rotating set of "rakes" that can be raised or lowered. These rotating rakes smooth out the mash as it enters the lauter tub and makes an even filter bed. Undissolved particles in the mash settle to the false floor of the lauter tub. Once settled, the liquid wort can be drawn off with the aid of hot "sparging" water, which rinses the wort off the grain. The undissolved mash is then collected and sent to the nearby Miracle Feed Company, where it is processed into a highly nutritious livestock feed.

The drawn-off wort then enters the brew kettle, where it boils for two hours. This boiling stabilizes the wort by killing off bacteria, deactivating enzymes, and coagulating any still undissolved particles. During this boiling, hops are introduced to the wort to enhance its flavor by extraction of desirable hop components. Boiling also increases the concentration of the wort through evaporation. Once boiled, the hops and trub (coagulated sediment) are separated out by whirlpool action in a special vessel. The hot wort is then cooled and aerated.

FIGURE E1 The brewing process as followed at the Winston-Salem plant of the Stroh Brewery Company.

Fermentation and Finishing

Only after yeast has been introduced to the cooled wort and fermentation is complete can the product be called beer. The yeast that is introduced to the 50-foot-long fermentation tanks transforms maltose, glucose, and other sugars in the wort to alcohol and carbon dioxide. Stroh's fermentation is accomplished by a patented process called "accurate balanced fermentation." During fermentation, carbon dioxide gas is collected and purified. After fermenting has finished and the

A control panel in Stroh's Winston-Salem brewhouse. *(Courtesy of Stroh Brewery Company)*

A brew kettle in Stroh's Winston-Salem brewhouse. *(Courtesy of Stroh Brewery Company)*

yeast has been separated from the beer by centrifuge, the carbon dioxide is reintroduced to the beer (carbonation), and the beer is chilled.

Once fermentation is complete and the yeast separated, the remaining finishing consists of a string of storage and filtering steps. The chief aging occurs in the ruh cellar, where the beer is held for between 7 and 21 days. Once properly aged, the beer is filtered several times through diatomaceous earth. Final storage occurs in what is called the "government cellar." Beer typically spends less than 1 day in the government cellar, the time largely dependent on packaging needs.

Out of the government cellar, the beer flows to the keg, canning, and bottling lines.

Canning, Bottling, and Kegging

The Winston-Salem brewery operated six canning lines, three bottling lines, and a keg line. Each line performed essentially the same functions: (1) filling and capping and (2) pasteurizing (for the non-draft beers). Cans and bottles were also boxed into six-packs and cases, and cases were placed on pallets for shipping by truck or rail. The process from filling to palletizing ran continuously, with no significant buildup of in-process inventories unless a piece of equipment in the line broke down. The key piece of equipment on the line was the filler (an investment of $400,000)—the limiting element for capacity. All of the machines that followed had rated capacities in excess of the filler; so any equipment breakdown after the filler did not necessitate shutting down the entire line. Small reservoirs of work-in-process were held at several places along the line in order to keep things moving in case one part of the line had to be shut down temporarily (such as a shutdown to remove a broken bottle).

The can lines could run at 1600 cans per minute, the bottling lines at 900 bottles per minute, and the keg line at 340 half-barrels per hour. With six canning lines, several brands brewed at the plant could be canned at the same time. Alternatively, the same beer could be packaged in three different size cans (12 oz., 16 oz., and 24 oz.) at the same time. Three bottling lines were needed not only to match the demand for bottles but also to permit bottles of different shapes and sizes to be run at the same time. A canning line shift required 5 workers, while a bottling line shift required 14.

Warehousing

The Winston-Salem plant preferred to load the beer directly from the line into railcars or trucks rather than warehouse it. (See the plant layout in Figure E2.) In fact, about half of the plant's output was shipped without any storage in the warehouse. The warehouse's fully enclosed railroad docks could store thirty 50-foot freight cars. In addition, 20 truck loading docks were available. The warehouse was designed so that output could be shipped by either rail or truck. The warehouse stored some brands that were not produced at the plant. Also, 10-ounce cans were not filled here. These items had to be supplied by other Stroh plants.

Loading the Plant

Order Taking

Stroh's Winston-Salem brewery served approximately 200 wholesalers stretching over the entire eastern seaboard from New England to some parts of Florida and inland to Michigan, Indiana, Kentucky, and some parts of Tennessee.

The kegging line at Stroh's Winston-Salem plant. *(Courtesy of Stroh Brewery Company)*

A wholesaler generally handled one of the major national brands and perhaps a smaller, regional brand. Each wholesaler serviced a range of retail accounts (such as liquor stores, bars, grocery stores) within a specified geographic area.

At the middle of each month, every wholesaler placed an order for delivery next month. This procedure meant that the brewery had lead times of two to six weeks for each order. The order, entered either directly by computer or mailed in, specified item, quantity, and date (sometimes hour) for delivery of the beer ordered. The brewery offered a remarkable diversity of items. Over 100 different brands of beer were brewed at the plant, among them: Stroh's, Stroh Light, Old Milwaukee, Old Milwaukee Light, Old Milwaukee Non-Alcoholic, Schlitz, Schlitz Light, Schlitz Malt Liquor, Piels, Piels Light, Goebel, Goebel Light, Schaefer, Schaefer Light, Red Bull, and Silver Thunder. Old Milwaukee accounted for 37 percent of production and Schlitz Malt Liquor for 30 percent, with the other brands dividing up the remaining 33 percent of the brewery's capacity. This beer could be packaged in cans, bottles, or kegs of various sizes, with different lids and in different kinds of cardboard cartons. In all, there were 759 beer and packaging variations that a wholesaler could order. Wholesalers could pick up their order by truck, paying the expenses themselves, or they could have the plant load a special Stroh-assigned rail freight car and direct it to the wholesaler's own rail siding. The truck option offered greater speed and reliability of delivery than rail, thereby cutting down on the inventory the wholesaler had to carry, but it cost considerably more. About 20 percent of the plant's volume was shipped by rail and 80 percent by truck.

The Winston-Salem plant monitored the inventory positions of each of its wholesalers, and it followed trends in the marketplace as well (such as promo-

1. Fuel oil tanks
2. Fire protection water tank and pumps
3. Liquid adjunct tanks
4. Grain storage
5. Grains drying
6. Brew house
7. Brew supplies
8. Government cellar
9. Ruh storage cellar
10. Filtration cellar
11. Fermentation cellar
12. Offices
13. Keg area
14. Warehouse
15. Packaging
16. Can warehouse
17. Can warehouse
18. Truck docks
19. Distribution offices
20. Railroad tracks
21. Schlitz Avenue
22. Parking

FIGURE E2 Layout of the Winston-Salem plant of the Stroh Brewery Company.

tional campaigns and their effect). The plant sometimes made suggestions to its wholesalers on what and how much to order, especially if it felt strongly that a wholesaler might not have ordered correctly.

Production Planning

Production planning was intimately related to order taking and was performed in the same department. (See the organization chart in Figure E3.) The role of the production planners was to figure out how the brewery could best fill the orders placed by its wholesalers. A good production plan was one that satisfied all of the wholesalers' demands with (1) little repositioning of the requested delivery dates, (2) few changes in the workforce, and (3) full usage of the existing equipment.

Planning and scheduling production for each month meant determining (1) how much beer of which type was required and the timing of its delivery and packaging and (2) the precise sequencing of lines and beer/packaging combinations on each line.

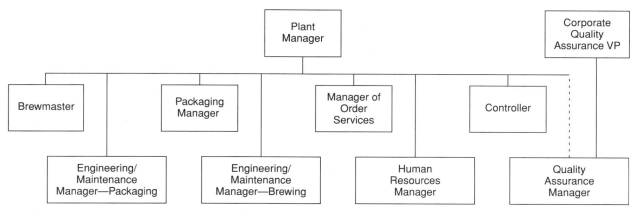

FIGURE E3 Organization chart for the Winston-Salem plant of the Stroh Brewery Company.

Because it took a month to brew beer, the brewmaster had to produce to a forecast of sales rather than to customer order. This production to forecast was a key reason why the plant kept close tabs on retail activity and made buying suggestions to its wholesalers. The packaging of beer, on the other hand, could be, and was in fact, done to customer order.

In planning packaging for any given month, it was advantageous to:

1. Group runs of the same beers together, such as packaging Old Milwaukee on several lines at the same time.

2. Group similar packaging sizes and types together, such as running all quart bottles at the same time rather than interspersing them among other production runs.

3. Run similar lines at the same time, such as running two can lines in tandem. To run a second line, given the first was running, required only four more workers rather than the eight it took to run the line by itself.

4. Run a canning line together with the keg line, since the joint workforce for such a combination could then be shifted en masse to a bottling line if need be. In that way, the groups working on any line would not have to be split up and reassembled as often.

Once the next month's wholesaler orders were received, the production planners went to work to schedule the production to fulfill that demand. This scheduling was accomplished manually, using trial and error but with reference to decision rules like the four mentioned here. After the production plan became "final," the wholesalers' delivery dates and order quantities were acknowledged on a week-by-week basis, giving the wholesalers two weeks' notice. About 70 percent of the wholesalers' original orders were acknowledged without any changes in dates or quantities. For the other 30 percent, all quantities were filled with timing dislocations that were always less than two weeks. Fully 99 percent of all the acknowledged orders were shipped on time.

Wholesalers could request changes in the schedule after their initial orders had been placed. This meant calling a production coordinator who could change the production plan or arrange swaps between wholesalers (since the brewery was aware of all wholesaler inventory positions). Major modifications of the production plan rarely had to be made. Minor adjustments were made about twice a week, but these occurred normally for production problems such as a machine breakdown. The production plan was declared fixed as to labor content one week in advance of production. It was declared fixed as to packaging variations only one day in advance of production. About one shift's production was kept as a safety stock so that snafus in demand, production, or logistics would not necessarily affect delivery.

The production plan had another role somewhat different from the weekly scheduling of machines to match orders exactly. This role had to do with anticipating the seasonality of beer drinking. There was a definite seasonal trend to beer sales. Demand peaked from May through September, with the height of the peak accounting for sales roughly double those of the winter trough. Because Stroh's pasteurized beer had no living organisms in it (milk has 500 per milliliter), the beer did not spoil. (The draft beer was specially filtered so that it, too, had no living organisms in it.) The brewery could therefore cushion itself somewhat for the peak season demand by building up inventories, both in its own warehouse and in the warehouses of its wholesalers. In this way, the brewery did not have to hire or lay off as many workers during the period when demand was changing abruptly. The brewery and its wholesalers built up some inventories during the late spring and ran them down as summer progressed.

Because beer tasted best when it was fresh, it was company policy to hold no packaged beer at the brewery that was older than 21 days. The policy for wholesalers was not to hold any beer longer than 60 days. These policies helped to ensure that consumers enjoyed a fresh product.

The precise production schedule for the various lines depended in large measure on the time it took to accomplish various changeovers with the equipment. There were three key types of changeovers:

1. *Beer changeovers.* When a different beer was to be packaged, the pipes leading to the line from the government cellars had to be cleaned out by a "blow back" of beer to the cellars, using carbon dioxide. Only then could the new beer travel the pipes to the filling machine. For most beer switches, this changeover could be accomplished in 15 minutes, quicker than that for lines close to the government cellars and longer than that for lines far from the cellars. Because of the significantly different composition of light beers, a changeover to or from light beer involved, in addition to a "blow back" with carbon dioxide, flushing the pipes and the filling machine bowl with water. Thus, when light beer was run, the changeover entailed 20 or 25 minutes to prepare the line for the beer and a similar amount of time to clean up the line once it was run.

2. *Packaging changeovers.* On the canning lines, the chief packaging changeovers involved either a change of can lids or a change of case carton. The "ecology lid," where the tab was pushed down into the can and remained attached, was used exclusively, but these lids could carry special tax-paid statements for various states, and thus can lid changes had to be made. There were many major carton possibilities: a standard case of 24 made up of four six-packs and a fully enclosed box of 12, 18, 24, or 36 loose cans. Other carton possibilities were also possible. A change of lids took 5 to 10 minutes on average, while a change of case cartons could take several hours.

The only packaging change for the bottling lines involved a switch of cartons for the 7-ounce bottles, a changeover that averaged 10 minutes.

3. *Container changeovers.* The most complex and time-consuming changeover involved a switch of container sizes—for example, from 12-ounce to 16-ounce cans or from 20-ounce bottles to 22-ounce ones. (Three can sizes were possible—12,

16, and 24 ounces—and six bottle sizes—12, 20, 22, 32, 38, and 40 ounces.) Such changes involved resetting the filling equipment, the lid placement or bottle crowning equipment, the labeling equipment, and the cartoning equipment. Typically, an entire shift was devoted to these changeovers.

On a typical day, for example, a 12-ounce can line would make 10 to 15 lid or beer changeovers, a 16-ounce can line would make 8 such changeovers, and a quart bottling line would make 6 such changeovers.

The extent of container changeovers depended on the season. There were two basic types of can changeovers and two basic types of bottle changeovers. In the summer, the cycles shown in Table E1 prevailed for these can and bottle lines.

Given changeovers of various sorts and mechanical and other problems, can and bottle lines could not operate all the time. For the most part, the line efficiencies ran about 80 and 85 percent. Changeovers accounted for between 5 and 8 percent of the difference between these efficiencies and 100 percent.

Purchasing

The purchasing function for the plant was housed in the same department that handled order taking and production planning. This arrangement made sense since the production plan implied, in a straightforward way, the material needs for the entire process.

All of the brewery's major material inputs (malt, adjuncts, cans, bottles, cardboard) were purchased on long-term contracts from major suppliers. These contracts were all negotiated by Stroh's headquarters staff in Detroit. The Winston-Salem plant negotiated on its own only those contracts for materials and services that went into the maintenance of the brewery itself and were not an integral part of the final product. Still, there were plant-specific negotiations for 2500 contracts

TABLE E1 Container changeovers for can and bottle lines during summer (Stroh Brewing Company)

Line	Shifts Per Cycle
Can Line	
Type A 12-ounce cans	Line devoted to 12-ounce cans: no changes
Type B 16-ounce cans 24-ounce cans	15 shifts 6 shifts[a]
Bottle Lines	
Type A 12-ounce nonreturnables	15 shifts[a]
Type B 12 ounce 20 ounce, 22 ounce 32-ounce or 40-ounce bottles	20 shifts 15 shifts 6 shifts[a]

[a]Cycle then repeats.

each year. Also, even though Detroit headquarters may have negotiated for a specific material, there was often a direct supplier-brewery relationship. This was particularly true for cans and bottles. Cans were supplied by American National Can located near the brewery, and bottles were provided by three outside sources: Anchor, Foster-Forbes, and Owens-Illinois.

The brewery placed orders for these major materials in much the same way that Stroh's wholesalers placed orders with the brewery. For example, the July order for cans or bottles would be placed on June 10. At that time, the brewery would place a firm four-week order and an estimate of the succeeding four weeks' demand.

The inventory levels for any one of these major materials depended crucially on the dependability of the supplier. If the supplier had proven reliable and no special circumstances intervened, the brewery would want to hold only enough of the material to last until the next delivery. As it was, special circumstances were continually intervening, and so the brewery often adjusted the amount it ordered to take advantage of volume discounts in price or seasonal differences in sales or expectations about a strike in the supplier's plant. Some typical inventory levels for major materials were:

Bottles	1–2 days of production
Malt	5–7 days
Cans	1 week
Cardboard cases	1 week
Bottle labels	1 month

The Workforce

The brewery currently employed about 500 people, producing on three shifts a day, 5 days a week. Of these, about 70 were salaried (managers and staff) and 430 were paid hourly. The hourly workers were represented by a union, the International Brotherhood of Teamsters.

Most of the workforce had been hired from within a 50-mile radius. Half of the salaried workers were drawn from other Stroh breweries, but none of the hourly workers came from other Stroh breweries, mainly because they had to be volunteers and had to pay for their own move. During plant start-up a strong effort was made to hire persons so that there was a representative mix of ages, races, and sexes.

The hourly workers were divided into two main groups: the production workers who brewed and packaged the beer, and the engineering and maintenance workers who cared for and fixed the plant's equipment. The maintenance workers were paid about 5 percent more than the production workers, since their jobs required greater expertise and wider skills.

Once in a department (brewing, packaging, engineering/maintenance), workers tended to stay, often doing the same job. This status quo was frequently by choice, since workers who complained of boredom were generally shifted to more complex jobs or made relief workers (spelling other workers who were taking breaks). Advancement through the ranks and into management was possible, especially in brewing and packaging, although the odds were short. Most movement among the hourly employees was between shifts; such moves were based on seniority.

Control and Evaluation of the Operation

Quality Assurance

Quality assurance (QA) at the brewery was an important activity, employing 30 people in three separate labs: microbiology, brewing, and packaging. The staff at those labs performed 1100 separate tests, many of them repetitions of the same test, on each batch of beer brewed at the plant. QA staff worked round the clock, seven days a week. Quality assurance had the authority to stop operations at any point in the process. The QA manager was responsible for dealing with and rectifying any customer complaints.

Here are two examples of the specifications that the QA staff tested for, one set by the corporation's brewing staff and the other set by the corporation's packaging staff:

A worker inspecting cans of Schlitz along Stroh's Winston-Salem canning line. *(Courtesy of Stroh Brewery Company)*

1. The brewing staff had set a standard of 16 million yeast cells (+ or − 2 million) per milliliter of beer during fermentation. Quality assurance tested for this standard twice for every fermentation tank's batch. The test had to be completed within the first four hours of fermentation so that any necessary corrective measures could be taken. The test was accomplished by taking a 4-ounce sample from the tank, diluting it in three steps, and then counting yeast cells by microscope.

2. The packaging staff had established a standard that the air content in a 12-ounce can of beer be no more than 0.66 cubic centimeter, because oxygen caused flavor instability in the beer. The QA staff tested for this standard by checking each canning line five times per shift, taking three cans from each line each time. If the cans were off specification, the QA staff would quarantine all the line's beer up to the last good check and then systematically inspect the quarantined lot until the beginning of the off-specification beer was encountered. The beer that passed inspection was released, and the beer that failed inspection was discarded. As it turned out, about 98 percent of any quarantined beer was eventually released as good product.

Rarely did any of the batches of beer fail to satisfy standards, but the quality assurance department prided itself on its vigilance. It viewed itself as the early warning station for detecting any encroaching degradations of the process's integrity.

Information Flows Within the Process

Most of the information flows within the process were directed from the top down. If the process was working smoothly, workers needed to be informed of only routine things, such as the changeover in a line from one beer to another or the shifting from one line to another. Most jobs did not vary that much anyway, and so the information that was transmitted could be sparse without any detrimental effect.

Top management was eager, however, for the thoughts of the workers on all matters of plant operations. The plant had begun a total quality management (TQM) program that was involving the workforce in process improvements. Of particular concern were breakdowns in the process. After worker signals of process breakdown, the engineering and maintenance force would be called in. These troubleshooting jobs were generally regarded as the most complex at the brewery and the most pressure-filled. A good engineering/maintenance department was a real asset and a chief way to keep costs low by maintaining high speed and high yields. The TQM program was also instituting supplier certifications to improve quality even more.

Evaluating Plant Performance

Each week management at the brewery developed an operations summary that listed goals and actual results for an entire list of performance measures such as productivity (barrels per worker), cost per barrel, packaging line efficiencies, material losses, beer losses, beer rejected by QA, deliveries made on time, shipment errors, wholesaler complaints, and worker absenteeism. Each week, too, the plant's beer was evaluated by taste tests in Detroit and elsewhere. More than any other test, this was the one the plant always wanted to pass.

In many respects, the plant's performance could be fine-tuned only from week to week. The major elements of plant performance were either already decided (plant design) or beyond the scope of plant management (the plant's sales volume). As the plant manager admitted: "The heaviest decision in our industry is capital equipment investment." Major cost and quality advances were very much a function of the equipment the company's design people in Detroit decided to incorporate into the plant.

Over the past 20 to 25 years, breweries had also been built larger than before. There were real cost savings implied by larger brewery size: vats and tanks could be larger and still make quality beer at lower cost per barrel, and packaging line speed and capacity could be used fully. The size for the Winston-Salem brewery was determined as a sort of "lowest common denominator" for different "lumpy" capital investments. Specifically, the plant's lauter tub could process 3 million barrels of beer a year, and the mandatory assortment of packaging lines (lines for kegs, cans, one-way bottles, and returnable bottles) could process 5.2 million to 6 million barrels a year. With the addition of other canning lines and another bottling line, packaging capacity could then precisely match the output of two lauter tubs—hence a brewery capacity of 6 million barrels a year.

What the plant manager worried about depended a lot on volume. As he noted, "Volume solves everything." When volume was high, all the manager had to worry about was whether the workers would accept the necessary overtime and whether maintenance could hold everything together. At capacity, quality and meeting shipments were chief concerns, with product cost lower in priority. When sales volume dropped, however, meeting cost targets became relatively more important, and that meant tightening up on staff and laying off workers. The plant was operated as a cost center, since it had no responsibilities for revenue raising (e.g., no marketing at the plant) and its geographic market area was fixed. Plant management was concerned chiefly for the maintenance of the plant and the motivation of the workforce; with them came good-quality beer, high yields, and on-time shipments.

PART TWO: DISCUSSION

The Stroh Brewery Company is in no way responsible for the following views and presentation. They remain solely the responsibility of the author.

The Process Flow

Much of the Stroh brewery's operation is reminiscent of the continuous flow process at International Paper's Androscoggin Mill. Even though there are about 759 beer and packaging variations, most of these modifications require setup times that are small in comparison with the run length. The process flow is well defined, and every product goes through the same steps in the process. (See Figure E1 for a process flow chart.) Over time, equipment advances have speeded up the process and have driven labor out of the product's value.

The job contents of the direct labor in the process are of two kinds, polar extremes. Most workers have well-delineated tasks, most of which are repeated time and again as the product is manufactured. These jobs, typically, are not very demanding. At the other extreme lies the brewmaster. Despite great strides in automation and control, the brewmaster's duties still lie within the realm of art. Brewing is still imperfectly known enough to require great experience to produce a quality product.

Requiring nearly comparable levels of skill and experience are the plant engineers. Plant engineering and maintenance are crucial to an operation such as a brewery, where the capital investment is enormous and the success of the process depends on meeting quality standards and delivery schedules and on maintaining high yields of output. All of these goals are influenced importantly by the design and upkeep of the equipment in the plant. Moreover, all of the equipment must be functioning smoothly for any of the product to meet its specifications. Breakdowns or below-specification performance of any of the equipment is likely to lead to poor quality, poor shipment performance, or excessively high costs (such as low packaging speeds).

Despite these important similarities to the continuous flow process at the Androscoggin Mill, the Stroh brewery is not strictly a continuous flow operation. This is true primarily because the brewing phase of the process is done on a batch basis. True, these batches are large, but it is only because of their sequencing and the accumulation of a work-in-process inventory just before packaging that the batch operation in brewing can supply a steady flow of beer to the continuous flow that is packaging. The work-in-process inventories in the ruh and government cellars separate the two different types of processes. Without such an inventory, even though the daily or weekly capacities of the two processes (brewing and packaging) may be matched perfectly, the lumpiness of the batch flow operation's output cycle would cause severe problems for the smooth-running continuous flow operation.

The Information Flow

The inventory between brewing and packaging does more than even out production. It also separates the information needs of the two processes. The brewmaster need only know how much beer of which kind to brew, and the packaging department need only know what, when, and how much it is to package.

Moreover, the timing of the information flows is much different. The precise packaging department schedule is set as final only one day prior to packaging. Up to that time, adjustments to the schedule can be accepted. Needless to say, the brewmaster cannot react so quickly. Because it takes about a month to brew a batch of beer, the brewmaster can work only to an estimate of demand, not from firm wholesale orders. The work-in-process inventory between brewing and packaging, then, acts as a safety stock of beer as well, so that last-minute changes in demand can be accommodated. It also serves as the dividing line between production triggered by estimate (brewing) and production triggered by firm orders (packaging). This difference in information requirements, as much as anything else, sets aside the Stroh brewery as a hybrid (batch/continuous flow) process.

The separation of information needs and flows at the brewery is depicted in an information flow diagram (Figure E4). Note that the information basically flows in only one direction (top down) except for the usual signaling of equipment breakdowns and acknowledgments of orders shipped. In this way, the information flows are reminiscent of the Androscoggin Mill.

Capacity Measures

The capacity of the brewery is a firm and easily understood number, 6 million barrels of beer a year. Barring a major breakdown of equipment, the capacity figure is primarily what the existing plant and equipment permit, although the product mix and scheduling had some impact on capacity. Other than to maintain the equipment and keep quality up, the plant can pull only so many levers to increase the quantity of good product brewed and packaged.

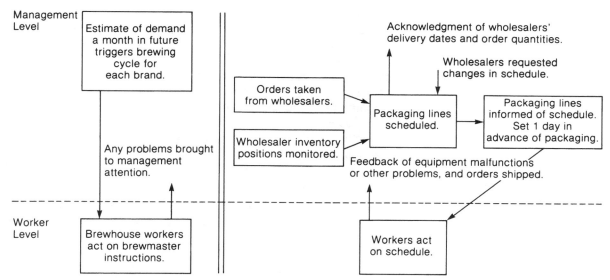

FIGURE E4 An information flow diagram of the Winston-Salem plant of the Stroh Brewery Company.

By the same token, capacity utilization is a well-defined concept. The capacity of any piece of equipment is known because it was engineered that way, and the current capacity is also easily measured. Moreover, because the plant's designers want to leave as little waste or spare capacity unused as possible, the capacity utilization for any single piece of equipment is often very close to the capacity utilization figure for the process itself. Since the process's capacity utilization is determined by the bottleneck operation, one can say that all equipment capacities are likely to lie close to the bottleneck capacity.

Standards and Incentives

The standards that matter at the Stroh brewery are not the type of standards that managers of batch or job shop operations get concerned about. Labor standards (output per worker per unit of time) do not exist at the brewery. Rather, it is machine standards (units processed per hour) and quality standards that capture managers' attention and influence their behavior. These are the standards management strives to meet.

Similarly, labor incentives are absent from the brewery. The plant's output is so overwhelmingly related to machine performance rather than worker performance that worker incentive schemes make little sense.

Demands of the Process on the Workers

The process at this Stroh brewery places a variety of demands on a variety of different work groups within the brewery. Art, science, and routine are all found. For the brewhouse workers, even with the panels of controls that now abound, the brewing process still requires art, a "feel" and a "taste" for what makes quality beer. In many breweries, it still is true that the brewmaster's skills have been handed down from generation to generation.

While science may not have overtaken all aspects of the brewing art, it rules the quality assurance operations of the brewery itself (although the Detroit taste test is still the single most important check on the brewery's quality performance). Science is evident everywhere in quality assurance, from the chemistry involved to the statistical sampling. The training for the quality assurance department can thus be long and rigorous.

Science and art are mixed in the plant's maintenance activities, which are an important and prestigious activity. The capital intensity of the process dictates heavy reliance on maintenance and the ability to troubleshoot problems quickly so as not to waste time and output needlessly. Only with the line jobs in packaging does routine best characterize the process. Still, switching from canning to bottling to kegging provides a measure of diversity in the job from day to day.

Demands of the Process on Management

Stroh's Winston-Salem brewery and International Paper's Androscoggin Mill place many of the same kinds of demands on management. The high degree of capital intensity they both share dictate concern for (1) selection of the proper technology and (2) the balancing of capacities in all segments of the process. Over time, technological advance has dictated numerous advances in the process itself (centrifuges, stainless steel tanks, panels of process controls) and in the scale of the process (larger tanks than ever before). The design, choice, and matching of equipment are critical decisions for a brewer like Stroh.

Scheduling production, while a nontrivial matter, is not as critical to a brewery's success as it is to a job shop. As important, or even more so, as the positioning of orders within any work shift or within any week's production is the accurate forecasting of demand. A Stroh wholesaler who is out of a particular beer or package risks that the consumer will merely choose a different brand. It is up to the brewery to track sales reliably and to forecast sales, especially seasonal sales, accurately.

Good forecasting also plays a significant role in managing suppliers' deliveries and inventories (e.g., cans and bottles) well. Since individual breweries do not negotiate price, delivery becomes the key aspect of brewery-supplier contact.

Hybrid Processes

Hybrid processes, mixes of two or more of the purer process types (job shop, batch flow, line flow, continuous flow), are common occurrences. Numerous plants are organized with line or continuous flow processes on their front ends, say, to assemble a product or to package it. On their back ends, these plants often have components fabricated or materials processed by job shop or batch flow processes. Much of food processing, drug manufacture, many complex, assembled consumer items (such as appliances and furniture), and other products combine production of components in lots with assembly/packaging in lines—the kind of hybrid process represented by the Stroh brewery.

Questions

1. What similarities are there between the Stroh brewery operation and the Androscoggin Mill operation? What dissimilarities?
2. What did Stroh consider to be the elements of the satisfactory production plan and the requirements for good package planning? What particular elements of Stroh's hybrid process planning might be applicable to the hybrid process in general? Why?

3. Describe how quality control may differ between the two main processes involved in a brewery.

4. Compare and contrast the demands of the process on Stroh workers and management with the demands on the same groups in two other processes you have studied.

5. It was stated that the brewery had a capacity of 6 million barrels of beer per year. If the plant were to can, bottle, and keg 6 million barrels in a year, what would be the capacity utilization of the packaging equipment, given the speeds mentioned in the case? Feel free to make assumptions about the relative demands for cans, bottles, and kegs.

6. How could the capacity of the brewing process itself be increased without a physical expansion of the brewery? How attractive is such a change?

7. Given the chapter's information on the relative demands of different brands and the summer cycle of container changeovers, concoct a month's production schedule for each major Stroh company brand. In an average week, what fraction of time would be devoted to changeovers of various types?

Situation for Study E-1
Country Gelatin Company

Thomas Brewer is the plant manager for Country Gelatin Company, maker of powdered gelatins for human consumption. The main component of gelatin is collagen, a fibrous substance that is mostly protein. Steerhide, a major source of collagen, is the main ingredient in the gelatin powder produced at Country's Kansas City, Kansas, plant.

Figure E5 shows the process that Country uses to produce its gelatin. First, the steerhides are treated (acid is added to remove the hair, then neutralized), weighed, and put into storage. Enough steerhide is treated at one time to provide two days' worth of production. The hides are then stored for about two weeks so that they begin to "break down" and can be blended with other ingredients. This storage is called "aging."

FIGURE E5 The production process at Country Gelatin Company.

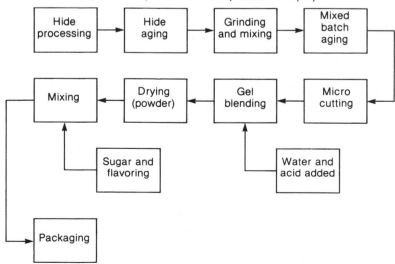

Once several batches of steerhides (1500 kilograms each) have aged properly, enough batches are ground (to about the consistency of hamburger) to run one week's production. These mixed batches (5500 kilograms each) are then aged again for a few days before they are mixed into a gel blend (8000 kilograms, of which about half is water). One gel blend is enough for one day's production of gelatin.

After being mixed and aged, the mixed batch undergoes microcutting, a process that cuts the material into very small pieces. It then is mixed with water and an acid to form the gel blend. Next the gel blend is forced through a dryer to make it a powder. Under proper conditions, the powder can be stored almost indefinitely, until it is needed for final production.

Final production consists of two stages. First, the powder is mixed with sugar and a powdered flavoring (unless the final product is to be an unflavored gelatin); second, the product is measured and packaged. Final production, although continuous, is done to customer order. All stages in the process are highly mechanized, and workers are needed only to monitor the machines.

Tom feels that quality control at Country can be adequately handled by three types of highly trained process control workers: solutions technicians, powder technicians, and line technicians. The solutions technician is responsible for the proper acid balance, salts, density, percent of solids, and the like of the gel blend. The powder technician's main responsibility is proper mixing of the final product—that is, the proper proportion of powder, sugars, and flavoring. The line technician is responsible for packaging.

Tom is wondering how he should schedule production at the various stages in the process, including the scheduling of labor and machines. In addition, he is uncertain how much inventory should be carried, and in what form. He feels he could begin to answer his concerns about scheduling and inventory control by (1) analyzing the characteristics of the process, and (2) asking himself what aspects of the process would help him in scheduling production and controlling inventories and which ones would hinder him.

Situation for Study E-2
Buchanan Tobacco Company

Buchanan Tobacco employed 2000 people in a plant that stretched 15 acres. Ten different cigarette brands were made at the site, each with its own blend of bright, burley, and Turkish tobaccos and various other flavorings.

After the tobacco (the whole dried leaf) had been purchased by the company's buyers at various tobacco markets, it was brought to the stemmeries. Here it was cleaned with moist air and dried, and the stems were removed. The tobacco was then cut into small pieces and stored for two to three years in hogsheads before being brought to the plant for blending. The hogsheads were loaded onto flatbed tractor-trailers, and the tobacco arrived at the west end of the building in the containers in which it was aged.

In the blending area, the tobaccos were blended and flavorants were added in order to produce the correct blend for each brand of cigarettes. At each stage in the blending process, the tobacco was exposed to certain relative humidities and temperatures. At the completion of each stage, the blended tobacco was aged through drying. This aging allowed the tobacco to absorb moisture and flavorants.

After being aged, the tobacco went through the "casing and cutting" process, where certain liquids (casings) were added and the tobacco was shredded and blended for the particular brands being made. A pneumatic vacuum system transported the blended tobaccos to one of the 100 cigarette-making machines (makers) designated for its brand. Each maker required one operator.

The sealed vacuum tubes ran above the machines, and so the tobacco fell to the bottom of the makers by gravity. The tobacco entered at the rate of 10 pounds per minute. The action of turning drums pulled the tobacco up through the machine. This action also vacuumed out dust and particles such as stems. As the tobacco came out of this section of the maker, it entered a small tube at such a constant rate that one continuous rod of tobacco was formed; this rod stretched almost the length of the machine.

At this point, the paper was wrapped around the tobacco. The paper, which was produced by a subsidiary, came in rolls over 6 miles long. Each roll contained enough paper for 95,000 cigarettes. The paper was threaded through the machine, and the cigarette brand name was printed on it. As the paper was folded around the continuous rod of tobacco, a wheel applied glue to one edge. The paper was then sealed around the rod of tobacco.

After sealing, the continuous cigarette was cut by a revolving knife, which cut 4100 cigarettes per minute and was timed to cut the exact length required.

The cut cigarettes next went to a drum. Vacuum pressure held the cigarettes on the drum as they slid into pockets. Simultaneously, the filters for the cigarettes, which were made in another area of the building and were precut to the appropriate size, were blown over on a tube. The cigarettes in the pockets were directly opposite each other, and a filter simply fell between them so that a cigarette, double-length filter, and another cigarette were all sealed together. At this point, the double cigarette passed over a sealer, and the filter was sealed to the paper on both ends. At the same time, corking paper, which was fed from a roll into the maker, was cut to the proper length and wrapped around the filter by the action of the drums. The "tipping" picked up enough glue to cause it to adhere to the filter. The double cigarette was then moved to a knife and cut into two 80-millimeter filtered cigarettes.

There were various automatic quality checks during the making process. Any cigarette with a defect would be automatically rejected. Common defects found at this point included air leaks and pin holes. All defective cigarettes were broken down and completely recycled through the process.

Immediately after cutting, the cigarettes that passed inspection were moved on a belt, with cigarettes on the back part of the drum being turned so that all were now facing the same direction. This belt carried the cigarettes to a special reservoir that created a buffer between the making and packing processes.

This reservoir loaded cigarettes onto a conveyor for up to 17 minutes. If the maker went down, the packer could continue running for up to 17 minutes by using the reserve cigarettes from overhead. If the packer went down, the process simply reversed and cigarettes fed onto the conveyor directly from the maker. If either machine was inoperable for more than 17 minutes, both machines had to be shut down.

From this point, the cigarettes were fed by gravity into the packing machine or packer. As the cigarettes were fed into the machine, they automatically fell into three rows of 7, 6, and 7 cigarettes. A plunger pushed the 20 cigarettes into a foil pocket, which was formed as a series of turning drums took the foil that was fed off a roll and wrapped it around a form identical in shape and size to a pack of cigarettes. This foil was the interior of a pack of cigarettes.

Next, the label was taken from the front of the machine and formed into a pack and sealer was applied. Another plunger pushed the foiled pack into the label. A stamper picked up glue and applied a closure (stamp) to the pack. The pack slid on chains to the film machine.

The film fed off of a roll and was cut to the desired length to wrap a pack. Just before the pack was pushed into the film, the tear tape was laid across the film and sealed to it. Mechanical folders folded the film around the pack and electric heaters caused it to seal.

The packer packaged 210 packs of cigarettes a minute (4200 cigarettes); it was operating at a slightly faster rate than the maker. There were approximately 110 packers in the plant, each one operated by one worker.

The packaged cigarettes were then fed on conveyor belts past an inspector. The inspector looked for missing closures, missing tape, or any other defective packaging. Packs were fed to the inspector from two packers; therefore, an inspector saw about 25,000 packs an hour.

After the visual inspection, the packs proceeded on belts to the carton boxer machine. There were approximately 50 carton boxers, each one receiving from two packers; thus, two belts came together at the boxer. The cartons were fed down by a series of rollers and automatically opened. The packs from the two belts (five packs from each belt) lined up. The pressure from the last pack activated a switch, which in turn activated the plunger, pushing 10 packs into a carton. The flaps of the carton were turned down by guides. When the carton emerged at the back of the boxer, it was sealed. At this point, an electronic inspector (operating on the basis of the metal in the foil) was used to detect missing tape or packs. The carton boxer's speed was determined by the speed of the packers, but generally it boxed 200 packs, or 20 cartons, per minute.

Next, the cartons proceeded up the elevator to the carton conveyor and down to the case packer. Usually at least five packers sent cartons to a single case packer; however, a single case packer could receive from as many as 20 packers. There were 5 case packers at the plant.

Flattened cases were stacked and fed down through one end of the machine, where guides opened them automatically. The cases had been preprinted with the brand name, but print was now applied to the cases to specify the date and the name of the plant. Cartons came down overhead slides from the carton collector and were conveyed into the back of the machine. The cartons were stacked in layers. As soon as 10 rows of 6 cartons each had accumulated, a switch was activated to plunge the 60 cartons into one case. Thus each case contained 12,000 cigarettes. The filled case was then moved forward. Glue was applied from rollers to the end flaps. When the machine cycled again, these flaps were sealed down with pressure. The case stayed in this compartment until the glue was dried and sealed, which was less than a minute. Each caser had the capacity of packing approximately five cases per minute.

The sealed cases crossed an automatic scale before going up an elevator. This scale inspected for light cases; being underweight indicated that a pack or carton was missing. A heavy case was not rejected, because extra weight merely indicated the presence of collected moisture.

After reaching the top of the case elevator, the case traveled on a conveyor to the transfer room. Here all brands were assembled on pallets by brand. Each pallet had an identification number, which the computer married to the brand's code number to permit tracking these cases to the warehouse. After the cases had been palletized, elevators lifted the pallets to the conveyor to the shipping center. All of the shipping was done from the new, completely computerized central distribution center. The cigarettes were produced strictly to order. Everything produced during the day was shipped out at night so that there was virtually no work-in-process or finished goods inventory.

1. Diagram the process flow.

2. Speculate, as best you can, on the flows of information in the process.

3. Why might this operation be classed as a hybrid? What type of hybrid is it and how does it compare with the Stroh brewery?

4. What do you see as key challenges for management in this process?

5. What kinds of changes to the process would occur as new makers are purchased with speeds twice as great or more than those already in the plant?

A Worker-Paced Line Flow Process and a Service Factory

Burger King Restaurant
Route 37
Noblesville, Indiana

(Courtesy of Burger King Corporation)

The Burger King Restaurant on Route 37 in Noblesville, Indiana, was one of over 8000 fast-food restaurants operated worldwide by Burger King Corporation, a wholly owned subsidiary of Grand Metropolitan, and by the corporation's franchisees. Service was available from 5:45 A.M. to 1 A.M. every day. The dining room was open from 5:45 A.M. until 11 P.M., Sunday through Thursday, and from 5:45 A.M.

until midnight on Fridays and Saturdays. Breakfast was available from the opening until 10:30 A.M. and consisted of a choice of bacon, ham, and sausage bagels, biscuits, and Croissan'wiches®, with or without eggs or cheese, French toast sticks, biscuits with gravy, hash browns, and a scrambled egg platter. The regular menu consisted of a wide selection of hamburger sandwiches (regular hamburger and cheeseburger; a special Whopper® sandwich with or without cheese; Whopper Jr.®; double burger, double cheeseburger, and double Whopper®; and a bacon double cheeseburger) as well as some specialty sandwiches (chicken, ham and cheese, fish), BK Broilers® (broiled chicken sandwiches), Chicken Tenders™, and prepacked salads. To accompany these selections, the restaurant offered various choices: french fries, onion rings, soft drinks, shakes, apple pie, and other seasonal pies. Occasionally, there were promotional items.

The restaurant, the highest sales volume Burger King in Indiana, was located on Route 37, a busy thoroughfare between Marion and Indianapolis. The restaurant was opened in May 1987 on the site of a former farm. The restaurant was owned and operated by a franchisee, Douglas Brucker of Marion.

The restaurant was rectangular, freestanding on 2 acres, and was constructed mainly of wood planks, bricks, and glass. The building was situated toward the front of the lot, freeing the sides and rear for 64 parking spaces. A "drive-thru" was operated on one side of the restaurant, with the order board at the rear and the pickup window toward the front. Within the restaurant 96 seats (either benches or freestanding chairs) were arranged in groups. There were 16 tables of four, 1 table of three, 8 tables of two, and 13 single places within the restaurant. The eating area was tastefully appointed in oak wood, with a handsome color scheme, an atrium off to the side of the main eating area, ceiling fans, and many hanging plants. In the eating areas there were service counters for napkins, straws, and so on, and several large trash cans for customer use. The rest rooms were lo-

The dining area. (*Courtesy of Burger King Corporation*)

cated next to the main door. The eating area occupied about half of the restaurant's square footage; the other half was occupied by the counter, the kitchen, and the storage area.

PART ONE: PROCESS DESCRIPTION

Restaurant Operations

Order Taking (The Front Counter)

After entering the restaurant, customers walked between the railings of the queuing line (or, as Burger King calls it, the "customer guidance system"). While awaiting their turns to state their order at the counter, they could consult the brightly lit menu above the counter area. At the right-hand side of the counter were two cash registers with screens (point-of-sale devices). An order taker greeted each customer there and took the order. As the customer spoke, the order taker keyed the contents of the order on a register (e.g., pressed the key for the Whopper®—a large hamburger with lettuce, tomato, onions, pickles, ketchup, and mayonnaise), read the printed total for the order, took the customer's payment, and gave the customer change and a receipt that listed the order. Each register could accommodate one or two cashiers simultaneously and could handle multiple transactions at the same time.

At the other end of the counter, a printer printed a duplicate copy of the order. Using this copy, an expediter proceeded to assemble the order. Assembling the order meant going to the counter and the chutes that lay between the front counter and the kitchen to gather the sandwiches, fries, or other items that flowed from the kitchen. When shakes were ordered, the expediter was responsible for drawing them from the nearby dispensing machine. After assembling the kitchen items of the order, the expediter presented them to the customer either on a tray

The front counter as seen from the dining room. *(Courtesy of Burger King Corporation)*

(for inside use) or in a bag (to go). The expediter also gave cups to the customer so that he or she could fill them with the desired soft drinks, tea, or coffee.

Several features of the front counter's operation merit highlighting. The most important feature was the split made in the duties of the order takers and expediters. The system in use at the Noblesville Burger King was known as the "multiconventional" lineup. It was a throwback to the early years of Burger King when the "conventional" lineup was used. That system consisted of a single line of customers served by a single cash register where orders were taken. Expediters assembled the orders and presented them to the customers farther along the counter. The present system operated in much the same way, although many more orders could be taken at the same time, and several expediters could handle those orders. The multiconventional system was thus far faster than the old system.

The multiconventional lineup was a more radical change from the "hospitality lineup" that had replaced the old conventional system. With the hospitality lineup, cash registers were evenly spaced across the entire front counter and customers had to choose which of several lines they wished to wait in. Cashiers both took orders and assembled them. The hospitality lineup, although somewhat more labor intensive than the old conventional lineup, could handle peak hour demand more efficiently than the older system. With the advent of the multiconventional lineup, however, the labor intensity of the hospitality lineup was reduced without sacrificing its peak-period capacity advantages. Customers preferred the multiconventional lineup as well. With a single line, they did not risk becoming annoyed because some other line was moving faster than theirs. In addition, they were frequently better prepared to give their order to the order taker, and this speeded up the process for everyone.

Another feature of the front counter's operations involved self-service drink dispensers where customers could fix their drinks precisely the way they wanted

The front counter as seen from the kitchen. *(Courtesy of Burger King Corporation)*

(whether lots of ice or no ice). By moving the drink dispensers out of the kitchen, time and some labor costs were also saved. Because free refills were possible, materials costs were somewhat higher, but not appreciably so.

Order Filling (The Kitchen)

Burger King differed from McDonald's and some other fast-food restaurants in that comparatively little finished goods inventory was kept; sandwiches were assembled continuously. While certain orders might not have been delivered as quickly as when larger inventories were kept, this approach offered the distinct advantage of producing to order when appropriate. As an old Burger King slogan put it, you can "have it your way," say, by ordering a Whopper® with double cheese and mustard but no pickle, or a hamburger with extra onions.

Providing this kind of customer order variation with minimum customer waiting demanded a production system that was extraordinarily flexible. In fact, two kinds of flexibility were required: flexibility to meet special customer orders and flexibility to meet large surges in customer demand during lunch or dinner hours. Many aspects of the production system contributed to this flexibility.

The "Line": Layout and Job Descriptions

The process of making sandwiches and filling orders at Burger King was explicitly recognized as an assembly line. Production of the hamburger sandwiches (burgers, for short) followed a straight path from the back of the kitchen to the front counter. Along this path were a series of workstations (see Figure F1).

Any of the various burgers was begun either by taking a broiled meat patty and toasted bun out of an environmentally controlled holding compartment called a "steamer" or by placing a frozen meat patty (Whopper®-size or regular) and bun onto the chain drag at the feed end of a specially constructed, gas-fired broiler at the back of the kitchen. The meat patties were drawn from a freezer be-

FIGURE F1 Layout of the Noblesville Burger King. The circled numbers indicate the sequence of additions of workers to the kitchen as demand increases.

The fry station. *(Courtesy of Burger King Corporation)*

low the broiler. The broiler cooked the meat at approximately 800°F, allowing the grease to drip into a special compartment, and it also toasted the bun.

Next in the assembly line came the "board," where buns and meat were transformed into Whopper® sandwiches, burgers, Whopper Jr.® sandwiches, double cheeseburgers, and the like. This was the key portion of the line, where the burger could be assembled "your way." The board itself was a long, stainless-steel table in the center of which were bins of condiments (refrigerated cheese slices, bacon, pickles, onion, sliced tomatoes, shredded lettuce, mayonnaise) kept at room temperature. Below the table were racks for holding spare quantities of condiments and supplies and also places for waste disposal. There were two work areas, one on each side of the center inventory of condiments. Above each side were two microwave ovens that could be used for keeping assembled sandwiches hot, stacks of various wrappers into which the sandwiches were placed, and a special series of touch controls that were part of the information flow system of the kitchen (more on this later). Beyond the board, on the pickup counter, were chutes that held completed sandwiches ready for assembly into customer orders.

On one side of this main burger assembly line were the frying vats and the specialty sandwich board. The four frying vats were computer controlled, two just for french fries and two for other products (such as onion rings, chicken sandwich portions, Chicken Tenders™, or fish portions). Near the frying vats were racks of thawed or thawing french fries (one- to two-hour thaw times maximum). Behind the frying vats was the specialty sandwich board, which had its own assortment of condiments, buns, and wrappers. To one side of the specialty sandwich board were two warmers (one for items such as cooked chicken patties and the other for Chicken Tenders™) and to the other side was a bun toaster.

On the other side of the main burger assembly line were the automatic drink machines for the drive-thru operation. A worker simply placed an ice-filled cup under the appropriate drink spout and pressed a button for small, regular, or large drinks; the machine then dispensed the proper quantity of soft drink, freeing the worker to do something else while the cup was being filled. The shake machine (for chocolate, vanilla, and strawberry) was located nearby, close to both the drive-thru window and the front counter.

Around the periphery of the kitchen were sinks and storage areas for food and supplies. There were also cooler and freezer rooms, an office, a training room, and a crew room where workers could congregate.

The Drive-Thru Operation

Because the drive-thru at the Noblesville Burger King accounted for approximately 50 percent of the restaurant's business, its smooth operation was critical. Work assignments at the drive-thru depended on how busy the restaurant was. In very slow times, a single worker (order taker/expediter) could handle the drive-thru alone. When business picked up, two people were assigned to the drive-thru—one as an order taker and one as an expediter. At peak times, five workers were assigned to the drive-thru: order taker, window pusher, expediter, drink assembler, and cashier. (The Noblesville Burger King had two windows in the drive-thru lane, the first to handle the money and the second to "push out" the order.)

Peak Versus Nonpeak Operation

Employees were allocated to the workstations at the restaurant according to the pace of demand. When demand was slow, a smaller crew operated the restaurant: an order taker/expediter at the front counter, a drive-thru order taker/expediter, and two kitchen workers. One worker took the broiler and the burger board, while one worked at the fry station and the specialty board. At peak times, there were as many as 18 employees working in the restaurant plus two or three managers. Management knew from historical data exactly when the peak hours would be at the Noblesville restaurant and so could plan worker arrivals.

Pitching patties into the continuous chain broiler. *(Courtesy of Burger King Corporation)*

Before the daily peaks in demand at lunch and dinner, considerable preparations were made, such as stocking the freezer under the broiler with hamburger patties, taking frozen fries out for thawing, and slicing tomatoes. If things worked as planned, minimal restocking would be needed during the peaks.

As demand picked up, more workers were added, and job assignments became more specialized. In slow times, for example, one worker split duties between the fry station and the specialty sandwich board; during peak periods there were separate workers for these two work areas. During slow periods, one worker handled the broiler and all burger sandwich preparation; during peak times, one worker "fed" the broiler, one or two "caught" patties and buns and monitored the steamer, and up to four workers assembled sandwiches at the burger board. At the Noblesville Burger King, the burger board was divided during peak times into cheese and noncheese sides. (At other Burger Kings, this division might be Whopper®-size sandwiches on one side and small sandwiches on the other. Such a split frequently depended on the composition of demand at the particular restaurant.) During peak periods as well, two workers helped keep the dining area clean.

During very slow periods, much of the sandwich and drink production was triggered by the customer order itself. The burger given to the customer might actually be the one placed on the broiler chain in response to punching in the order. Some items could be held in inventory. An inventory of the most popular sandwiches (such as regular burgers and Whoppers®) was usually kept in the chutes, but only for 10 minutes; if no customer requested them, they were discarded. Each sandwich wrapper was marked with a "time to discard." The system used the numbers pointed to by the minute hand on the clock. Thus a Whopper® wrapped at 20 minutes after the hour (the 4 on the clockface) would have a 6 marked on the wrapper, because at 30 minutes after the hour (the 6 on the clockface) its 10-minute hold time would have expired. French fries were handled in a special way. Fries took approximately 2 minutes and 30 seconds to cook—too long to have a customer wait. As a result, fries had to be waiting in finished goods inventory. Here, too, the restaurant kept track of the time fries were waiting. If no one claimed fries within 7 minutes, they were discarded. (The fry station computers helped by keeping track of the time between batches so that fries were not sitting out too long.)

As demand picked up, it became more and more likely that a finished goods inventory of the major burgers and specialty sandwiches would be kept and that the broiler feeder would be loading the broiler in response to the inventory situation rather than in response to the particular orders displayed on the video screens. To guide production and to maintain inventory levels as demand increased, the Noblesville Burger King operated "stock level charts." There were four stock level charts—one each for the broiler-steamer, sandwich board, specialty sandwich board, and specialty sandwich warmer. The chart featured a stock-level light indicator on which there were seven lights. Corresponding to each light was a volume of sales range to which were pegged inventory standards for the various items. Each change in the level (e.g., from level 4 to level 5 or from level 6 to peak) was announced by a special bell and the light switched so that all workers could infer, for example, how many sandwiches of particular types should be in the finished goods chutes and how many patties and buns should be in the steamer. The workers at the board were constantly tracking how many sandwiches were in each chute as well as keeping an eye on the video screen for any special order variations entered by the cashiers. When a worker finished such an order, he or she pressed one of the special touch controls above the station (mentioned ear-

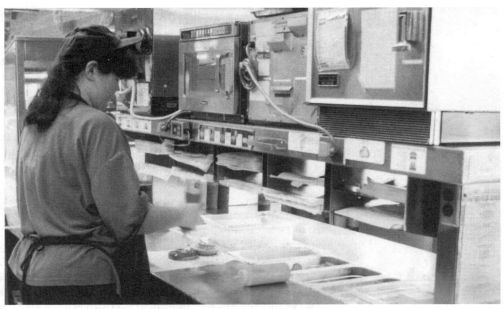

At the burger board. *(Courtesy of Burger King Corporation)*

lier), which removed the call for that sandwich from the video screen. The worker then marked the wrapper to identify it to the expediters.

For the manager, the choice of a "level" represented a trade-off between meeting service standards with quick deliveries, on the one hand, and keeping too much in inventory and risking waste on the other. The manager always wanted to raise the level just before a surge in demand and to lower it just before the surge evaporated.

Coping with Bottlenecks

Surges in demand or runs on particular items could strain the production system and cause it to miss its established service standards. Three service standards were routinely tracked: (1) door-to-door time—the time elapsed from the moment the customer entered a line to place an order until the customer was served; (2) drive-thru time—the time elapsed from the arrival of a car in line until the customer was served; and (3) drive-thru transaction time—the time elapsed between a car's arrival at the pickup window and its receipt of the order. The Noblesville Burger King restaurant tried to keep these service standards at company-mandated levels: 3 minutes average for the door-to-door and drive-thru times and 30 seconds average for the drive-thru transaction time. This last time was tracked automatically by the store's computer.

To reach these goals consistently the restaurant's managers had to avoid bottlenecks in production. By providing both guidance to the crew and a set of spare hands, a manager could help ensure a smooth operation. (The Noblesville Burger King's sales volumes were high enough to warrant the creation of a "production leader" position for work in the kitchen, and a head cashier position. These workers were active in guiding the crew and anticipating bottlenecks.) During peak hours especially, it was not uncommon to see the production leader or a manager stepping up to the board to assemble a sandwich or drawing a shake from the machine or bagging fries or replenishing materials. The managers also encouraged crew teamwork. For example, workers with some slack time helped those who were overloaded—a cheese sandwich worker might assemble some noncheese burgers. In fact, the manager's mandate for each of the workers was (1) to be aware of which "level" was being operated and what was on the video screen, (2) to be aware of any materials that would soon be out of stock, (3) to keep the workstation clean, and (4) to help anyone needing help. This mandate to keep production smooth and efficient placed special demands on a manager. The manager's job was not only to break any current bottlenecks but also to anticipate any potential ones. The manager constantly sought information from the workers on where bottlenecks were, how many cars were in line, which materials were running low, and encouraged them to handle as much of any surge in demand as possible themselves.

Adequate prepeak period preparation also meant a great deal in coping with bottlenecks. If the shake machine was not completely filled with ingredients or if the cash register tape was close to running out, the operation was in danger of some bottlenecks that might affect service adversely. The restaurant manager had to check the status of items like these to be sure that incomplete preparation did not detract from the success of the operation.

Purchasing and Materials Management

For any item, the quantity ordered was the amount needed to bring the restaurant's existing inventory up to a certain established level. This level was the quantity of the item the manager expected to be used between receipt of the order and receipt of the next order (three to five days at a maximum) plus a safety stock amount equal to 20 percent of the expected usage. This safety stock helped ensure that the entire menu was always available. The expected usage was calculated from the previous week's demand but was adjusted to reflect special trends or such conditions as holidays, school vacations, and newspaper promotions.

Orders were typically placed one day in advance of delivery. Materials were generally received in the morning. All materials were dated on receipt, and the oldest materials were always used first. However, usage levels were so high that the restaurant never needed to worry about spoilage, even for produce or dairy products. Orders for meat, paper products, and certain other supplies were placed three times a week with the Louisville regional office of King Distribution Services, one of Burger King's supply subsidiaries. Fresh produce was ordered from either King Distribution Services or an independent supplier six days a week. Baked goods were ordered five days a week.

The Workforce

The restaurant employed 45 workers. A typical worker put in 35 to 40 hours each week, spread over 5 or 6 days. Most lived in the area of the restaurant. At night and on weekends, high school students and second-job workers were often employed. The area was considered one that was hard to find staff for.

The crew for the Noblesville Burger King was hand-picked by the assistant managers. Almost none had worked at a Burger King before. Workers were paid for the hours worked, with overtime given after 40 hours each week. The average hourly wage was $6.60, with some workers receiving a minimum wage of $5.25 and the best-performing workers receiving $7.50. The fringe benefit package was modest. Labor turnover at the restaurant ran at 100 percent.

A worker's hours were likely to differ from day to day, although there was a set crew for the breakfast shift. The schedule for any week, however, was worked out about a week in advance. The schedule did try to reflect worker preferences about the amount and timing of their work. Most work assignments were shuffled daily. The prime reason for shuffling assignments was to promote worker cross-training, which increased the operation's flexibility. A manager might also be forced to shuffle assignments because of worker scheduling or absentee problems. For these reasons, the order taker knew how the kitchen operated, and the kitchen knew how to take orders. The cross-training also had the welcome benefit of heightening the tolerance any worker had for the momentary troubles of other workers.

The daily rise and fall of peak and off-peak demand required continual changes in crew size, so that neither too few nor too many workers worked at any one time. The flexibility needed in the schedule was achieved by using the part-time labor force and by scheduling their arrivals and departures at different times. Some, for example, reported to work just 15 minutes or so before the noon rush hour. Workers worked at least 3 to 4 hours at a time. A worker's departure from the restaurant was at the discretion of the manager. If sales were light, the manager could let some of the workers out early; if demand was heavy, it was understood that workers would be asked to stay past the scheduled departure time. The best crew, however, was generally scheduled for the peak times on Friday and Saturday.

The production leaders and the head cashier were responsible for training new workers. There were seven main stations on which to be trained (sandwich board, specialty sandwich board, fry station, broiler-steamer, order taker/cashier, drive-thru, and hostess [clean-up]). Training for any one of these stations took about three hours and consisted of reading some prepared material, watching a videotape on the station's work, doing a worksheet based on that video, reading a manual on procedures on the workstation, watching the trainer demonstrate procedures at the workstation, performing on a trial basis from one to two hours, tak-

The drive-thru window as seen from the kitchen. *(Courtesy of Burger King Corporation)*

ing a written test, and then having performance evaluated by the trainer. A new worker trained first on the broiler and steamer and then progressed to every station in the kitchen, finally winding up at the front counter and drive-thru operations. The fry station and the burger sandwich board were generally acknowledged to be the toughest tasks at the restaurant.

Quality

Periodically, about once a quarter, a team from the corporation would visit the restaurant unannounced to perform a quality inspection. They used a form for rating the food, the service, the appearance of the restaurant, and some other factors. In addition, the district manager for the franchise made weekly visits to the restaurant to audit quality. Twice a year, management performed a three-day restaurant operations consultation during which every aspect of the restaurant's operation on every shift was analyzed. The results of such audits were taken very seriously. In addition, much of the managers' time was spent in the dining room talking with customers and assessing how well the service was being delivered.

Management

The Noblesville Burger King was a franchise store. It was part of the company's Lakes area. Supervising the Noblesville Burger King were a manager and six assistant managers. One of these seven was always at the restaurant. During peak times managers would overlap, so that two or three sets of extra hands and eyes were available for breaking bottlenecks. The six assistant managers worked five days a week, but on a rotating shift.

Any manager's primary responsibility was to ensure that a good-quality product was promptly served in a clean environment within company guidelines. Although a manager's ability to control costs was valued, meeting the corporation's service, quality, and cleanliness goals came first. Meeting these goals meant developing the capabilities of the production crew and maintaining its morale. Thus the manager was first and foremost a crew foreman, teaching new hires, guiding work assignments, checking quality, breaking bottlenecks, and providing an example for the crew. Layered on these responsibilities were others—ordering materials, receiving deliveries, checking and posting standards of performance (such as the door-to-door or transaction times), checking on the preparations for the day and for the peak periods, and scheduling the part-time workforce. Of the restaurant's six assistant managers, three specialized in the functions of ordering, scheduling, and breakfast operations.

Burger King headquarters provided restaurant managers with a number of aids. Chief among these aids for the week-by-week operation of the restaurant were the charts, formulas, and decision rules for scheduling the workforce, given the restaurant's particular configuration. The corporation had developed aids that showed, for different sales levels and hours of operation, how much labor each restaurant should have and where that labor ought to be assigned. These charts, formulas, and decision rules greatly aided the managers in controlling labor costs, which was the second highest cost that could be controlled.

The restaurant's POS system (computer/cash register network) was also a useful management tool. From the computer, the manager could obtain information, by half-hour increments, on sales, product mix, and discounts. The POS system also kept track of the restaurant's service standard performance.

Facilities and Technology

This Burger King was a design called BK87. According to Larry Levensky, the franchisee's district manager, the BK87 was an excellent design for a high-volume restaurant. The layout was very efficient, workers did not waste many steps in performing the tasks required of them, materials were readily available, and there was ample storage space. Workers at nonpeak times could easily cover more than one workstation.

In addition, the Noblesville Burger King included several technological improvements that had been initiated by the corporation over the years. For example, computerized frying vats had been installed with temperature probes that automatically adjusted the frying times so that french fries or other fried foods were cooked perfectly. Buzzers indicated when the fries should be shaken or removed from the vats. The automatic drink machines were another advance; these permitted workers to engage in other tasks while soft drink cups were being filled automatically. The shake machine mixed shakes automatically as well. The addition of TV screens to indicate variations on the standard sandwiches was another advance; these reduced the cacophony that could strike the kitchen during peak periods. The kitchen included a breakfast grill and hood, a specially designed unit that could be set up for the breakfast business and then transformed into a work area the rest of the day. The heat chutes for finished sandwiches were coated with Teflon and were enclosed to keep the sandwiches warmer. The extra window for the drive-thru was still another innovation, helping to cut 12 seconds off the line time for drive-thru customers. Burger King was continually inventing new ways for delivering better service.

PART TWO: DISCUSSION

The Burger King Corporation is in no way responsible for the following views and presentation. They remain solely the responsibility of the author.

The Flow of the Process and of Information

In most service industries, the time delay between service provision and service consumption is necessarily very short. Put another way, one can rarely inventory a service, at least not for very long. Hotel room–nights cannot be inventoried, nor can timely tips on the stock market, nor can tasty hamburgers. Hence a whole degree of freedom is removed from the service manager, which heightens the importance of capacity choice in most service industries.

It is also frequently the case that services must be particularly flexible so that they can be customized to individual consumer needs. Think of the travel agent, the salesperson, the cab driver, and, yes, the fast-food restaurant.

These two basic features of many service businesses place substantial demands on the process design and information systems of an enterprise like Burger King. Flexibility in both product and volume is paramount, and Burger King has adopted some classic policies for yielding such flexibility.

Figure F2 is a process flow diagram for assembling an order. It is simple, and that is one of its advantages. Responsibilities are clearly demarcated, and yet all of the key tasks for customizing the hamburger or specialty sandwich rest with the worker who actually assembles the sandwich at the board. This fact, in turn, simplifies the information flow so that only one worker need pay strict attention to

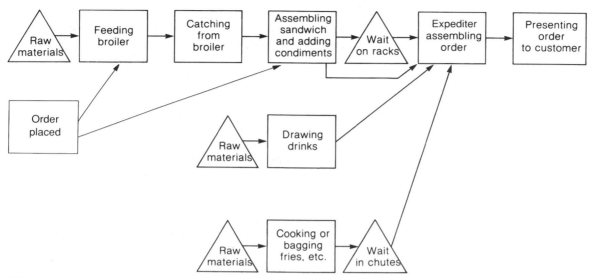

FIGURE F2 A process flow diagram (nonpeak period) for the Noblesville Burger King restaurant's kitchen operations.

the punch-in of a special order. (An information flow diagram is found in Figure F3.) In this way, with a clear delineation of tasks and direct information flows, rapid product changes can be facilitated.

Flexibility in changing production volumes is achieved by a continual rebalancing of the sandwich production line. The time pattern of demand is well known from past experience, and this knowledge has permitted the staggering of work hours for the part-time workforce so that varying numbers can be on hand at any one time. The workforce ebbs and flows from 3 during slack periods to 20 during peak periods. As more workers are added, the job contents narrow and, importantly, the flow of information changes. No longer is production keyed completely to the punch-in of the order. More and more, production is keyed to the levels of the finished goods inventory and of the work-in-process inventory of broiled burgers and toasted buns. Instead of reacting to the order punched in, the broiler feeder reacts to the manager's posted list of burgers to be held as work-in-process, feeding the broiler so as to maintain the desired inventory level. Similarly, the

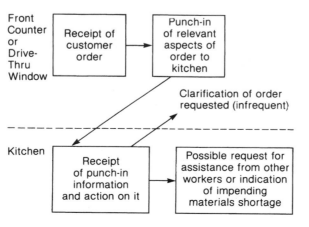

FIGURE F3 An information flow diagram (nonpeak period) for the Noblesville Burger King restaurant.

board workers respond to the level of finished goods inventory, although these board workers must also respond to any special orders that are punched in. Special orders, of course, must take precedence over the maintenance of the finished goods inventory. The peak period changes in the process and information flow diagrams are pictured in Figure F4.

Demands of the Process on the Workforce

The flexibility of the Burger King fast-food operation demands flexibility from its workers. The job contents and the production pace vary markedly throughout any worker's shift during the day, requiring a special tolerance. Workers on a machine-paced assembly line get used to the rhythm of the conveyor. But, on a worker-paced line, and particularly one in a service industry, any rhythm may soon dissolve.

What is especially true of worker-paced lines is that the crew on the line views itself as a team, largely because they are so dependent on one another. This fact often permits worker-paced lines where the demand is steady (unlike at a fast-food restaurant) to be paid according to a group incentive scheme. Some standard of production—X units per time period—is established and the crew on the line, if it can better the standard, is paid extra for doing so. This kind of group incentive pay scheme can tie a crew together as a team even more thoroughly than usual.

Demands of the Process on Management

An operation like a Burger King restaurant places specific demands on management both because it is a service operation and because it is a worker-paced line

FIGURE F4 Process and information flow diagrams (peak period) for the Noblesville Burger King restaurant.

flow process. As a line flow process, many of the issues that were discussed in Tour D with respect to Carrier Corporation surface:

Balance of the line

Materials management

Technological advance

Capacity planning

Product design

Workforce management

Managers of worker-paced lines should be sensitive to all these issues, since to fall down on any one could seriously jeopardize the entire operation.

The issue of technological advance is particularly acute, since such an advance may enable a smoother, more regular flow of the product. After all, a worker-paced line flow usually remains worker- rather than machine-paced because there is as yet no easy way to guard against a succession of overcycle conditions striking a worker all at once (such as a run on "Whoppers®, hold the pickles"). If the mix of product options can somehow be smoothed out or if particular advances can be made in product or workstation design, a worker-paced line can easily be transformed into a machine-paced line. In other words, the worker-paced line is somewhat more vulnerable to radical, rather than incremental, change than is a machine-paced one.

The technological changes evident at the Noblesville Burger King all contributed to a smoother flow of product. The automatic drink machines, the computerized frying vats, the TV monitors of information, and even the new BK87 layout all act to speed up and smooth the delivery process.

A Burger King's status as a service operation only heightens the importance of capacity planning, since service firms cannot ordinarily inventory their product. The new BK87 design is testament to the importance the corporation assigns to planning capacity. The importance of workforce management is also heightened, because the worker-customer interaction is part of the service. Ordinarily, one cannot hide the service process as readily as one can hide the manufacturing process. Keeping the workforce productive and interested in their jobs is a key challenge for managers in service operations.

Questions

1. Visit a fast-food restaurant with a friend to perform an experiment. While one of you times the other's entry and exit and the time from the placing of the order to its receipt, the other should observe how many workers are actually involved with the order. Visit the fast-food restaurant at a slack time and at a peak time, and compare the differences in time and number of workers.

2. Watch for bottlenecks the next time you are in a fast-food restaurant (or any worker-paced service operation). Where do they arise and why? How might they be remedied?

3. Suppose that Burger King were to introduce a new type of sandwich. What aspects of the restaurant's operations would be affected, and how?

4. Why is flexibility one of the key features for success in a worker-paced assembly line operation such as Burger King?

5. How would you define capacity at a Burger King? What factors influence the establishment of a limit to capacity?

6. Would you prefer to work on a machine-paced assembly line or a worker-paced one? Why? Which would you prefer to supervise? Why?

7. Visit a Burger King close to you. It is unlikely to be a brand new one with all the advances incorporated into the Noblesville Burger King. Consider the ways by which the Burger King you visit could be modernized. Consider as well what could be done at the restaurant to increase capacity as sales increase. Prepare plans of action that specify which things ought to be done, and in what order, to modernize the restaurant and/or increase its capacity. Defend your choices.

8. Consider an alternative kitchen layout to the one at the Noblesville Burger King. In what ways is your alternative better or worse than the one discussed in the tour?

Situation for Study F-1
Legacy Homes

Tom Stoddard had been employed part-time as a "rough carpenter" by Legacy Homes while he completed his degree at Interstate Tech University. After his graduation, Legacy hired Tom as a construction superintendent; this job combined the duties of foreman, scheduler, and expediter.

By building only to order, Legacy took a conservative approach to the ups and downs typical of the home construction industry. Legacy offered a limited number of home designs; Tables F1 and F2 show the work involved on most of

TABLE F1 Crew size and times for various tasks (Legacy Homes)

Task	Description	Work Type*	Minimum/Maximum Crew Size	Days to Complete (with Minimum Crew)
1	Concrete footer	A	2–4	1.00
2	Foundation	F	Subcontract	1.00
3	Grading	A	2–4	0.50
4	Framing	B	5–8	2.60
5	Roofing	F	Subcontract	1.00
6	Concrete	A/B	3–5	1.50
7	Wiring	C	2–4	1.00
8	Furnace and ducts	C	2–4	2.25
9	Plumbing	C	2–3	2.50
10	Insulation	B	1–3	2.25
11	Dry wall	F	Subcontract	1.00
12	Siding	F	Subcontract	5.50
13	Sewer line	A	2–3	2.00
14	Painting	F	Subcontract	1.50
15	Finish carpentry	D	2–4	2.50
16	Tile	D	1–2	5.00
17	Electrical trim	C	1–2	1.50
18	Finish plumbing	C	1–2	3.50
19	Heating trim	C	1–3	2.50
20	Carpeting	F	Subcontract	2.00
21	Cleanup	E	1–3	2.00

*A, excavate; B, rough carpentry; C, plumbing, heating, electrical; D, finish carpentry; E, part-time cleanup; F, subcontract.

TABLE F2 Precedence relationship (Legacy Homes)

Job	Preceding Operation(s)
1	
2	1
3	2
4	3
5	4
6	2
7	4
8	5
9	5
10	7, 8, 9
11	10
12	10
13	9
14	11
15	14
16	14
17	14
18	15
19	14
20	6, 12, 13, 16, 17, 18, 19
21	20

them—usually about 90 days' worth. When a buyer arranged a home loan from a lending institution, the local practice was to allow the construction company to receive the money in partial payments (cash draws) depending on the degree of completion of the home. Thus, for Legacy to receive the money, Tom needed to finish a home as fast as possible.

Legacy had a nucleus crew of highly skilled workers that it wanted to keep working most of the time. Other workers could be hired to supplement this crew when necessary. Table F3 shows this crew and the various tasks they were capable of performing. Each crew member knew well a primary function such as plumbing but could be counted on to help with other functions such as rough carpentry. The crew who installed the plumbing, for example, also installed the heating and electricity. This overlap of skills was possible for two reasons: (1) Most of the work on a Legacy house was rather straightforward and did not entail the total skill requirements of journeymen in any of the trades, and (2) Legacy hired nonunion workers.

Table F1 shows the minimum and maximum crew sizes for completing each task. For example, task 8 requires a minimum of two workers because one person working alone cannot position the furnace or handle the ductwork; two people working on separate houses would take much longer to complete their work on both houses than if they worked together on one house at a time. At the maximum crew size, of course, it can happen that workers interfere with each other's work. Tom assumed that additional workers could work at the same rate as workers already on the job; he therefore scaled the number of workers up or down proportionately. For example, in task 1 if two workers can do the job in 1 day (i.e., 2 labor-days are required), three workers can do the job in $\frac{2}{3}$ day (2 labor-days di-

TABLE F3 Labor force (Legacy Homes)		
Type of Work	*Current Labor Available*	*Tasks Performed**
A Excavate	3	1, 3, 6, 13
B Rough carpentry	5	4, 6, 10
C Plumbing, heating, electrical	4	7, 8, 9, 17, 18, 19
D Finish carpentry	2	15, 16
E Part-time cleanup	1	21
F Subcontract		2, 5, 11, 12, 14, 20

*See Table F1 for an explanation of these numbers.

vided by three workers available), and four workers can do it in ½ a day. All operations have been designed to require a low level of skill; thus, any worker can shift to another operation with only a negligible loss of efficiency. Usually one worker is used as parts chaser and relief. The supervisor can help with the parts chasing but is not expected to take part in operations except as a troubleshooter.

Although the products (houses) do not move, Tom feels that the principles of worker-paced lines can be applied with beneficial results.

1. Design a process flow for Tom.
2. What is the minimum time requirement to build a house? How many houses should be being built to keep the permanent crew busy? What is the maximum number of houses that should be under construction at one time?
3. Is the workforce balanced? If not, which crew sizes should be changed?
4. Design an information flow for Tom.
5. Set up a sequence for raw material flow for Tom.

Situation for Study F-2
Small City Newspaper

Small City Newspaper (SCN) was a family-owned paper with a circulation of 43,000 in the morning and 22,000 in the evening. There were three editions of the morning paper and two editions of the afternoon paper; the earlier editions of each paper were for delivery farther away.

Newspapers have two content inputs: news and advertising. For SCN, as with most daily newspapers, advertising determined the size of each issue, which in turn affected the length of the production run. To maintain an average of 43 percent news content and 57 percent advertising, the number of columns of news was allocated according to the number of columns of advertising sold for a particular issue. A minimum number of news columns (front page, sports, editorial, comics, and so on) was required for the morning paper (96 total columns) and for the evening paper (80 total columns). Information about the number of columns of advertising was communicated to the editors and the production manager by the advertising department.

Advertising was divided into three categories: display, classified, and national. Display was used primarily by local retailers and ad agencies, who often had camera-ready copy prepared for the pasteup department. On occasion, the advertising and art departments worked with the customer in preparing the advertisement. Three days' lead time was generally required of the client when placing a display ad; however, flexibility in this procedure allowed for changes to be made until press time. Classified ads had to be submitted by 5:00 P.M. the previous day and could be prepared for pasteup on the computer. National advertising copy was usually camera-ready and followed much the same procedure as the display ads. To expedite the use of both display and national ad copy, an inventory of these ads was maintained.

The morning news department had a staff of 40: city desk, copy desk/AP wire service, sports, style, editorial, and cartoon. The afternoon paper had a staff of 22 (no cartoonist). The library kept microfilmed copies of newspapers, publicity brochures, and a master file of news clippings (filed alphabetically) on important individuals. A personal computer that was tied into the Associated Press news retrieval system was also located in the library.

The managing editor assigned reporters and photographers to cover newsworthy events. Editorials as well as style and feature articles had the earliest deadlines (5:00 P.M. for the morning paper and 9:00 A.M. for the afternoon paper) and so were often written the day before they were to be published. Front page stories and sports coverage demanded up-to-date reporting; the deadlines for these articles were 11:00 P.M. for the morning paper and 11:00 A.M. for the afternoon paper.

Flexibility in the entire operation was a must, to allow for reporting late-breaking news. Because these stories could significantly disrupt the process, reporters were encouraged to prepare as much of their other copy as far in advance of press time as possible. To facilitate this, the newspaper had adopted a flexible time schedule for its reporters, who were generally on the job from 3:00 P.M. to midnight (for the morning paper) and from 7:00 A.M. to 4:00 P.M. (for the afternoon paper). In spite of this effort, half of the newspaper was made up in the two hours before press time.

Generally, a reporter composed a story at a video display terminal (VDT). The story appeared on a screen (CRT) as it was typed. Errors could easily be corrected, and additions and deletions did not affect the rest of the story. Typewritten copy could enter the computer through the use of an optical character reader (OCR), which sensed typewritten copy if it was prepared in a compatible typeface. Once the reporter was satisfied with the story, a single key command put the story in line in the computer. If this was done close to the deadline and the reporter considered the story to be especially important, the reporter could supersede this queue by notifying the editor.

The editor had a list of all stories in the queue. He accessed the stories and made revisions using special keyboard commands. Once he was satisfied, the editor added the headline via the keyboard, specifying the type size of the heading (in points), and designated where the story should go in the paper. The story was then transferred by computer to page pasteup, where a hard copy was printed.

Syndicated features and wire service copy were transmitted to the paper in a form compatible with the VDT system, replacing the old teletypewriter and eliminating the need for rekeyboarding. At the copy desk these stories were reviewed and a determination was made concerning which stories to use; then the copy was forwarded by computer to page pasteup. The laser photo service was another external input. Photographs were beamed to the newspaper along with a subtitle and/or a short explanation. The photo came to the paper ready for pasteup.

Advertising copy, news stories, and photographs were pieced together on a page the size of a newspaper page. Reusable bylines and photos of syndicated columnists were kept at the pasteup tables. Efforts were made to smooth the flow through pasteup by having advertising, feature articles, and as much of the news as possible to pasteup as early as possible. The pasteup operation for the morning paper normally ran from 5:30 P.M. to 11:00 P.M. Pasteup for the afternoon paper generally ran from 8:00 A.M. to 11:30 A.M. The time difference for the papers was due to the latter's smaller size and the advance preparation the morning paper pasteup had to do for its Sunday edition. Changes for the final edition of each paper could be made after the presses began the earlier edition(s).

Once the pages had been laid out, they were photographed. An aluminum-backed, polymer-coated plate was placed in an exposure unit beneath the page negative. After a 45- to 70-second exposure, it was put through a wash unit, which used water and a small amount of biodegradable defoaming agent to remove the nonexposed polymer areas. After drying, the plate had a raised mirror image surface, which was curved to fit the rotary press cylinder. One page could pass through the engraving process in 22 minutes standard time, though several plates could pass through simultaneously. Once the plates had been prepared, a press room employee picked them up on the fourth floor and carried them to the press on the first floor.

The current printing process replaced several steps of the old letterpress system. It was compatible with both the rotary press and the offset press systems. An offset press, although it wasted as much as 4 percent newsprint per run, offered computerized printing capabilities, better quality of print, and flexibility with the use of color.

Press runs for the morning paper were approximately as follows: first edition (outlying counties) 12:10 to 12:40 A.M, second edition (adjacent county) 1:00 to 1:25 A.M., and final edition (city) 1:45 to 3:20 A.M. Press runs for the afternoon paper were approximately as follows: first edition (all counties, except the immediate one) 12:50 to 1:30 P.M., and final edition 2:15 to 3:15 P.M. The capacity of the press was 80 pages (16 per deck) per run. When full color was used, only 64 pages could be printed per run, because two half-decks had to be devoted to overlap the four colors necessary for full color. To circumvent this bottleneck, the Sunday feature section was printed on Saturday and many of the inserts were preprinted during slack time. The Sunday comics, for example, were printed externally and were delivered early in the week.

The press cylinders were on the first floor. Rolls of newsprint were loaded on the press in the basement, and the cutting and folding mechanism was on the second floor. The newly printed newspaper was carried by conveyor to the mailroom.

Maintenance could be performed by disconnecting the individual decks; however, all five were operated simultaneously by a central drive system. A problem with the electrically powered drive unit, which had happened recently, could prevent the press from operating. Fortunately, this situation was corrected in time to get the paper out, but it pointed up a weakness in the functioning of the entire operation.

In the mailroom, the sections and inserts were assembled. The papers were counted, bundled, labeled, and dropped through a chute to an alley where they were picked up by carriers or were trucked to drop points.

Timely delivery was very important. The evening newspaper had to reach the customer before the evening TV newscast, or it would not be read. The morning paper had to be to the carriers (who usually held day jobs) in time for them to make deliveries before they went to work. In meeting these objectives, the earlier editions of the morning paper were to leave the headquarters by 2:00 A.M. and the final edition was to be to the drop points by 4:00 A.M. The earlier afternoon edition was to be ready to go by 1:30 P.M., with the final edition due at the drop points by 3:30 P.M.

1. Diagram the process and information flows for this process.

2. In what ways is this a worker-paced line flow operation and in what ways, if any, is it not?

3. How do the concepts of line balance and rebalance apply to this situation?

A Service Shop

Ogle–Tucker Buick
Auto Service and Repair
Indianapolis, Indiana

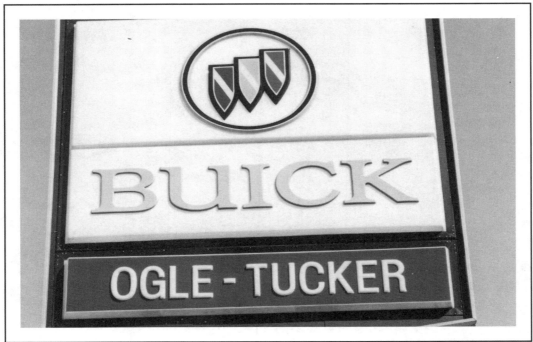

(Courtesy of Ogle–Tucker Buick)

Ogle–Tucker Buick was located on Keystone Avenue in northeast Indianapolis. It was located on 7.25 acres of land and occupied 43,000 square feet of space. The service department consisted of 27 stalls available in the service area, 24 stalls in the body shop, 6000 square feet dedicated to parts storage, and the associated office space for these operations.

The dealership was owned by Robert Ogle and Thomas Tucker, who had grown up on farms and had moved to Indianapolis after World War II. The dealership had been at its current location since 1969. It sold Buick cars exclusively.

Ogle–Tucker Buick was one of the top 100 Buick dealers in the nation, as rated by General Motors. It was a four-time Best in Class dealership, most recently in the last year, which meant that it had passed certain stringent requirements associated with its sales and service abilities and the satisfaction of customers.

PART ONE: PROCESS DESCRIPTION

Writing the Service Order

The service operation began at 7:00 A.M., Monday through Friday. At that time, the two service advisers who were responsible for developing the repair orders began greeting the customers who had lined up for service. The service advisers' responsibilities were to detail (1) the symptoms of the problem experienced by the customer, and/or (2) the work the customer wanted to have performed. This called for skillful listening by the service adviser and the knack for asking the right questions to glean the proper symptoms to explain to the mechanic assigned. The service adviser was also responsible for suggesting additional services the customer might want but had not thought of, such as oil changes, new brake linings, or front-end alignments. The service adviser was the operation's chief contact with the customer through the service process. If the customer needed to be informed about the progress on his car, or that additional work was needed, or that the car might not be ready on time, the service adviser communicated that information.

Upon greeting the customer, the service adviser logged in necessary identification information to the service department's computer, and a customized repair order form was generated (Figure G1). When the customer finished detailing the work to be done on the car, he or she signed the repair order, giving the service operation authorization to work on the car. The service adviser then assigned a control number to the job and placed an oaktag control number on the rearview mirror of the car and also attached a tag with the same number on the keys to the car.

The repair order consisted of four paper "soft" copies plus an oaktag back "hard copy." The four soft copies were of different colors. The top, white copy, was the accounting copy. The yellow sheet was the customer's copy. The pink sheet was

Stop here for service. *(Courtesy of Ogle–Tucker Buick)*

```
VID#?F1424428                          ** SERVICE HISTORY **

O P E R A T I O N    TECH  ADV  MILES   R.O.#   DATE      O P E R A T I O N    TECH  ADV  MILES   R.O.#   DATE
1-LUBE               C008  66   276088  100247  022096    99-TIRE REP.         C027  66   249034  82089   081694
2-OIL CHANGE                                              52-REPLACE BELTS     C027  93   247674  81075   071894
3-OIL FILTER CHANGE                                        4-CARB OVERHAUL     C014  66   246958  80720   070794
5-TUNE ENGINE        C006  66   274745  99614   020596    94-DIAGNOSTIC TIME   C034  93   245932  80196   062394
6-EMISSION SERVICE                                                             93   238682  76159   022494
18-TUNE & ENG ADJ                                         WOC-K7535
84-ACCESSORIES REPR  C067  66   272216  98124   121495    42-DIFF REPAIR       C067  82   235008  73355   120893
7-BALANCE WHEELS     C011  66   268902  95873   102595    93-MISCELLANEOUS     C027
                           66   268902  95872   102595                         93   230230  70232   081993
44-TRANS REPAIR      W067  52   268902  95872   101495    58-WATER PUMP        C002  93   215586  61956   120992
WOC-K7000                                                 WOC-006001
11-SERVICE TRANSMISSION C067 93 267106  95101   092295    65-AIR COND REPAIR   C003  82   211397  58684   090292
85-BULB REPLACE      C012  66   264757  93531   080895    64-AIR COND SERVICE  C003  93   208839  57250   071792
83-BATTERY REPLACE   C034  66   255020  86154   121994    29-RELINE BRAKES REAR C016 82   204750  55378   052692
31-BRAKE REPAIR      C011  66   252353  84354   102594    86-ALT. REP.         C011  55   196398  51815   020692

                                       ** SERVICE MENU **
OPERATION  GROUP:  1     * -MILEAGE **-MONTHS         OPERATION  GROUP:  1     * -MILEAGE **-MONTHS
RECOMMENDED SERVICE     PARTS LABOR  TOTAL    HRS    RECOMMENDED SERVICE     PARTS LABOR  TOTAL    HRS
** 8-ROTATE TIRES
** 9-2 WHEEL ALIGNMENT
**10-4 WHEEL ALIGNMENT
**12-PACK WHEEL BEARINGS
**13-SERVICE BRAKES

                                       ** RECALL  CAMPAIGNS **
RECALL NAME          RECALL DESCRIPTION              RECALL NAME          RECALL DESCRIPTION
85 C18               ENGINE PROM EMISSIONS

WELCOME TO OGLE TUCKER BUICK          WHERE GOOD SERVICE          NEVER GOES OUT OF STYLE
```

OGLE-TUCKER BUICK, Inc.-Indianapolis, Indiana 46240

R.O. NO. **101990**

DATE	VEH. CTL. NO.	R.O. NO.
04/11/96	F1424428	101990

PHONE WHEN READY
YES ☐
NO ☐
LICENSE NO.

TERMS: STRICTLY CASH UNLESS ARRANGEMENTS MADE
I hereby authorize the repair work hereinafter set forth to be done along with the necessary material and agree that you are not responsible for loss or damage to vehicle or articles left in vehicle in case of fire, theft or any other cause beyond your control or for any delays caused by unavailability of parts or delays in parts shipments by the supplier or transporter. I hereby grant you and/or your employees permission to operate the vehicle herein described on streets, highways or elsewhere for the purpose of testing and/or inspection. An express mechanic's lien is hereby acknowledged on above vehicle to secure the amount of repairs thereto.

X

DISCLAIMER OF WARRANTIES
The seller, OGLE-TUCKER BUICK, INC., hereby expressly disclaims all warranties; either express or implied, including any implied warranty of merchantability or fitness for a particular purpose, and OGLE-TUCKER BUICK, INC. neither assumes nor authorizes any other person to assume for it any liability in connection with the sale.

LUBRICATION	☐
CHANGE OIL	☐
CHANGE OIL FILTER CART.	☐
CARB. OVERHAUL	☐
TUNE ENGINE	☐
EMISSION CONTROL SERV.	☐
BALANCE WHEELS	☐ x ☐
FRONT END ALIGN.	☐
SERVICE TRANSMISSION	☐
PK. BRG. ☐ CLEAN SERV.	☐

NAME SCOTT,MARVIN B
ADDRESS --- AAA ---
7431 MALIARD CT

CITY/STATE	ZIP CODE
INDPLS., IN	46260

PHONE-BUS.	RES.	DELIVERY DATE	DELIVERY MILES
283-9464	259-1102	01/01/85	99999

CUSTOMER LABOR RATE IS FIGURED AT
$ _____ PER FLAT RATE HOUR.

VEHICLE IDENT. NO.	CUSTOMER NO.	ACTUAL MILES
1G4CW6935F1424428	41067	25400

MODEL/DESC.	TIME REC'D	PR	TIME PROM.	SVC. ADV.	WARRANTY CLAIM NO.
85 PA	10:06				

C	QTY	ITEM NO.	DESCRIPTION	SALE

A TIME COMPLAINT
FAIL CODE | TECH | CAUSE
CORRECTION
OPER.

B TIME COMPLAINT
FAIL CODE | TECH | CAUSE
CORRECTION
OPER.

C TIME COMPLAINT
FAIL CODE | TECH | CAUSE
CORRECTION
OPER.

D TIME COMPLAINT
FAIL CODE | TECH | CAUSE
CORRECTION
OPER.

TIRES
ENGINE OIL
DIFFERENTIAL LUBE
TRANSMISSION OIL
SUBLET REPAIR

Ogle-Tucker
INDIANAPOLIS BUICK INDIANA

7250 NORTH KEYSTONE AVENUE
P.O. BOX 40297
INDIANAPOLIS, INDIANA 46240
TELEPHONE 257-2271

Thank you for this opportunity to serve you. It is our aim to perform all the repairs requested on this repair order to your complete satisfaction. If our service was satisfactory tell your friends, if not, please tell us immediately. · Thank you

	SALE
LABOR-MECHANICAL	
LABOR-BODY SHOP	
SUBLET REPAIRS	
PARTS-MECHANICAL	
TIRES	
GAS, OIL, GREASE	
PAINT & MATERIAL	
WARRANTY DEDUCTIBLE	
SUPPLIES	
TAX	
CASH SALE	

FIGURE G1 A repair order.

kept with any warranty parts to aid any audit by Buick of warranty claims. The green sheet was a control copy that was used by the person who checked by phone with customers on their satisfaction with their repaired cars and was then routed back to the service manager, whose secretary filed them. After the service adviser filled out the repair order, he detached the green sheet and sent the other soft copies, together with the hard copy, to the dispatcher in the "tower." Detaching the green sheet at this time was a control so that mechanics could not enter work that was not ordered by the customer.

Dispatching

The service adviser sent the repair order into the dispatching office (the tower), the nerve center for the service operation. Here the dispatcher (the tower operator) logged in the control number, the name of the customer, the type of car, the time the service adviser promised the car for delivery, the repair order number, and the work that was to be done, together with the number of the mechanic who was supposed to do that work. Figure G2 shows a dispatcher's route sheet.

Jobs were classified by category. The categories included lubrication and filter changes, tune-ups, front-end work, rear axle work, transmission work, brake work, and the like. Ogle–Tucker's mechanics (termed "technicians" at the dealership) were specialized by task. For example, one did transmission work exclusively, two did front-end work, three handled tune-ups, while others devoted themselves to other tasks. When the tower operator logged in a repair, he noted which technician in which specialty was to do the job. When that job was completed, another technician might take over the car to work on a different aspect of its service or repair. An x-ed out entry on the route sheet meant that the technician had completed his work.

Routine items such as tune-ups and oil changes could be assigned to technicians without requiring a diagnosis about what was wrong. For a number of cars,

The dispatcher's tower and the main desk for the service advisers. *(Courtesy of Ogle–Tucker Buick)*

NAME 3/29	YEAR AND MAKE	LOCATOR NUMBER	TIME PROMISED HOUR	WAIT		WRITER	REPAIR ORDER NUMBER		LUBE	TUNE-UP	AIR CONDITIONING	ELECTRICAL	FRONT END	BRAKES	REAR AXLE	EXHAUST	ENGINE HEAVY DUTY	TRANSMISSION	COOLING	BODY SHOP	WASH/WAX	SUBLET	MISCELLANEOUS	REMARKS
Stippler	96 Regal	025	X	X	⑧	S	476		X						X								X	
Wadsworth	85 Elec.	021	X	X	①	T	477		X			X											X	
Murphy	92 Les	027	X	X	⑩	T	478						X										X	
Kline	81 Park	026	X	X	①	S	479		X		X													
Bull	93 Les	028	X	X	⑤	T	482		X															
Fields	52 Road	021	X	X	㉗	S	481	X			X												X	
Woo	95 Park	030	X	X	③	T	482							X										
Arison	52 Riv	032	X	X	②	T	483																X	
McDonald	81 Les	051	X	X	㊺	S	484			X								X						
McIlvaine	91 Cent	054	X	X	⑨	S	485				X													
Mays	86 Cont	033	X	X	⑦	T	486																X	
Bone	93 Regal	035	X	X	㉔	S	487		X					X									X	
Leslie	93 Cont	036	X	X	④	T	486																X	
Dutts	94 Les	037	X	X	㉓	S	489		X					X										
Wilson	95 Park	038	X	X	⑥	T	490		X															
Germany OTBI #205	ex. Les	042	X	X	㊱	S	491				X			X										
Lowe	95 Lark	040	X	X	⑤	S	492																X	
Gouman	88 Les	042	X	X	㊼	S	493				X													
Turner	89 Park	041	X	X	⑰	S	494		X															
O'Brien	94 Les	041	X	X	⑱	T	495											X						
Ray	94 Regal	044	X	X	⑪	S	496		X															
Kiley	91 Park	045	X	X	⑬	T	497		X															
OTBI #983	95 Reg	6144	X	X	㉛	T	498		X															
Traylor	95 Cont	046	X	X	ⓒ	S	499															X		
Houston			X			T	500																	Theft
Sherman	92 Les	049	X	X	㉕	T	501		X														X	
Clack	95 Park	050	X	X	㉒	T	504		X			X												
Glanzman	93 Regal	048	X	X	⑭	S	505																X	
Thompson	95 Park	051	X	X	㊳	T	504	X	X			X		X										
Bocock	93 Regal	052	X	X	⑯	S	505							X	X									
Bridges	94 Les	053	X	X	⑲	T	506		X															
Patton	89 Cent	054	X	X	㉖	S	507											X						
Keller	91 Cont	055	X	X	㊷	T	508		X									X				X		
Turner	85 Park	043	X	X	㉓	S	505				X													
OTBI #963A	90 Caprice	056	X	X	㉔	S	510	X		X														
OTBI #982	95 Camaro	058	X	X	⑧	S	518		X															
OTBI #985	95 Cad	059	X	X	㉛	S	512		X															
OTBI #987	94 C+D	060	X	X	㉞	S	513		X															
OTBI #062	94 Cad	062	X	X	⑩	S	514		X															
Jabot	89 Cent	063	X	X	㉘	T	515				X													
OTBI #984	TRK	063	X	X	㉙	S	516		X															
England	84 Regal	064	X	X	㊵	T	517		X													X		
Miller	96 Les	065	X	X	㊹	S	518		X															
Giralia	94 Cont	067	X	X	㉝	T	519															X 3		
Schermerhorn	91 Les	068	X	X	㉟	T	520		X															
Leslie	93 Cent	036	X	X	㊸	T	521																X	
OTBI #983	95 Regal	066	X	X	㊼	S	522																X	
Hill	89 Torn	071	X	X	㊽	S	523				X		X											
Stiles	84 Hyundai	070	X	X	⑧	T	524		X															
Matchett	93 Les	073	X	X	㊺	T	525		X															

FIGURE G2 Dispatcher's route sheet.

however, some diagnostic work had to be done before the car could be fixed. Whether diagnostic work was needed was generally determined from the service adviser's wording on the repair order. Key words such as "hesitating sometimes," "occasionally stalling," and so on, were tip-offs. Technicians were responsible for diagnosing problems as well as fixing them. On particularly tough assignments, the service manager was consulted. The dealership referred to the "3 C's" of "complaint, cause, and correction" that were listed on the repair order. The service adviser was responsible for detailing the complaint and the technician was responsible for determining the cause and performing the correction.

Shop Operations and the Workforce

The service floor had 27 stalls that were divided among the 13 technicians (and one apprentice) currently employed. Most technicians were assigned two stalls. Most of the shop's technicians (mechanics) had some postsecondary school education, generally technical school training, and they frequently had a rich family heritage of working on mechanical things. The better-established mechanics could make over $50,000 a year and carried at least $20,000 worth of their own tools. Established technicians earned a higher total income than younger technicians who did not have as many tools or as much knowledge. Younger technicians built up their collections of tools on a continual basis. Tool salespeople came to the shop every week to peddle their tools and collect payments from any technicians who were buying tools on credit.

The technicians were paid on a flat-rate basis. A manual indicated what the time standard should be for every particular kind of job. The technician was paid according to the standard for the job and not according to the time spent on it. Thus, if he spent less time than that indicated in the manual the technician could "beat the book" and earn increased wages. If he spent more time at the job than indicated, the technician would not earn as much. Any rework was directed back to the technician on an unpaid basis, and the shop's policy was that any rework had priority over other work. There were also some skill-level differences incorporated into the wage structure. The most inexperienced worker received $10.50 for every "flag hour" (standard hour), and the most experienced worker earned $17.50. Thus a technician could earn more annually in two ways: (1) by improving his skill level or (2) by being more efficient. When technicians had to wait for a part, it was to their advantage to go to the tower operator and get assigned some quick work that they could perform while waiting. In this way technicians were able to convert more of the time they were in the shop into flag hours for which they earned income.

After a mechanic finished working on a car, he road tested it, and if satisfied, wrote the mileage on the back of the repair order's hard copy and filled in both the cause of the complaint and the correction he made. He then returned the repair order to the tower. There, the dispatcher reviewed what the technician had written, and in consultation with a standard reference, determined what the flag hours should be for the repairs made. The dispatcher then filled in and attached a gummed segment of the time sheet (Figure G3) to the back of the hard copy.

The repair order was routed to the cashier for payment and accounting, the pink copies were retained by the service advisers, and the hard copies filed. White and green copies were filed by repair order number; hard copies were filed by car serial number. Customers returning for their cars went to the cashier to pay, and there received the yellow copies of the annotated repair orders and the keys to

A line of service bays. *(Courtesy of Ogle–Tucker Buick)*

their cars. Within a few days of repair, customers were called by the dealership and asked to comment on the quality of their repair. If customers were not at home, a letter was sent. Postcard surveys were also left in each car repaired, with customers encouraged to mail their responses back in. The service manager viewed these customer surveys as an important aspect of the service department's operation.

Cars typically arrived during the morning. On an average day, 70 cars might be worked on, with a typical range of from 40 to 85. The day's chief period of stress came between 4 P.M. and 6 P.M., when most people came to pick up their cars. This was when customer complaints surfaced about cars not being ready or

A service bay with an oil change in progress. *(Courtesy of Ogle–Tucker Buick)*

FIGURE G3 A worker's time chart.

(Courtesy of Ogle–Tucker Buick)

about the bill being too high. The service advisers were pulled in many different directions during this time.

Quality Control

Quality was enhanced in several ways. There were, of course, the road tests done on each car. And because technicians had to do rework for no pay, there was an incentive to do things right the first time.

Shoddy workmanship was grounds for termination. If, in the opinion of the service manager, there were three instances in one month where poor workman-

A technician repairing brakes. *(Courtesy of Ogle–Tucker Buick)*

ship was involved with no mitigating circumstances, the technician was terminated. The technicians, of course, were alert to this policy, and each instance of shoddy workmanship was discussed between the service manager and the technician.

From time to time, technicians were sent to training schools, usually either in Indianapolis or in Cincinnati, where the zone's main training center was located. Most schools lasted between two and four days. The dealership paid for the school's fees plus food, lodging, and transportation. Technicians were also encouraged to take the twice yearly Automotive Service Excellence tests for accreditation in major aspects of automotive service and repair.

The Parts Department

The parts department employed six people: a manager, a computer operator, a truck driver, and three countermen. The parts department was charged with purchasing all the parts used by the technicians, maintaining that inventory, handling damaged parts, and filing claims and other returns. The department maintained an inventory of $275,000 worth of parts, an inventory that turned over three times a year. In a typical day perhaps 300 parts would be used to serve the needs of the technicians in the shop, but only two or three of those parts would be out of stock and have to be special ordered.

The parts department could place orders with General Motors Service Parts Operations (GMSPO), outside jobbers, or other dealers. The parts department liked to turn a part around (sell it) every 30 days, but with an actual inventory turn ratio of around three they were only able to turn parts on the average every 120 days. Exactly which parts should be purchased at any time was determined jointly by the parts department and a computer program developed by Reynolds and Reynolds. The computer system and its software were reasonably standard for the industry. This computer software used past sales histories to generate suggestions for which items should be purchased to replenish the inventory. Each day, the parts department manager made sure that parts that had been used or sold were removed from the perpetual inventory record kept by the computer. In this way the computer knew what was needed for replenishment, although the parts de-

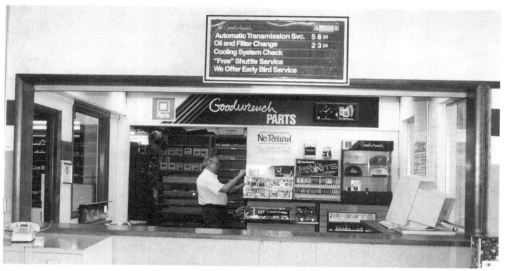

The parts counter. *(Courtesy of Ogle–Tucker Buick)*

partment manager could override the suggestions made by the computer to take into account special circumstances.

There were several ways by which parts were ordered in the GM Service Parts Operation. The system had been altered significantly in March 1996. The goal was to put more parts closer to the customer so that more repairs could be done in the same day. This required improved inventory management, logistics, and transportation. Orders were made electronically over GM's Rapid 2000 computer network.

1. *Daily Replenishment Orders (DROs).* The DRO was the regular way to order parts. Parts were ordered every day through the Rapid 2000 computer network. Parts ordered through DROs received a 3.75 percent purchase discount and a 6 percent credit on returned parts. The credit was useful because it permitted Ogle–Tucker to return slow-moving parts at no cost, thereby improving the way the dealership's inventory dollars were spent.

There were several other ways to order parts. These were more costly than stock orders, but provided faster service.

2. *Customer Special Orders (CSOs).* If Ogle–Tucker did not have a part and could not procure the part from a local source (e.g., another dealer), a CSO could be initiated. CSO orders were handled faster than stock orders; GM checked the six closest depots in that region for parts. CSOs received the same 3.75 percent discount and 6 percent credit on returned parts as the DROs. (The distribution channel for parts went through three types of depots. The most local were termed Parts Distribution Centers [PDCs], the closest being in Chicago. The next level up, Field Processing Centers, carried more inventory. Lansing, Michigan, was the nearest Field Processing Center. The last resort were the parts plants themselves, controlled from Flint, Michigan.)

3. *Customer Special Order—3.* If the customer's car was inoperative, a CSO-3 could be initiated for an overnight delivery. The dealer paid the freight charge for such an order.

4. *SPAC (Special Parts Assistance Center) special orders.* If all else failed, and if GM had a formal customer complaint, SPAC could be initiated. A SPAC special order called for action within 48 hours and dealers across the country could get involved.

5. *Partech*. For problem parts, Partech could be consulted. Partech helped with part number problems such as no part number or part number misprints in catalogs.

6. *Other dealers*. Ogle–Tucker also bought parts from other dealers through informal relationships. The parts manager sometimes phoned other dealerships and asked whether they had specific parts that could be shipped by bus or some other means. Typically, the cost was dealer cost plus 22 to 25 percent.

General Motors provided several incentives to dealers to carry a broad assortment of parts. For example, dealers could get a 2 percent credit on the parts they ordered if they utilized the Rapid 2000 system effectively and stocked at least 90 percent of the Required Parts (667 in number for Buick) as indicated in the Stocking Guide.

Within the first floor storage area of the parts department, there were both small bins and large bins. In the upstairs area, bulk materials such as sheet metal parts were stored. Parts were stored in numerical order by group number. For example, 2000 series numbers were for electrical parts, 3000 series numbers for fuel and exhaust, 4000 series numbers for transmission and brake parts, and so forth. Ordering parts, however, depended not on the group number, but on a specific part number of six to eight digits in length. The workers at each counter were responsible for identifying the proper part for the job, tracking it down in the storage room, and delivering it to the technician or the purchaser, with the proper paperwork done. At each counter, there were manuals for each model or body type of Buick. Each manual had both text and illustrations to aid the search. Prices were kept on the computer. When a part was billed out, the computer automatically deducted it from inventory and kept its accounting straight.

Body Shop

The body shop's major task was to repair cars that had been in accidents. These cars had smashed some sheet metal parts or even the car's frame itself. The shop employed nine: a manager, four bodymen, a painter, a painter's helper, a car washer, and a porter (who did waxing, detailing, and kept the shop clean). There were 15 stalls designated for the four bodymen and 9 stalls for the painter. The dealership had recently installed a paint mix room that could mix the proper colors for any car, including those whose paint jobs had faded with age.

The body shop was a full-service body shop that could handle both ordinary sheet metal tasks and framework—the shop was equipped with the hydraulics, chains, and other equipment necessary to straighten automobile frames. The dealership provided benches, welding equipment, painting equipment, some special tools, and the consumables such as sandpaper that were used in the course of the shop's work. Each bodyman, however, owned his own tools, which were valued between $15,000 and $20,000.

The bodymen typically worked on two cars at any one time, one that could be classified as a "heavy hit" and one that demanded much lighter work. Often the major job proceeded in fits and starts as parts became available. The smaller job thus served to keep him fully occupied. The painter often worked on six or seven cars in a day.

Within the body shop, the bodymen continually helped one another with problems, such as opening smashed doors or attaching frame straightening equipment. Even though they were paid for their individual work, they recognized the need for assistance when one of them ran into trouble. Within the paint shop, the painter was aided by a helper who did much of the required sanding and the tap-

A car being painted in the body shop. *(Courtesy of Ogle–Tucker Buick)*

ing of those parts of the car that were not to receive paint. The painter was primarily responsible for "shooting" the paint and ordering supplies. The other two were mainly cleanup people.

The typical car spent one or two days in body repair and two to three days in painting. (Painting required the application of a base coat and a clear coat, with time in between for drying, sanding, and rubbing out.) Some cars with major damage spent much longer in the shop. They required much more work and were sometimes delayed until parts were received. Typically, the body shop did not begin work on an automobile until all the parts were received. Thus, if the owner could still drive the automobile, he or she continued to drive it until all the parts were received and an appointment was scheduled. However, if the car had sustained major damage and could not be driven, it remained outside the shop until all the parts were available. With major damage, however, there was always a substantial chance that hidden damage would be revealed as the car was worked on. Hidden damage took even more time to fix and often required the purchase of additional parts. This took time, especially if the car was a foreign make.

The body shop had two constituencies: car owners and their insurance companies. Almost all of the shop's work was paid for out of insurance claims, which meant that the shop had to agree with the insurance companies about how much a particular job was worth. The estimates by both the insurance companies and the shop itself were aided by reference to standard books that periodically updated prices and gave standards on the time it should take to remedy certain problems. The shop, in particular, followed the "Mitchell Crash Book" and had very few disputes with insurance company adjusters. Most of the disputes centered around which parts ought to be straightened rather than replaced. (It was standard practice to replace a smashed part with a brand-new one on new cars, whereas on older cars, the existing parts were more often straightened or replaced with used parts of the same kind and quality as used on the car.) The shop contacted insurance adjusters either by telephone or when adjusters came by to check jobs in progress or to obtain estimates for potential jobs.

Adjusters could not insist that repairs be made by a particular body shop, but they could recommend shops. Thus, keeping the insurance adjusters happy was an important aspect of the body shop's efforts. The body shop manager kept the adjusters up to date on what was happening and indicated when hidden damage was found. They could check this type of damage themselves and then reach agreement with the shop on a supplement to the original estimate. The shop tried to do its work quickly. Often the insurance company had to pay for rental cars for inconvenienced owners. Thus, the quicker the work was done, the more likely the insurance company would not have to pay extended rental charges. To make life easier for the adjusters when they came to visit, the body shop maintained a small office and stocked it with supplies and a telephone.

The body shop manager also spent considerable time with car owners. Typically, there were many occasions for such customer contact. The first occurred if an estimate of the damage was requested. An estimate was made by systematically examining the car, in the same fashion as an insurance company adjuster, and by using the pertinent information in the crash book. Once the owner received the estimate, the body shop manager typically followed up by phone to answer any questions about the estimate or about the insurance process itself. Often in these follow-up calls the shop was informed that it or some other shop had been selected to do the work. However, sometimes it took two or three follow-up calls before a determination was reached about what to do with the car.

After the car was brought in, the body shop manager went over with the owner what was going to happen and what the probable time for repair would be. The body shop manager instructed owners to call the shop before the car was due, in case there were any schedule problems, hidden damage, or the like. When the car was ready, he went over the car in detail with the owner, telling the owner what had been done and letting the owner check the quality. The shop delivered cars to owners in as close to showroom condition as possible. Every car was road tested and thoroughly cleaned.

How Workers Were Paid

The technicians in the main shop, the bodymen, the parts department countermen, and the service advisers were paid in different ways. As discussed previously, technicians were paid on the basis of a flat-rate hour. The best technicians generally were the fast ones. They were the best at diagnosing problems, they did not squander time, and they knew exactly how to do each job. Technicians could also receive "spiffs," bonuses for working more than a set number of flat-rate hours. A bonus of 25¢ per hour was paid each week to technicians who had more than 35 hours of time logged. A bonus of 50¢ per hour was paid to those with over 40 hours, a bonus of 75¢ per hour went to those with over 45 flat-rate hours, and $1 per hour went to those with over 50 flat-rate hours for the week. The service manager sometimes deducted from these bonuses for quality problems that were clearly traced to shoddy workmanship.

The bodymen and painter were paid in a similar way. If they were able to beat the standards set for their work, they were able to make more money. If they could not meet the standard, they made less. Some standards naturally were looser than others. In the body shop, for example, sheet metal standards were generally looser than other types of work: thus, sheet metal jobs were the most prized.

The parts countermen were paid a salary, although they received a bonus if sales reached some target level. Service advisers were paid commission. That is, they got a set percentage of the service business brought in. This was an incentive for them not only to do a good job so that people were satisfied but also to suggest additional repairs that the owner might not have thought of. They also received spiffs for special sales (e.g., tires, antennas) that were documented on their pink job order sheets.

The Duties of the Service Manager

The service manager was constantly on the move. In the early mornings and in the late afternoons his main interactions were with customers. He helped the service advisers at the start of the day so that particularly concerned and/or aggressive customers could be handled individually by him. This saved time for the service advisers and contributed to a routine flow of cars into the shop. In the late afternoon, the service manager spent time with customers who complained about work or registered dissatisfaction with the size of the bill. He listened to customers and then, typically, educated them as to the real problems with their cars and/or the reasons for the costs charged.

During the day the service manager made the rounds of the repair floor, the body shop, and the parts department. He checked the dispatching and the efficiency of technicians. He did diagnostic work and road tested completed cars. On heavy days the service manager was particularly stressed. The tasks were the same, but heavier days were more demanding on everyone, especially if the shop was shorthanded.

Promotions and Specials

The flow of work into both the service area and the body shop was not even from day to day or month to month. People drove their cars more during the summer months and thus incurred more repair problems during that time. Periodically, in an effort to smooth the flow of work it received, the dealership publicized some service specials. These were typically cut-rate prices on services such as oil changes and lubrications, cooling system winterizing, or total paint jobs. These specials were timed so that they did not interfere with normally busy periods.

PART TWO: DISCUSSION

Ogle–Tucker Buick is in no way responsible for the following views and presentation. They remain solely the responsibility of the author.

The Flow of the Process and of Information

Figures G4 and G5 display process flow and information flow diagrams for a car in the course of its repair at Ogle–Tucker Buick. Similar diagrams could be drawn for the operation of the body shop or indeed for the operation of the parts department. (The development of those diagrams are left as exercises at the end of this tour.) Note that the customer's car may wait at almost any point in the process. The only wait shown in the diagram is between logging in the job and its diagnosis; it is but one of many such waits that could exist. What is most striking about the flow of the process and of information at Ogle–Tucker versus a service factory like Burger King is the extent to which there is communication between customer and management and between management and technicians. Because of the customization

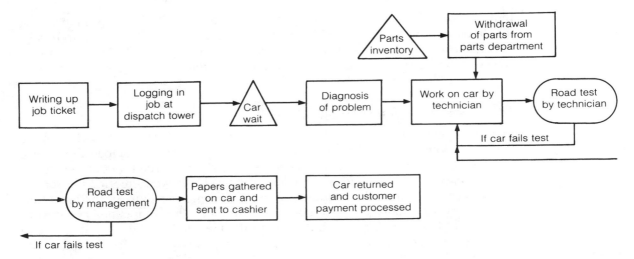

Note: The car may wait between any of the process steps shown and not simply between the log-in of the job and the diagnosis of any problem.

FIGURE G4 Process flow diagram that follows a car in the course of its repair at Ogle–Tucker Buick, Indianapolis, Indiana.

that is required in auto repair, the flow of information at Ogle–Tucker is much more frequent and less structured than that at a Burger King. Management is very much an intermediary between the customer and the technician. At the same time, management is also very much the source of control for the process.

One can see from this information flow diagram why peak days are so tough on management. There are no shortcuts in the information flows that must occur on busy days. The only source of help is to draw on others, such as calling on the service advisers to do road tests or to give diagnostic work to technicians themselves.

Of interest is the fact that Ogle–Tucker represents an example of a fixed position layout, where materials are brought to a particular location.

Demands of the Process on the Workforce

Most of the repair workers at Ogle–Tucker Buick are paid on an incentive basis. The technicians, bodymen, and painters all are paid according to the ratio of their

FIGURE G5 Information flow for a car in the course of its repair at Ogle–Tucker Buick.

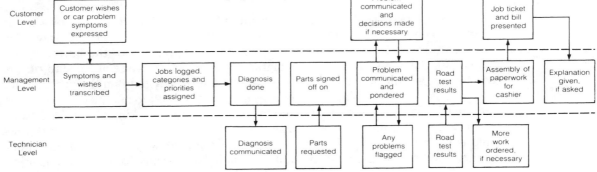

performance relative to a time standard. The base wage against which that ratio is applied depends on their level of skill, which in turn depends on their willingness to learn and the experience they have accumulated. If a technician wants to get ahead and if he wants to be able to be promoted to more prestigious jobs in the shop, he must be willing to go to school. The increasing sophistication of cars demands this. The increasing sophistication of auto repair work is reflected in the fact that Ogle–Tucker's mechanics are not called mechanics but technicians. The use of that term is a reflection of how the workforce and management alike consider the demands of the job.

Working hard as a technician means more than simply beating the standard as set in the book. Working hard also means being able to juggle several different jobs at once so that little time is spent waiting for parts or otherwise removed from the actual repair job. In this regard, the technician is responsible for the pace of his own work. That pace is not dictated by the dispatcher nor by the flow of work along a line. The pace is dictated solely by the technician and his level of skill and effort.

The high level of individual responsibility evident for the technician job carries over to the considerable inventory of tools that everyone is expected to carry. Indeed, the capital-to-labor ratio implied by this tool inventory is not too much above 1 ($20,000 plus in tools and perhaps $30,000 in annual wages, for an average technician) without counting any of the plant, equipment, or parts that are made available to the technicians by the dealership itself. As owners of their tools, technicians are almost like independent operators rather than employees of the company. They have considerable freedom to come and go on their own, for they are paid only for what they do and not for how many hours they spend in the shop per day. Nevertheless, being part of a dealership's service operation has its advantages. The work is steady, training is provided, and the technician does not have any of the headaches that would be involved in establishing and directing a business.

Ogle–Tucker represents a significant contrast to a Burger King. The jobs involved in auto repair are more individual and varying, and, despite some specialization within the workforce, there are fewer job niches. Although some teamwork is required, the element of teamwork at the dealership is much less than that which has to apply in a service factory.

Demands of the Process on Management

As the information flow diagram leads one to suspect, auto repair places some significant demands on management. Some of those demands deal with the control of the process, which essentially means control over the rather independent operators. The elements of control include dispatching, diagnosis, the periodic checking of efficiencies, and the quality checks made for both part ordering and road testing. Control over the workforce is a continual endeavor, and one that is fairly loosely defined.

In addition, management must deal with complaints from technicians about their pay or what has been assigned to them. Management must also keep track of the training possibilities for the technicians and who should be assigned to which school.

Monitoring technician training is just one aspect of keeping up to date. Other aspects deal with equipment and information. The use of computers is now standard in most auto dealerships, and computer facilities are steadily being improved. This permits more of the paperwork and information needs of the dealership to be put on computer. Keeping up to date with the increasing sophistication of cars requires added investments in plant and equipment and in manuals and documentation. It is important for management to have the right kind of equipment and enough of it so that workers are not cramped for space or equipment and thus do not impede the capacity of the shop. An important aspect of the capital requirements of the dealership is the parts department. Dealers, of course, want to have enough of the right parts available so that they do not stock out too often, but they do not want to drown in inventory. The use of the computer helped to strike this balance, as did the discipline that was applied in keeping track of the parts on hand.

Another whole realm of management effort is devoted to dealing with customers. Managers were in repeated contact with customers—taking orders, handling complaints, and explaining the shop's actions. Senior managers, in particular, were safety valves for the service advisers so that when all the service advisers were occupied with customers, the flow of the process could continue unabated.

Management is also responsible for generating a steady flow of work into the shop. That means trying to perk up business in the off-peak times of the year through promotions and specials. And, once a customer does come in, the service adviser informs the customer about other services that his or her car could really use.

Questions

1. How does the payment scheme for the shop's technicians compare with other incentive pay schemes discussed in previous tours?
2. How does the Ogle–Tucker Buick dispatcher compare with the foreman at Norcen Industries?
3. Why are the various copies of the repair order split the way they are?
4. What kinds of parts orders suggested by the parts department's computer program would likely be overridden by the parts manager?
5. Why was the parts manager so dedicated to daily updating the perpetual inventory records kept of each part?
6. In what ways was managing the body shop similar to managing the service shop? In what ways were they different?
7. In what ways is the Ogle–Tucker service manager's job like that of the Noblesville Burger King manager? In what ways is it different?
8. Develop process and information flow diagrams for the body shop.
9. Develop process and information flow diagrams for the parts department.

Situation for Study G-1
Big City Hospital Emergency Room

The emergency room of the Big City Hospital served about 100 patients a day. Some patients' arrivals were unannounced. Others, however, were announced through communication with ambulance drivers or physicians. The pattern of admission was routine except for patients who were obviously in medical distress.

Each patient entering the emergency room was met by one of two clerks at the front desk. The clerk was the first to assess whether the patient needed immediate medical attention. The clerk would announce "patient here" over the loudspeaker and a triage nurse would take over, reviewing the paperwork that had been done, taking the patient's vital signs, and gathering additional information. The triage nurse then determined whether the patient had to be seen by a physician immediately or whether he or she could wait. If a patient arrived by ambulance, the communication from the ambulance would indicate an estimated time of arrival and some word of the patient's condition. If the patient could give some preliminary information on arrival to the clerk, that would be done; if not, the patient was wheeled directly into the emergency room treatment area.

There were several treatment areas to the emergency room. These included the acute trauma room; a large open area with seven bed slots with curtains to close off each of the slots; four other, separate holding slots; an ear, nose, and throat room; an OB-GYN room; a cast room; and a family room. The acute trauma room was kept always set up in anticipation of a patient with a severe problem. Up to 20 people could be mobilized to help stabilize a patient in acute trauma.

The open area with the seven bed slots was used for general admission patients. If the patient's condition warranted continual observation, he or she was placed near the nursing station. Patients not needing constant surveillance were placed at more of a distance. The ear, nose, and throat; the OB-GYN; and the cast rooms were used for isolating patients with those conditions. The family room was used either for psychiatric patients or for the families of patients who were critically ill.

Once patients were seen by the triage nurse and then by the resident nurse, they were evaluated by a surgical or medical intern, and, if necessary, by an attending resident or physician. Upon examination, the patients were either treated and discharged or admitted to the main part of the hospital. The time goal for admitting, treating, and discharging a patient was four hours. Nurses handled any transfers to other areas of the hospital.

Each patient generated substantial amounts of paperwork: personal medical history, notes from physicians and nurses, diagnoses, orders and instructions, laboratory tests performed, and any supplies used. This paperwork was necessary for recording instructions to be used by other hospital personnel, or by departments for billing and for the creation of a permanent medical record. Given these various purposes, the record forms included space for personal data, the nature of the complaint, the physician's name, the type of insurance, notes from the physician, orders from the physician, diagnosis from the physician, and instructions for the discharge. Separate records were kept for nursing, the physicians, and insurance. Lab work was tracked using individual tickets that were kept grouped with the emergency room reports. After a specific time, these reports were entered in the hospital computer for storage.

1. Diagram the process flow.
2. Diagram the information flow.
3. How would you determine how the emergency room ought to be staffed with clerks, nurses, and physicians?

Mass Service

Lazarus Department Store
Castleton Square Mall
Indianapolis, Indiana

(Courtesy of Lazarus—Castleton Square)

The Lazarus department store at the Castleton Square Mall was one of 49 stores of that name that the company operated throughout the Midwest. It was one of 9 Lazarus stores in Indiana and the largest one in the state. Lazarus itself was a part of the Rich's-Lazarus-Goldsmith's group within Federated Department Stores, a major retail company headquartered in Cincinnati that included such well-known stores as Bloomingdale's, Burdines, Jordan Marsh, and Macy's. The department store was founded in 1851 by Simon Lazarus in Columbus, Ohio, and through the years had combined with four other stores: Shillito's in Cincinnati, Joseph Horne in Pittsburgh, Rike's in Dayton, and Blocks in Indianapolis. Over the years it had pioneered a number of retail innovations: one-price policies to eliminate price dickering, the arrangement of clothing by size rather than price, liberal return policies, and in the Midwest, electric lights, elevators, and air-conditioning.

The Castleton Square store was built in 1974 and remodeled in 1986. It occupied 312,000 square feet of space on three levels, and was a key anchor to a large shopping mall. Six hundred people worked at the store. It carried a broad assortment of merchandise: clothing, housewares, cosmetics, gifts, linens, furniture, electronics, jewelry, carpets, and more. The store was typically open from 10 A.M. to 9 P.M., Mondays through Saturdays, and from 12 noon to 6 P.M. on Sundays.

PART ONE: SERVICE PROCESS DESCRIPTION

Layout

The ambiance and design of a department store was recognized as an important feature in attracting customers and generating sales. A good layout accomplishes several things. It provides excitement for the shopping experience. The customer is led in a logical progression from one area to another. A good layout allows a store to present its merchandise in an accessible manner, to change the fashion statements each season, and to present the merchandise assortment in a meaningful way and thereby to maximize each area's sales potential.

Of the Castleton store's three floors, the first floor was by far the largest. The first floor housed what was known as the "center core"—cosmetics, feminine accessories (e.g., handbags, jewelry, sunglasses), women's shoes, and intimate apparel—as well as other women's sportswear and dress departments, and mens-

The cosmetics department. *(Courtesy of Lazarus—Castleton Square)*

wear of all sorts. The second floor displayed housewares, textiles (e.g., linens), children's clothes, china/silver/crystal, the bakery, the café, the hair salon, and furs. The third floor was home to furniture, carpets, electronics, and watch repair. (See Figure H1.)

The store's main entrance from the interior of the mall opened onto a variety of cosmetics counters. Cosmetics sales are important to any department store and the cosmetics counters played an important role in inviting customers into the store. Once at cosmetics, the customer could then move easily to feminine accessories—handbags and sunglasses to the left and jewelry to the right. Beyond the feminine accessories were better sportswear (Jones New York, Liz Claiborne) straight ahead, shoes and the juniors' departments to the left, and moderate sportswear to the right. Catching one's eye along the walls were bright, attractive clothes from floor to ceiling, helping to draw the shopper into those departments of the store. As the shopper moved farther along the main aisle, she passed special displays for Calvin Klein and for Charter Club (the Federated Department Stores' own high-quality brand) and several "swing areas" whose merchandise varied with the season. Farther along was the sizable menswear department.

The store's main entrance from the parking lot opened onto that menswear department. This entrance was a common way for many people to enter the mall itself and so it was heavily trafficked. At the center of menswear were the various "collections"—Nautica, Polo, Hilfiger—so that one could not enter or leave the store without passing by these renowned brands. Surrounding these centrally located collections were the Sports Forum (Nike, Reebok, Russell Athletic), dress shirts and ties, men's suits, and more standard men's clothes. Further to one side were men's accessories—underwear, socks, leather goods—and men's pants (Dockers, jeans).

This layout put the fast-moving items, and those items more likely to be impulse purchases, near the main aisles. Associated items were generally located in adjacent areas. Considerable care was taken in the decision of what to put adjacent to what, so that a logical flow of merchandise would be presented to the cus-

A Charter Club display. *(Courtesy of Lazarus—Castleton Square)*

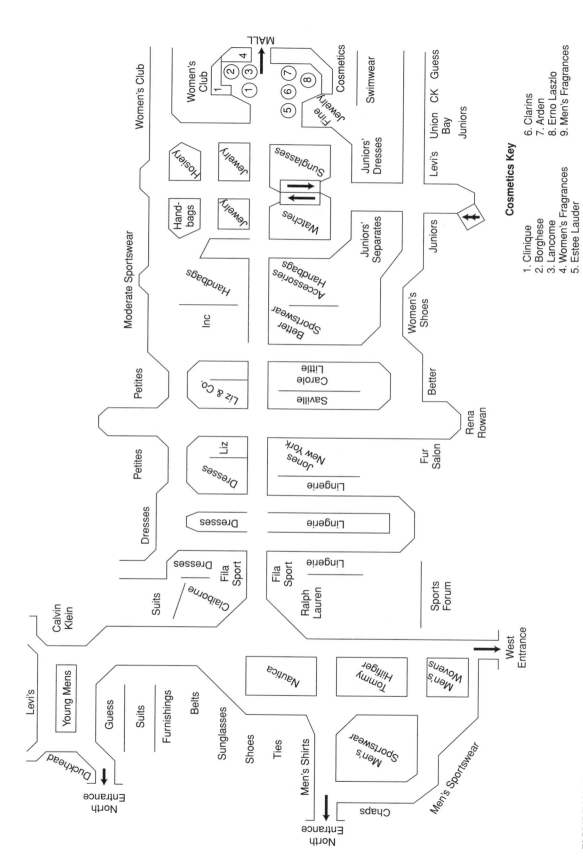

FIGURE H1 Lazarus—Castleton Square
A. first-floor layout.

Cosmetics Key

1. Clinique
2. Borghese
3. Lancome
4. Women's Fragrances
5. Estee Lauder
6. Clarins
7. Arden
8. Erno Laszlo
9. Men's Fragrances

FIGURE H1 Lazarus—Castleton Square
B. second-floor layout.

The main aisle on the first floor, going from cosmetics to menswear. (Courtesy of Lazarus—Castleton Square)

tomer. Items whose purchase was likely to be the reason for the shopper's trip (destination items such as shoes or dresses or men's socks) were often at the edges of the store with appealing displays to help draw the customer into those areas.

Some departments within the store generated substantially greater sales per square foot than others. For example, cosmetics sales per square foot were almost twice the store's average, and feminine accessories were 40 percent above the store's average. Housewares, on the other hand, accounted for sales per square foot that were only 80 percent of the average. In part, these numbers were driven by the space available for each department. Petites was viewed as "underspaced," and it generated sales per square foot that were 20 percent greater than the storewide average. The spacious menswear area, however, while generating more sales that any other menswear department in the metropolitan area, still had sales per square foot that were only 60 percent of the storewide average.

The Workforce

The organization chart for the Castleton Square store is displayed in Figure H2. Reporting to the store's manager were three assistant store managers for merchandising and one assistant store manager who oversaw human relations and operations, including the warehouse, loss prevention, the restaurant, and alterations. Also reporting to the store manager were the manager of visuals (store props and the display of merchandise), and the sales manager of that most important department within the store, cosmetics. Under each of the store's assistant managers were a variety of sales managers for different areas of the store.

Salespeople, known as selling associates, reported to work starting 30 minutes before the opening of the store, which was usually 10 A.M. How long they worked depended on whether they were full- or part-time employees. A typical assignment might call for 8 hours on the selling floor with 45 minutes additional for a meal and 30 minutes for a break. Full-time associates could be scheduled for 35 or more hours a week, whereas part-time associates might work 15 or 20 hours a week, or more, if absenteeism or business needs demanded it. There was also a

FIGURE H2 Organization chart for the Lazarus store at Castleton Square Mall.

category of "contingents" who worked a flexible schedule, often in different areas of the store. Associates punched a time clock upon arrival at the store, and picked up relevant transactions-related materials at the gift wrap window, which was the point in the store that was open anytime the store itself was open.

The schedules for the selling associates were determined at least 10 days in advance of each week. The schedule was set initially by a computer program that matched staff availability against the expected sales and traffic patterns in each department, so that no department was either under- or overstaffed. The computer-generated schedule was adjusted to reflect special considerations (e.g., promotions, inventory taking) for which it was not initially programmed. Figure H3 displays the schedule for the Intimate Apparel department's sales associates for a week, and it also shows the coverage the department has for mornings, afternoons, and evenings during that week.

The selling associates' duties were varied. Not only were they responsible for providing help and advice to shoppers and for ringing up sales, but they were also responsible for unloading the racks and carts of new merchandise that the warehouse associates had brought from the receiving docks, for signing, for replacing tickets in their areas, for repricing merchandise, for keeping the merchandise attractively arranged, and for securing merchandise against shoplifting with electronic and other devices.

The selling associates met with their supervisors, the sales managers, for brief morning meetings four times each week. These two-way communication meetings alerted the associates to special promotions or procedures that were applicable to that day's operations. The supervisor for each department would also occasionally bring out short videos to these meetings with specific product information to keep the associates up to date. There were rooms in the back office area that kept all the product information for the associates and that kept the associates posted on goals, policies, advancement opportunities, service projects, and the like.

Women's shoes. *(Courtesy of Lazarus—Castleton Square)*

```
                          LAZARUS CASTLETON #80
                DEPARTMENT WEEKLY SCHEDULE -- Week of 04/20/96
           AREA :  7 - MARLENE ALBERSHARDT    DEPARTMENT :  201 - INTIMATE
                SEASON :   1 - NORMAL WEEK

Run Date: 04/03/96                                                   Page:   1
                                       START/STOP/MEAL TIMES
                       Tot.hrs.
                       for week
Employee   Name
========   ====================   ========  =======  =======  =======  =======  =======  =======  =======
                                             04/14    04/15    04/16    04/17    04/18    04/19    04/20

FULL-TIME EMPLOYEES
-------------------
                                              SUN      MON      TUE      WED      THU      FRI      SAT
   640995  LINK, SHERRY            37:30    11:30am   9:30am            1:00pm   9:30am  12:45pm
                                    6:15pm   6:00pm     OFF    9:15pm   6:00pm   9:15pm     OFF
                                             1:00pm            4:15pm  12:45pm   4:15pm

                                              SUN      MON      TUE      WED      THU      FRI      SAT
   762120  MANDRESH, CASSANDRA     37:45              1:00pm   9:30am            9:30am   1:00pm   9:30am
                                      OFF    9:15pm   6:00pm            6:00pm   9:15pm   5:30pm
                                             5:00pm   1:00pm            1:30pm   5:00pm  12:45pm

                                              SUN      MON      TUE      WED      THU      FRI      SAT
   583021  MILLER, SHARON          0:00**       OFF      OFF      OFF      OFF      OFF      OFF      OFF


PART-TIME EMPLOYEES
-------------------
                                              SUN      MON      TUE      WED      THU      FRI      SAT
   315895  BACON, LIZETTE          24:15                      9:30am   9:30am   9:30am   9:30am   5:00pm
                                      OFF             2:30pm   2:30pm   2:30pm   2:30pm   9:15pm

                                              SUN      MON      TUE      WED      THU      FRI      SAT
   384917  COOK, BARBARA           11:45                      5:00pm                             1:00pm
                                      OFF      OFF    9:15pm     OFF      OFF      OFF    9:15pm
                                                                                         5:15pm

                                              SUN      MON      TUE      WED      THU      FRI      SAT
  1234567  CRAVENS, SUZANNE        25:15    11:30am   9:30am   9:30am                    9:30am
                                    6:15pm   5:00pm   5:00pm                     2:30pm     OFF
                                             3:00pm   2:15pm

                                              SUN      MON      TUE      WED      THU      FRI      SAT
   250209  ERHART, KIM             27:15              5:30pm            9:30am            9:30am   1:00pm
                                                      9:15pm     OFF    6:00pm     OFF    5:00pm   9:15pm
                                                                                                  5:00pm

                                              SUN      MON      TUE      WED      THU      FRI      SAT
   319970  LANCASTER, BABS         17:15    11:30am  11:00am                     9:30am
                                    6:15pm   4:00pm     OFF      OFF    3:00pm     OFF      OFF

                                              SUN      MON      TUE      WED      THU      FRI      SAT
   324137  MEES,JEAN               10:00                                         6:00pm            9:30am
                                      OFF      OFF      OFF      OFF    9:15pm     OFF    5:00pm
                                                                                         1:30pm
```

FIGURE H3 The schedule for the sales associates of the Intimate Apparel department and the coverage the department has for each day.

```
                        LAZARUS CASTLETON #80
                DEPARTMENT WEEKLY SCHEDULE -- Week of 04/20/96
           AREA :   7 - MARLENE ALBERSHARDT    DEPARTMENT :  201 - INTIMATE
                    SEASON :  1 - NORMAL WEEK

Run Date: 04/03/96                                              Page:   2
                                       START/STOP/MEAL TIMES
                         Tot.hrs.
Employee   Name          for week
=========  ===================  ========  =======  =======  =======  =======  =======  =======  =======
                                          04/14    04/15    04/16    04/17    04/18    04/19    04/20
                                          SUN      MON      TUE      WED      THU      FRI      SAT
   404251  MERVER, JUDI          20:15    11:30am                    6:00pm   6:00pm            9:30am
                                          6:15pm            OFF       9:15pm   9:15pm            4:30pm


                                          SUN      MON      TUE      WED      THU      FRI      SAT
   567750  TEASLEY, NANCY        18:30             6:00pm   6:00pm            6:00pm   6:00pm   9:30am
                                                   9:15pm   9:15pm   OFF      9:15pm  `9:15pm   3:00pm



-------------------------------------------------------------------------------------------------
                         Week Total  SUN      MON      TUE      WED      THU      FRI      SAT

HOUR TOTALS :              229:45   27:00    34:00    27:00    24:15    35:45    36:00    45:45


COVERAGE :      (10:00)   MORNING     0        2        3        2        4        3        4
                (13:00)   AFTERNOON   4        4        3        3        4        5        6
                (21:00)   EVENING     0        3        2        2        3        3        3
-------------------------------------------------------------------------------------------------
```

FIGURE H3 (continued)

The store's various managers were responsible for the training of the associates, often on a one-to-one basis. There were manuals to orient the new associates to Lazarus and to describe to the associates how to sell effectively. In addition, there was a training room with a number of specially programmed computers that, acting as registers, introduced new associates to the proper way to handle

The bridal registry. *(Courtesy of Lazarus—Castleton Square)*

transactions, but also introduced them to the philosophies, procedures, and policies of Lazarus.

Selling associates were paid in a variety of ways, depending on the department in which they worked:

1. Typically, associates were part of a "sales performance plan." (See Figure H4.) These plans listed 10 categories of sales per hour with an associated rate of hourly pay. In any 6-month period (season), the associate's average sales would determine the applicable hourly rate. The goals differed by department. Thus, some associates were required to sell more dollars to earn the same pay as others, but because of the differences across departments (e.g., average price points and the nature of the sales encounter), this was viewed as just. Associate pay was determined afresh season to season, but in no case could an associate fall or rise any more than two pay categories from season to season, no matter how good, or ineffective, their sales in the preceding season had been.

2. Associates in cosmetics, one of the busiest places in the store, were paid a base plus a commission.

FIGURE H4 The sales performance plan for Men's Sportswear indicating the levels of sales needed to generate specific hourly wages.

Monthly guidelines are provided as well to help show what levels of sales per hour will qualify for each of the 10 standards.

80 Castleton Men's Sportswear	SELLING PRODUCTIVITY STANDARDS								Spring 1996	
	1	**2**	**3**	**4**	**5**	**6**	**7**	**8**	**9**	**Selling Cost**
Hourly Wage	$5.25	$5.65	$6.10	$6.60	$7.10	$7.60	$8.15	$8.75	$9.40	4.3%
Season Sales Per Hour Goal	$122	$133	$144	$155	$166	$176	$187	$198	$209	$224

	Monthly/Seasonal Sales Per Hour Guidelines						
Level	February	March	April	May	June	July	Spring 1996
1	$102	$126	$120	$125	$144	$107	$122
2	$111	$137	$131	$137	$156	$117	$133
3	$120	$148	$141	$148	$169	$126	$144
4	$129	$160	$152	$159	$182	$136	$155
5	$138	$171	$163	$170	$195	$145	$166
6	$147	$182	$173	$181	$207	$155	$177
7	$156	$193	$184	$192	$220	$164	$187
8	$165	$204	$194	$203	$233	$174	$198
9	$175	$216	$205	$214	$246	$183	$209
10							$225

Seasonal Sales per hour performance is measured against the SEASON GOAL ONLY.
Monthly sales per hour guidelines are provided as benchmarks only.

Page 559   1/26/96 9:49:21 AM   Area/Suffix: 07-02

3. Others were on a "draw" system whereby they drew a wage in advance against commissions they earned from their sales. Associates in the ladies' shoe, men's suits, electronics, furniture, and carpet departments operated on the draw system.

The planned storewide average rate of pay was $8.25 an hour, but this differed from department to department and, especially, from associate to associate. It mattered, too, whether the associate was on so-called productive, or nonproductive time. Productive time was the time when the store was open and associates could actually sell something; thus they stood to earn more. Nonproductive time was typically when the store was closed and there were no opportunities to make a sale. Activities such as restocking the shelves/racks were sometimes done on nonproductive time. Naturally, the more activities such as restocking could be done during the inevitable lulls in productive time, the better for all concerned.

Fringe benefits included paid vacations and holidays, medical and dental plans, a retirement program, discounts on store merchandise, a company credit union, and a matching charitable gifts program.

The turnover rate for selling associates was 59 percent per year, high for many industries, but low for much of the retailing industry. The Castleton Square store interviewed applicants on a continual basis, and associates were given bonuses for the successful hiring and retention of those whom they had referred to the store's human resources department. New opportunities for current associates in other areas of the store were posted in the associates' lounge; many of the long-standing associates had experience in a variety of the departments within the store.

Some associates were known as sales specialists because they had particular ties to branded products, such as various lines of cosmetics or of clothing. In the menswear department, there were 2 sales specialists each for Polo and Tommy Hilfiger, 1.5 for Nautica, and 1 for Claiborne. For meeting certain sales goals, these individuals could earn special benefits (known as "spiffs") from their sponsoring companies.

Peak Times

For special sales days and for the Christmas season, the store was open for longer hours. One-day sales days extended the hours from 8 A.M. to 10 P.M., while at Christmas, the hours were lengthened further, from 8 A.M. to 11 P.M. In past years the store would have hired an additional 150 to 300 people for the Christmas season, starting that hiring in late September or early October. More recently, Lazarus had taken a different approach. The store hired only about 100 or so associates for the holiday season and extended the hours of its part-time employees instead. This way, more knowledgeable people care for the store's customers and the demands on the store's managers for training and supervision are greatly reduced.

The Manager's Job

The store's cadre of managers over the various departments had what was acknowledged to be a hard job, but one that was diverse and fascinating, with no one day exactly like any other. Managers were responsible for a number of things:

1. *Hiring and retention of associates.* Managers were charged with hiring associates as well as training, scheduling, and evaluating them. Hiring was viewed as akin to casting in show business. Certain personalities were better at sales in certain areas versus others, and an associate's previous experience or interests could be useful to the store. For example, patience and broad knowledge were critical in the bridal shop where the registering of a single bride brought in an average of $600 in sales. Because of this, hiring was an important activity, and potential hires were judged on such things as friendliness, diplomacy, and the willingness to work a flexible work schedule, so that they could be at the store when customer traffic was high.

Although retail sales was notorious for high turnover, Lazarus did better than most because of its attractive employment package and its attention to retaining employees. Lazarus' managers were central to this effort. The clear communication of expectations and policies, accomplished in one-on-one meetings and in department meetings, was essential. Associates needed to know where they stood with respect to their sales goals and they needed to be trained in the techniques that would help them reach those goals. Managers provided this communication and they were also responsible for setting and maintaining a positive atmosphere in their departments. Managers were coaches to the sales associates, and role models too. Typically, a manager would spend 20 percent of her time selling within her department, displaying the kind of behavior that leads to successful sales results.

2. *Maintaining service levels.* There were elements to an associate's "service encounter" with the customer that were so important that managers kept track of them. These elements included the approach to the customer, critical product information, suggesting complementary items to go with the item the customer was interested in, asking whether the customer has a Lazarus charge, and thanking the customer, preferably by name (from looking at the charge card, for example). The store was subject to 40 "mystery" shopping incidents each month where sales associates were evaluated on a 100-point scale on these "service levels." Managers wanted to be sure that their sales associates kept up these service levels, to the level of at least 80 points.

3. *Managing and checking in the inventory.* The store neither wanted too much stock on hand nor too little. In addition, the daily deliveries into each department needed to be put on the shelves and racks in a timely fashion.

4. *Staff planning.* The sales associates' time in the store needed to be planned. Sales associates, to earn good money, had to be at the store when the business was there. That meant the typical associate worked four of six weekends on a rotating basis and one or two evenings each week.

5. *Visual merchandising.* Lazarus stressed the attractive display of its merchandise, on walls and in displays, preferably with an arresting, vertically oriented presentation.

6. *Paying attention to details.* There were a variety of details that any department was required to pay attention to, such as the spacing between racks (30″ for wheelchair access), the tidiness of the merchandise on the racks and shelves, and the condition of the fitting rooms.

7. *Covering for other managers.* When a manager had to be absent in an adjacent department, or when the schedule called for the store being open for longer hours (e.g., special sales, Christmas), managers had to cover for each other. This was known as the buddy system.

The Transaction—and Supporting It

At the heart of the store's operations was the sales transaction itself, and the information it generated. Scattered throughout the store in the various departments were 90 point-of-sale devices or registers. These registers were all tied into the store's computer, and via that computer, they were tied instantly to the computer at headquarters in Atlanta. Each transaction consisted of the following items of information: the type of payment to be made (cash or charge), the personnel identification number for the sales associate (the "associate number"), the department's number, the class of merchandise being sold, the stockkeeping unit number for the item (the "SKU number"), and the price for the item. (Vendors increasingly provided all the price tickets used in the store.) Once these bits of information were entered into the register, the sale could be completed, the drawer opened, and if change was required, change would be returned to the customer. With these registers, immediate credit information was available. Credit card numbers could be traced immediately and information relayed to the register on whether or not to complete the transaction. With the registers tied in to the company's computers, up-to-the-minute sales reports, or return reports, by department, could be generated at any time.

Supporting the store's transactions was a person in the vault room. This person was responsible for monitoring the $200 cash reserves for each register, for tracking the financial position of each register at the end of the day, and for making the daily deposit for the store.

Also in support of the store's transactions was a security office. This office housed the many monitors fed by the remote TV cameras mounted throughout

The Nautica collection in menswear. *(Courtesy of Lazarus—Castleton Square)*

the store. These movable cameras could be trained on any suspicious shopper and could follow him or her around the store. Instant communications capabilities could alert people on the shopping floor. Store security was responsible for about 30 apprehensions for shoplifting each month. Also in the security office was a special register that could be designated at will to mimic exactly what was occurring at any register in the store at any given moment. Thus, the precise item being purchased or the credit card number being used at any register could be checked immediately.

Managing and Controlling the Inventory

Buying

Buyers at the Rich's-Lazarus-Goldsmith's headquarters in Atlanta were responsible for purchasing the goods that the Castleton Square store sold. They knew, via the store's computer system, exactly what was selling at the store and their purchases reflected that information. The Castleton store had relatively little say in what was purchased, but it could offer suggestions, such as extra purchases of Indiana Pacers basketball apparel when the Pacers make the NBA playoffs.

Receiving

The day began early for those associates in the store's receiving area; they reported at 6:30, and their supervisors even earlier, to help prepare for the unloading of the one or two trucks that typically showed up at the store's docks during the night from Federated's Kemper Road warehouse in Cincinnati. Using a portable, rolling conveyor, the workforce unloaded each truck, first taking off the hanging goods packed in large cartons, and then the boxes of other merchandise. The workers then unpacked each box, putting the hanging goods on rolling racks

A display in the housewares department on the second floor. *(Courtesy of Lazarus—Castleton Square)*

(known as rails) for delivery to the various clothing departments throughout the store. Once the hanging goods were distributed, the other boxes were opened and their contents sorted and distributed. Because trucks arrived Tuesday through Saturday, the warehouse workers worked those days.

Much of the store's inventory was on display, but there were storerooms located throughout the store, particularly for items such as ladies' shoes. Other goods, such as lamps and linens, were stored in the warehouse on racks that went up 25 feet. Also stored in the warehouse were "fixtures" and props—the displays, racks, mannequins, and other apparatus—that were used to organize and display the merchandise in each of the store's departments.

This back-of-the-store area was home to a variety of other functions: customer pickup, the "send room" where items purchased (e.g., bridal gifts) were prepared to be sent to their recipients, a carpentry and maintenance shop, a hanger room where specially designed racks of hangers were kept to facilitate the sorting and use of hangers within the store, and an area for dealing with particular merchandise exceptions: returns of unsold items to vendors, returns of damaged goods to the Kemper Road warehouse, and the generation of replacement tickets for those items that needed to be repriced.

The receiving operation operated with very little paperwork. The warehouse did not have to check what it received against lists of what it was supposed to receive. Rather, it simply moved the merchandise from the trucks to the selling floor. About 99 percent of the deliveries made were accurate, anyway, and although a paper trail would have been useful to check on certain transactions, it was unnecessary for most of what was accomplished. Thus, the store received what it needed to replenish its stock, according to the sales information its computer system tracked, and what it needed to stock up for new merchandising initiatives or promotions. To reconcile the actual inventory on-hand against what its inventory tracking system thought was in the store, the store's management organized two physical inventories each year (January and June), where all of the merchandise in the store was counted. This activity, accomplished before and after business hours, took five days, from a Wednesday to a Sunday, moving systematically from department to department until everything was counted.

The receiving area had implemented a variety of productivity improvements in recent years. The unloading of trucks had been studied, and with the introduction of the portable conveyor and a zone system for staging the merchandise, this task was now done more quickly than ever before. The hanger room was a big advance and cut down on the sorting of hangers that in past times could be very time-consuming. Warehouse workers wore radio headsets to communicate with one another and to avoid unnecessary steps. The dearth of paperwork also greatly speeded up the receiving process.

Warehouse workers were paid by the hour. The starting pay was $6.60 an hour. Pay was competitive with other retail operations in the area.

Inventory Disciplines

Lazarus had a number of policies and procedures (disciplines) to keep its inventory secure and under control. For example, there were guidelines that kept expensive merchandise away from entry doors (especially entry doors near convenient parking). Some items might also be clipped to an electronic alarm system that would sound if they were removed by anyone other than the selling associate. Some garments carried inktags that could be removed only with special equipment and would otherwise ruin the garment if someone tried to remove them in

The Ralph Lauren Home Collection on the second floor. *(Courtesy of Lazarus—Castleton Square)*

any other way. The fitting rooms were visited each hour to remove and re-sort any items left there. These disciplines were followed scrupulously.

Evaluating the Store's Performance

The Castleton Square store was measured on both its sales and expense performance. Sales were measured in a variety of ways. A department's sales performance (dollars and percent of the store's entire business) was compared against the plan for it and against other stores. The store's performance was compared against others in Rich's-Lazarus-Goldsmith's or against others in the Federated Department Stores retail chain of companies.

Expenses were kept by ledger and each ledger had its own budget. There were ledgers for selling (e.g., the selling associates' pay); for visuals (e.g., signs, fixtures, displays); for human resources (e.g., hiring and training expenses); and for a number of others. Personnel expenses were tracked in terms of full-time equivalents (or full-hour equivalents) for the sake of comparability. Figure H5 is an accounting of the ready-to-wear dresses department.

In addition to financial reporting, the store's operations were audited six times a year by the corporation and every month by a Lazarus team.

PART TWO: DISCUSSION

Lazarus is in no way responsible for the following views or presentation. They remain solely the responsibility of the author.

The Flow of the Process and of Information

During the course of a day the sales associates at Lazarus do many things. The two chief processes in which they get involved are stocking, which occurs in the morning, and the sales transaction itself, which occurs all day long. Figure H6 diagrams both of those key processes. For the most part, these processes are fairly well

Source: IQ59-04-RptMaster
Report: 859-Detail

STORE ACCOUNT DETAIL

1/2/96 3:30:14 PM
Page 6 of 134

Castleton
Dresses/Multiple RTW
StoreAreaSuffix: 80-01-92

	Rate	Wage	Merit
Base:	$8.30	$332	$342
Build:	$8.30	$332	$342

BaseWeek: hrs/fhe's:	300	7.5
Staffing: FT/PT/CTG	6 3 2	
Productivity Code: (A-D):		A
Target Sales Per Hour:		$155
Merit Increase:		
Pct: 3.0% Week Effec:		-

Promotional Calendars:	
Sales:	RTW
Hours:	RTW
Comp Type:	SP
Acct Type:	1

Season Totals:	26 weeks	
Plan Sales:	$1,433.6	
Hours(Tot/Avg):	8022	309
FHE's (average):		7.7
Payroll:	$66,583	
Selling Cost %	4.6%	
Sales Per Hour:	$179	

PAYROLL COST | | | | | | | | | **PAYROLL COST**

	Sales	Hours	FHE's	Wages	Comm	Total	SPH	SC%			Sales	Hours	FHE's	Wages	Comm	Total	SPH	SC%
1-1	$31.9	291	7.3	$2,415	$0	$2,415	$110	7.6%	4-1		$80.3	360	9.0	$2,988	$0	$2,988	$223	3.7%
1-2	$51.3	309	7.7	$2,565	$0	$2,565	$166	5.0%	4-2		$48.3	300	7.5	$2,490	$0	$2,490	$161	5.2%
1-3	$44.0	300	7.5	$2,490	$0	$2,490	$147	5.7%	4-3		$55.3	300	7.5	$2,490	$0	$2,490	$184	4.5%
1-4	$39.0	300	7.5	$2,490	$0	$2,490	$130	6.4%	4-4		$56.9	300	7.5	$2,490	$0	$2,490	$190	4.4%
01	**$166.3**	**300**	**7.5**			**$9,960**	**139**	**6.0%**	**04**		**$240.9**	**315**	**7.9**			**$10,458**	**191**	**4.3%**
2-1	$38.5	309	7.7	$2,565	$0	$2,565	$125	6.7%	5-1		$56.9	312	7.8	$2,590	$0	$2,590	$183	4.5%
2-2	$33.9	300	7.5	$2,490	$0	$2,490	$113	7.3%	5-2		$66.8	330	8.2	$2,739	$0	$2,739	$202	4.1%
2-3	$100.6	360	9.0	$2,988	$0	$2,988	$280	3.0%	5-3		$49.3	300	7.5	$2,490	$0	$2,490	$164	5.1%
2-4	$88.6	348	8.7	$2,888	$0	$2,888	$255	3.3%	5-4		$34.1	300	7.5	$2,490	$0	$2,490	$114	7.3%
2-5	$85.4	345	8.6	$2,864	$0	$2,864	$247	3.4%	5-5		$40.6	291	7.3	$2,415	$0	$2,415	$140	5.9%
02	**$347.0**	**332**	**8.3**			**$13,795**	**209**	**4.0%**	**05**		**$247.7**	**307**	**7.7**			**$12,724**	**162**	**5.1%**
3-1	$54.8	285	7.1	$2,366	$0	$2,366	$192	4.3%	6-1		$45.4	300	7.5	$2,490	$0	$2,490	$151	5.5%
3-2	$88.0	300	7.5	$2,490	$0	$2,490	$293	2.8%	6-2		$60.0	300	7.5	$2,490	$0	$2,490	$200	4.2%
3-3	$46.4	300	7.5	$2,490	$0	$2,490	$155	5.4%	6-3		$47.2	291	7.3	$2,415	$0	$2,415	$162	5.1%
3-4	$52.1	300	7.5	$2,490	$0	$2,490	$174	4.8%	6-4		$37.8	291	7.3	$2,415	$0	$2,415	$130	6.4%
03	**$241.3**	**296**	**7.4**			**$9,836**	**204**	**4.1%**	6-5		$0.0		.0	$0	$0	$0		
									06		**$190.4**	**296**	**7.4**			**$9,811**	**161**	**5.2%**

FIGURE H5 A "Store Account Detail" for Ready-to-Wear Dresses.

Sales are indicated in thousands. FHE are full-hour equivalents. "Comm" stands for commissions that are not a part of this department's pay structure. SPH is sales per hour, and SC% is the "selling cost percent," the percent of sales accounted for by associate pay. The selling cost percent was expected to vary across departments.

FIGURE H6 Rough process flows for material receipt and for sales transactions at the Castleton Square store of Lazarus.

A. Material Receipt

Truck delivery → Sorting of truckload → Unpacking boxes, putting goods on rails → Delivery of hanging goods → Unpacking other boxes → Delivery to floor

B. Sales Transactions

Sales Cycle Repeated

Register opened → Presenting merchandise to customer and closing sale → Sale entry on register → Sale made → Register closed and balanced

Credit not approved

structured. While there is interaction between customer and sales associate during the transaction, particularly in the presentation of the merchandise and the closing of the sale, for the most part the process is a fairly standard one, well known to both parties. Similarly the stocking process is something that is a routine occurrence, day in and day out.

Information flows are also fairly standardized, although there are many different kinds of information that can be passed down from management to the sales associate and up from the sales associate to management. Figure H7 indicates some of the key information flows that can go both down and up in the organization. For the most part, the information flowing downward relates to merchandising shifts, whereas the information flowing upward deals with irregularities in the routine of the inventory and sales transactions.

Demands of the Process on the Workforce

Because Lazarus is open so many hours, one key demand on the workforce relates to the scheduling of everybody's work hours. Some evening and weekend work is typically required.

Another key demand relates to coping with the change that goes on around the employees all the time. Layouts are changing, inventory stock levels are changing, the character of the inventory is changing, and the workforce must cope with all of these changes. To help cope with these changes, there is considerable training. Workers not only are trained initially but also spend appreciable amounts of time week in and week out in training, both to improve their skills and to educate themselves about the merchandising changes in the store.

Another demand on the workforce is accuracy, both with respect to the transactions made and the inventory overseen. Such accuracy is crucial to the success of the store, and it is a routine to which they must apply themselves.

Demands of the Process on Management

Like the sales associates and others of the workforce, management must also adhere to and foster the importance of controls on transactions and inventory. The vault room and the security office are nerve centers for control.

Personnel functions are also extremely important, as indicated by the human resources department's status within the organization chart. Hiring—perhaps better termed "casting"—training, and advancement all consume a lot of management time and care. Sales associates' skills are critical to the sales volume that the store generates, and thus hiring and training are key functions of management.

The other key elements to sales increases are the layout itself and the presentation of merchandise. Good layout and good merchandise presentation de-

FIGURE H7 Examples of information flows at the Castleton Square store of Lazarus.

Types of Information Flows

1. Product information
2. Promotional information
3. Any changes to procedures
4. Schedules, including any absences that should trigger buddy system responses
5. Feedback on selling effectiveness and sales performance
6. Irregularities in the operations of the various departments within the store

pend not only on the analysis of sales figures but also on intuition and feel for the psychology of the sales situation. The worth of powerful fashion "statements" throughout the store is a clear indication of the art involved in a store's design and operation.

Because fashion can be so fickle and people's tastes can change so abruptly, it is important for the store to monitor sales and costs on a continual basis. Thus not only are there controls on the transaction and inventory levels themselves, but also controls on sales and selling costs. Store management has to be ready to examine these costs and use them to make decisions about staffing levels and the responsibilities of sales associates and support personnel within the store.

Questions

1. Visit a department store near you. In what ways is its layout similar to that of Lazarus? In what ways is it different?
2. One might suppose that theoretically, at least, departments ought to be given space in such proportions that the sales per square foot would be roughly the same anywhere in the store. Why is that point of view impractical?
3. Express some of the fashion statements you have observed at department stores. How does the store's layout, fixtures, and decor contribute to those statements?
4. What kinds of questions would you ask of a prospective employee to work in the Liz Claiborne shop? What characteristics would you look for? How would those characteristics and questions differ for someone working in the jewelry department?
5. What is the argument for paying sales associates on a commission basis? What is the argument for paying them on an hourly basis?
6. Lazarus does not have many controls on receiving inventory. Why are there not many controls?

Situation for Study H-1
Adams Convenience Store

The Adams Convenience Store, located on a major state artery, was open from 6 A.M. until midnight every day and sold grocery items, fast food, and gasoline. Gasoline, dispensed through self-service pumps, represented about 50 percent of total sales. Customers paid first and pumped afterward. All of the gasoline pumps were multiproduct dispensers that handled both leaded and unleaded gasoline.

The store was laid out as in Figure H8. Seventy percent of the people who entered the store to do something other than to pay for gasoline, bought some sort of beverage. The fast food available at the rear of the store was the highest-margin item for sale; gasoline was the lowest-margin item. The Adams Convenience Store offered hot dogs, sandwiches, pastries, coffee, and other food items. There were two peaks for food item demand: breakfast and the four to six, after-work period. Sales slowed in mid-morning, early afternoon, and late at night.

The store operated two shifts. The store manager was there to open the store in the morning and stayed during the first shift; the store's assistant manager handled the second shift. During the busiest period of each shift there were a total of four working in the store: two to handle the fast-food area and two to tend the registers. In addition to the manager and the assistant manager, there were two full-time workers and the remaining were part-time employees. Pay averaged just above the minimum wage, and turnover rates often ran as high as 300 percent a year.

FIGURE H8 Adams Convenience Store layout.

The manager and the assistant manager trained the others and determined which items met the company's definition for being short in supply and needing to be reordered. Orders were placed to a central Adams warehouse. The managers were also responsible for controls on cash and inventory so that everything was accounted for.

1. Why is the layout designed as it is? Give a rationale and explain what you think the typical traffic flow would be.

2. Why would the Adams Convenience Store invest in multiproduct gasoline pumps?

3. What do you see as the biggest challenges for the store's owners?

TOUR I

A Professional Service

Arthur Andersen LLP
Audit Services
Charlotte, North Carolina

(Courtesy of Arthur Andersen, Charlotte, North Carolina)

The Arthur Andersen Worldwide Organization was one of the world's leading professional service firms, with headquarters offices in Geneva, Switzerland, and in Chicago. As of early 1996, the firm employed 89,450 people worldwide and operated 358 offices in 74 countries. In the United States, Arthur Andersen LLP was the largest of the so-called "Big Six" accounting firms. The firm was operated as a partnership; that is, the firm was owned and managed by a group of partners (in 1996 the partners totaled 2685) who had been elected by other partners in the firm.

The Charlotte office was the administrative office that coordinated the practice for the two Carolinas, including Columbia, South Carolina; Greensboro,

North Carolina; and Raleigh, North Carolina. These four offices combined employed about 700 people, of whom approximately 600 were professionals and 100 were support personnel. Of the 700, roughly 500 worked in the Charlotte office, making it larger than any of its competitors in the region. The office served about 500 clients in a variety of industries.

PART ONE: PROCESS DESCRIPTION

Lines of Business

Although Arthur Andersen LLP was known as a Big Six accounting firm, it did more than provide classic auditing attest services (described in detail later). Its practice also included tax, consulting, and other business advisory services. Although this tour examines mainly the auditing practice of Arthur Andersen–Charlotte, the tax and consulting practices merit brief separate attention.

The Tax Practice

The tax practice in the Carolinas employed 83 professionals. It was an important component of the office's business and was well established in the firm at large. There were two major components to the tax practice. One dealt with client compliance issues—preparing returns for clients (both companies and individuals), representing clients at Internal Revenue Service reviews, and providing defense for any clients in legal matters involving taxation. The other component involved advice on business transactions that had significant tax implications, such as mergers and acquisitions, financial/industrial/real estate valuations, compensation and benefits consulting, and family wealth planning. This kind of work typically complemented that of investment bankers and lawyers. Tax work consisted of many short-term jobs that often had to be done quickly but that typically did not involve substantial resources over extended periods of time; consulting or auditing services were longer term. Although there was considerable demand for tax services all through the year, the peak demands naturally occurred each February through April.

The Consulting Practice

The Arthur Andersen Worldwide Organization was composed of two major branches of roughly equal size: Arthur Andersen and Andersen Consulting. Arthur Andersen provided the accounting and audit attest services described in this tour as well as the tax services described above. Arthur Andersen also provided a business consulting service that focused on strategy, technology, and processes. Typical activities here might include benchmarking, business process re-engineering, cost management, performance measurement, and quality management.

Andersen Consulting, for its part, was well-known for its prowess in information systems consulting and in management consulting. The mission of its practice was to help clients obtain the information they needed to plan and manage their organizations. The practice was broad-ranging and could include the development and installation of computer systems for financial and operations control of both manufacturing and service businesses. Much of Andersen Consulting's work was customized for the client and thus called for skill in drawing together the disparate elements of each project.

Andersen Consulting revenues in Charlotte were evenly divided among banking, manufacturing/textiles, health care, government work, and some miscel-

The reception area. *(Courtesy of Arthur Andersen, Charlotte, North Carolina)*

laneous businesses. The projects performed varied widely in their scope and duration, although many were accomplished for previous clients. Typical projects included the development of a new deposit system for bank customers and the installation of management information systems for a group of trucking companies. Of the 700 people working for Andersen in the Carolinas, about 370 worked for Andersen Consulting and 330 worked for Arthur Andersen.

Auditing Attest Services

All publicly held companies (those regulated by the Securities and Exchange Commission) are required to have independent, certified public accountants report whether their financial statements fairly represent their financial positions and results of operations. These reports are usually found in company annual reports (see Figure I1). Usually, these opinions, as they are known, are unqualified, but occasionally, accounting firms have to qualify them to alert shareholders to particular risks or problems in the financial statements of the company. Thus, these opinions are important safeguards to company shareholders. The "audit" was the procedure by which Arthur Andersen developed and substantiated reports about the financial records of their client companies.

Arthur Andersen's auditing methodology was designed to identify and concentrate on the risk areas of greatest exposure to a company's financial statements and the related key control elements put in place by management to mitigate the risks. It addressed risks in two stages.

The first stage focused on the principal external and internal factors influencing the client company's operations, such as the industry in which it operated, the nature and complexity of its businesses and products, the operational and financial planning and control activities of management, and management's attitudes toward risk control and financial reporting. Arthur Andersen had developed special computer software, WinPROCESS, to help plan cost-effective audits by focusing on the areas of high risk.

The second stage provided a systematic basis for evaluating individual internal controls over an organization's significant cycles of activity. Much as a

---

Report of Independent Public Accountants

To the Shareholders of International Paper Company:

We have audited the accompanying consolidated balance sheets of International Paper Company (a New York corporation) and subsidiaries as of December 31, 1994 and 1993, and the related consolidated statements of earnings, common shareholders' equity and cash flows for each of the three years ended December 31, 1994. These financial statements are the responsibility of the Company's management. Our responsibility is to express an opinion on these financial statements based on our audits.

We conducted our audits in accordance with generally accepted auditing standards. Those standards require that we plan and perform the audit to obtain reasonable assurance about whether the financial statements are free of material misstatement. An audit includes examining, on a test basis, evidence supporting the amounts and disclosures in the financial statements. An audit also includes assessing the accounting principles used and significant esti-

mates made by management, as well as evaluating the overall financial statement presentation. We believe that our audits provide a reasonable basis for our opinion.

In our opinion, the financial statements referred to above present fairly, in all material respects, the financial position of International Paper Company and subsidiaries as of December 31, 1994 and 1993, and the results of their operations and their cash flows for each of the three years ended December 31, 1994 in conformity with generally accepted accounting principles.

As explained in Notes 3 and 6 to the financial statements, effective January 1, 1994, the Company changed its method of accounting for start-up costs, and effective January 1, 1992, changed its method of accounting for income taxes.

Arthur Andersen LLP

New York, N.Y.
February 9, 1995

FIGURE II An opinion.

manufacturer is concerned about the integrity and capabilities of the manufacturing process, so, too, an Arthur Andersen auditor is concerned about the integrity and capability of the internal controls in the client company for capturing accurately all of the accounts billed and collected, the invoices to be paid, the expenses authorized, the inventory, and other data. This meant analyzing the operations of the client's computer system as well as the client's business procedures and controls; this was known as auditing "through" the computer rather than auditing "around" it.

The audit attest process could be broken into three major phases: the planning phase, the risk analysis phase, and the final phase. These different phases required different amounts of time and attention from the various members of the "engagement team" working on the audit.

The planning phase, for example, accounted for about 10 percent of the typical audit's effort, although much more than 10 percent of the time of the senior members of the engagement team. (For a typical audit, the senior members of the team were the partner in charge and the manager—the professional with rank just below partner, who had anywhere from 5 to 14 years of service. The manager was responsible for organizing the junior members of the engagement team and for handling the operational relationships with the client's management.) The planning phase was concerned with defining the scope of work to be done and its timing. It identified those risks that seemed to be important and those changes in the character of the business that ought to be scrutinized. Once the planning phase was over, the partner returned periodically to review progress, to help work through particular problems, and to monitor the quality of the work in progress.

The risk analysis phase was concerned with fact finding. In this phase, the junior members of the engagement team (i.e., the staff accountants, and the "seniors") investigated the paperwork, the computer, and the controls of the client company. They checked to see that the controls actually worked. Sometimes, they identified substantive problems that had to be dealt with by the senior members of the engagement team. This phase could range from perhaps 30 percent of the time and effort in a small audit to 60 percent of the time and effort in a large audit.

The final audit phase led to the generation of the report. This phase updated the results of the risk analysis phase, involved substantiation of year-end balances, and included a review of the client company's financial statements and their accompanying footnotes. For large audits, this final phase might account for only 30 percent of Arthur Andersen time and effort, whereas for smaller audits it could account for fully 60 percent.

The total professional time devoted to an audit by the Charlotte office could vary dramatically, from 80 hours each year for the smallest audits to over 5000 hours each year for the largest. The median amount of time consumed for an audit was estimated at about 500 hours each year. The calendar for an audit varied somewhat. For the largest audits, Arthur Andersen professionals were in and out of the client company all the time; they were often part of quarterly reviews of the client's business. At more typical audits, however, the planning phase was done about 6 months into each fiscal year, the specific risk analysis work was accomplished in months 7 through 11, and the final work was done in the first 3 months after the close of the fiscal year.

Although two thirds of the Charlotte office's audit work was repeat business, the office was always eager to attract new business. It secured this business by drafting a proposal to the target client company. This proposal discussed the key aspects of Arthur Andersen and what differentiated it from other accounting firms. It introduced the firm's other major clients in Charlotte and the services the entire office could provide a client company. It discussed in some detail the audit approach that Arthur Andersen planned to take. It profiled the personnel making up the engagement team, and it discussed how that personnel would be managed over time to provide the kind of continuity that was valued by clients. The proposal also established the fee schedule.

Managing the Practice

The Pyramid

Arthur Andersen's auditing practice in the Carolinas totaled 144 professionals. Of this number, there were 16 partners, 30 managers, and 104 seniors and staff accountants. In Charlotte itself, there were 8 partners, 1 senior manager, 14 managers, 16 seniors, and 26 staff accounts, for a total of 65 professionals. These different classifications could be depicted as a pyramid, with the staff accountants as the base and the partners at the top. Each engagement had its own pyramid, as well, with one or two partners at the top, one or more managers, and various seniors and staff accountants at the base.

Staff, seniors, and managers were all salaried positions. The partners were not salaried; their compensation depended on the profitability of the firm. If the partners were to make money, they had to use the salaried personnel of the firm effectively. This placed several demands on the partners: (1) effective scheduling of personnel so that everybody was working as much as possible but without excessive overtime (scheduling will be discussed later); and (2) fostering as much responsibility in the lower ranks as possible. Firm profitability was enhanced to the degree that effort and responsibility were thrust to lower levels of the pyramid

A manager's office. *(Courtesy of Arthur Andersen, Charlotte, North Carolina)*

(this was termed as having a broad-based pyramid). If the higher-paid senior members of an engagement team were free to perform other duties, such as bringing in additional business, everyone benefited and the firm as a whole would be profitable.

If a job could be run with a broad-based pyramid, it would likely be profitable. If, however, the pyramid were slender, it was likely not to be as profitable because the time of the senior members of the engagement team would not be as effectively leveraged as when the pyramid was broad.

Accounting firms like Arthur Andersen primarily operated on an "up-or-out" basis; professionals within the firm were either promoted to the next-higher rank or they left the firm. In a sense, the partners were the survivors, those who had proven themselves over the years by their performance and had demonstrated the qualities that made for effective partners.

There was considerable turnover at the lower levels of the pyramid. If one followed the path of new recruits in the Charlotte office, for example, one typically found that only about 50 percent of each new cohort of college recruits were still with the firm after 3 years, and that only about 25 percent of them were still with the firm after 6 years. After 10 years, the figure was 14 percent or so. Only about 9 percent reached partnership.

About three quarters of the time, professionals left the firm of their own volition. Some left for more attractive, higher-paying positions in other companies. Others left because of personal incompatibilities with the degree of overtime or travel, or because of other elements of life on the job. Some returned to school. The remainder left at the suggestion of the firm itself; those were split between professionals who lacked the technical ability to do the job and those who lacked some other personal qualities that were required. While an up-or-out system might be viewed as harsh, Arthur Andersen was famed for its concern for the placement of its accountants in other jobs, often with valued clients.

The pyramid concept raised several issues. Broad pyramids meant lower costs, but because they encouraged the delegation of responsibilities to lower levels of the pyramid, there were always quality control and cost-effectiveness issues associated with them. For example, staff might not have the capability or the training to do all that may be requested of them, or they might take a longer time than some more senior professionals in doing some job, thus raising the specter of cost-effectiveness. The design of an engagement team needed to keep these points in mind.

Another issue involved client perceptions. The accountants at client companies were knowledgeable about firm operations, since they were frequently former Big Six professionals themselves. Often they would prefer experienced personnel and staff who had worked on the audit before. The Charlotte office was careful about making its assignments and had to consider each client's preferences on staffing, but it also had to consider the development of its junior staff so that, over the years, the staff would work on a variety of audits and thus grow in their capabilities.

The Cycle of Business Planning

Given the labor intensity of auditing, business planning for the Charlotte office was very much an exercise in determining labor needs. The business plan for the audit practice started with a forecast of chargeable hours for the Carolinas' four offices. The area had been growing and Arthur Andersen had been developing additional clients, so chargeable hours were growing at a healthy clip.

Once a defensible forecast of chargeable hours was developed, "productivity factors" (i.e., average chargeable hours per person per year) were applied to determine how many people would be needed. The goal for the Charlotte office was an average of 1530 chargeable hours per person per year. That number differed by level within the pyramid: partners and managers generally had the fewest (about 1000 and 1200 hours, respectively) and seniors the most (between 1700 and 1800). Nonchargeable hours were taken up in a variety of activities, including training, marketing and sales promotion, community service, administrative tasks, and recruiting. Given the application of the productivity factors to the forecasted chargeable hours, the office figured out how many people it needed. This, in turn, determined how many new recruits were needed to make up for any personnel shortfalls.

The business plan's forecast of profitability depended on the fee structure as well as the manpower plan. With the growth of business in the Carolinas, there was heavy competition for new business. The Charlotte office took this into account in developing its fee structure to match its chargeable hour plan and its staffing plan.

Scheduling

As mentioned previously, personnel scheduling was a key determinant of the office's profitability. The Charlotte office had responsibility for scheduling not only its own operation but coordinating those of Greensboro, Raleigh, and Columbia as well. One manager-level professional was assigned full time to the scheduling and other division administration functions.

The scheduling process began with the managers in charge of the office's engagements. For each engagement, the manager indicated how many hours of

The computer network nerve center of Arthur Andersen's Charlotte operations. *(Courtesy of Arthur Andersen, Charlotte, North Carolina)*

which levels of professional were required and when during the year those hours, particularly the field work hours, were needed. The manager was also permitted to request specific people to be part of the engagement. This planning could often be done far in advance, due to the recurring nature of much of the office's business. Each December and January, a rough-cut schedule for the following May through April period was devised.

The allocation of people to jobs and of jobs to people was captured on the firm's Operations Management and Scheduling (OMS) System, which was usually dubbed the "railroad," after its long-time appearance on prior computer system printouts. The OMS was a relational database that could be used in a variety of ways. For example, OMS could indicate which personnel were scheduled for any engagement over the next year, or it could take any individual and indicate which jobs that individual was scheduled for over the next year and in which weeks the individual was either under- or over-scheduled. OMS also tracked the evaluations of each of the professionals. These evaluations, by the partner for the manager, and by the manager for the seniors and staff, were required for all the managers and for any staff working more than 80 hours on an engagement and for any seniors working more than 120 hours. (See Figure I2 for an example of what was filled out.)

The scheduling manager was responsible for pulling together the original schedule and then for adjusting it as time wore on and inevitable changes occurred, either because the nature or timing of the engagement had changed or because new work had been added to the office. Every Friday, "master plans" were distributed to all in the office. Two different sets were run: one showing the next 12 weeks, sent to the staff and seniors, and one showing the next 24 weeks, sent to the partners and managers. Highlighted on these master plans were personnel whose times were oversubscribed for particular weeks (see Figure I3.) The scheduler then needed to engage in some "horse trading" to resolve the conflicts. For example, perhaps an engagement could be delayed, or another auditer could be

ARTHUR ANDERSEN & CO.
ACCOUNTING AND AUDIT PRACTICE
STAFF PRELIMINARY EVALUATION FORM

NAME			CLIENT NAME OR ASSIGNMENT		PRELIM	
					FINAL	

CLASSIFICATION	LENGTH OF ASSIGNMENT	MTH	YR	MTH	YR	NUMBER OF PEOPLE SUPERVISED
	HOURS ____ FROM ____			TO ____		AA&CO. ____ CLIENT
COMPLEXITY			BASIS FOR EVALUATION			
COMPLEX ____ AVERAGE ____ EASY ____			EXTENSIVE ____ AVERAGE ____ LIMITED ____			

EXCEEDS (1)- Exceptional performance; greatly exceeds what is expected of individual in this classification.
MEETS HIGH (2)- Performance exceeds what is expected of individual in this classification.
MEETS (3)- Performance is at the level that would be expected of an individual in this classification.
MEETS LOW (4)- Performance minimally meets the requirements for someone in this classification. The individual has a deficiency or deficiencies which may hinder advancement beyond the present level.
DOES NOT MEET (5)- The individual does not meet the requirements for someone in this classification. The individual has a deficiency or deficiencies which will prohibit advancement beyond the present level.

I. BACKGROUND

A. Nature of Work Performed: (Describe the engagement including the staff member's areas of responsibility and any special skills required or developed on this engagement)

II. OVERALL PERFORMANCE (The detail performance assessment checklist on the reverse side of this form must be completed)

| EXCEEDS | | MEETS HIGH | | MEETS | | MEETS LOW | | | DOES NOT MEET |

This individual is ☐, is not ☐ ready for engagements with increased responsibility.

	Exceeds	Meets High	Meets	Meets Low	Does Not Meet	
I. UNDERSTANDING THE BUSINESS						
OVERALL RATING	1	2	3	4	5	NO BASIS
II. DEVELOPING AND MAINTAINING RELATIONSHIPS						
OVERALL RATING	1	2	3	4	5	NO BASIS
III. FACILITATING TEAMWORK						
OVERALL RATING	1	2	3	4	5	NO BASIS
IV. PROFESSIONAL/TECHNICAL COMPETENCE						
OVERALL RATING	1	2	3	4	5	NO BASIS
V. SELF-DEVELOPMENT						
OVERALL RATING	1	2	3	4	5	NO BASIS

III. Overall Strengths Demonstrated:

IV. Specific Actions that can enhance performance:

V. Manager comments on performance:

VI. Partner comments on performance:

VII. SIGNATURES

I have discussed this evaluation with the senior and have explained the performance expected in order for him/her to continue to progress.

evaluator Signature ____ Date

This evaluation has been discussed with me by the evaluator. I understand its content and the performance expected of me if I am to continue to progress.

Person Evaluated Signature ____ Date

Partner Review ____ Date   Manager Review (if different from evaluator) ____ Date

FIGURE 12 The evaluation form, as used at Arthur Andersen–Charlotte.

pulled in to do some of the work, or a tax specialist, who was required to do some auditing to earn a CPA, could be assigned to the job.

Naturally, the Charlotte office's profitability was greatest when everybody was fully scheduled and working, typically out in the field at client locations. The inexperienced staff accountants tended to have the most "open holes" in their schedules, and thus they were a constant concern for the scheduling manager. She reviewed the schedule continually to see whether all of the jobs being worked on were properly staffed. Were some projects in need of help? Were the Greensboro, Raleigh, and Columbia offices busy? Could professionals be swapped between offices? The Charlotte scheduler acted as the central clearinghouse for the staffing needs of all of the Carolinas' offices.

The scheduler was in repeated contact with the managers who oversaw the office's engagements. Those managers informed the scheduler of changes in their needs, and they occasionally lobbied her for particular professionals to work their engagements. Sometimes, staff and seniors would also lobby the scheduler for jobs in industries that they preferred or at clients that offered particular challenges. This was particularly true when new clients were added. An important task for the scheduler was balancing the training and development needs of staff accountants and seniors against the practice's need for their services and the client company's desires for continuity in the personnel assigned to them.

Office: 0025
Division: 015
Class: Senior

Personnel Scheduling
Master Schedule

Page: 1
As Of: 5/6/96
Prepared: 5/2/96

Personnel Name		5/6/96	5/13/96	5/20/96	5/27/96	6/3/96	6/10/96	6/17/96	6/24/96	7/1/96	7/8/96	7/15/96	7/22/96
AAA	AESR	111 40	222 16 111 8	333 24 222 16	222 16 333 16 Holiday 8	Training 40	333 24	444 40	444 40 111 8	Holiday 16 Vacation 8		111 24	111 24
BBB	AESR	555 40	666 40	555 40	555 24 Holiday 8	Training 40	777 40 888 24	777 40	Vacation 40	Vacation 24 Holiday 16	777 40 Training 32	888 24 777 16	888 24 555 16
CCC	AESR	001 24 002 16	002 40	003 40	Vacation 32 Holiday 8	Training 40	Vacation 40	003 40		Vacation 24 Holiday 16	004 40 Training 32	004 40	004 40
DDD	AESR	011 32 022 8	011 32	011 24 000 16	Vacation 32 Holiday 8	Training 40 011 32 Vacation 8	011 40	011 40	011 40	Holiday 16 Vacation 8	Training 32		
EEE	AESR	Vacation 40	Vacation 40	044 40	055 24 044 16 Holiday 8	Training 40				Vacation 24 Holiday 16	Training 32 Vacation 8	066 40 Vacation 24	066 40
FFF	AESR	Vacation 24 012 16	012 40		Holiday 8	Training 40		013 20	013 40	Holiday 16 Vacation 8	Training 32		
GGG	ASR	100 40	100 40	200 40	200 32 Holiday 8	Training 40	Vacation 8	300 40		Holiday 16 Vacation 8		Vacation 40	Vacation 40 400 40
HHH	ASR	501 40	501 40	502 40	503 32 Holiday 8	Training 40 503 16	502 40	502 40	503 40	Holiday 16 Vacation 8	Vacation 40	999 40 Vacation 16	504 40 999 40
III	ASR	601 24 Vacation 16	601 40	601 40	602 32 Holiday 8	Training 40	602 40	602 40	602 40	Holiday 16 Vacation 8 603 8		Vacation 40	Vacation 40
JJJ	ASR	701 40	702 40	702 40	702 32 703 8	Training 40	704 40	003 40		Vacation 24 Holiday 16	004 40	004 40	004 40

FIGURE I3 A portion of the master plan, known as the "railroad," as used at Arthur Andersen–Charlotte.

Notes:
1. Names are in letters—AAA, BBB
2. Companies have numbers such as 111, 222, 555, 001
3. Together in each box with the company are the hours per week devoted to each company, or to training, or to vacation
4. Shaded boxes have more than 40 hours committed
5. AESR = audit, experienced senior; ASR = audit senior

Personnel Policy

While profitability was tied to the pyramid and to the efficient scheduling of people, the Charlotte office's managing partner believed that in the long run, Arthur Andersen would be successful only if it served its clients well. His major concern was with the development of the professionals in the office and the culture in which they worked. Culture, of course, is an elusive concept, but a variety of indications of the Arthur Andersen culture could be cited:

- The Arthur Andersen motto: think straight, talk straight.
- No secrets were kept around the office.
- Teamwork and attention to detail were highly valued.
- Also valued was client service and the urgency in that. There was a "code red" program that called for some member of the engagement team to return a client's phone call

within 60 minutes, no matter where the engagement's lead partner or manager might find him or herself.

- The pride that Arthur Andersen had in having the widely acknowledged premier training program of any of the Big Six.

- The desire that Charlotte's managing partner had for everyone to have fun doing his or her job. In support of this, the goal was to have every professional assigned to the industry of his or her preference at least half the time.

- Each of the office's professionals was reviewed each year. Each professional filled out a form and then met with a partner to discuss his or her performance and career development.

Training

One of the partners was responsible for monitoring the training of all the audit professionals. Training at Arthur Andersen was done either within the local office or at the firm-wide level. To this end, the firm operated a training center in St. Charles, Illinois, and brought professionals from all over the world to it on a regular basis. Continuing professional education was required of all CPAs by the national and various states' accounting societies (120 hours over 3 years with no less than 20 hours per year in any year), so even partners and managers spent time in training. For the most part, partners and managers averaged at least 40 hours per year, and most staff accumulated between 150 and 200 hours of training, with 100 to 120 hours spent locally, and the balance at either the regional level or at the St. Charles campus. Seniors did not spend quite that much time, but they too spent a considerable amount of time in training.

Training was considered as important as a client assignment for the professionals in the office. The training plan was usually developed well in advance, and put out "on the railroad." Good attendance was viewed as important for career development. The slow period from April through August was the best time of the year for training, although training programs were scheduled throughout the year.

The training program was considerably varied. Some of the programs were basic for the first- and second-year professionals, but other programs were termed either intermediate or advanced. Some of these courses dealt with interpersonal relationships, marketing, effective presentations, and other aspects of management development. Still other courses had industry orientations, so that professionals could be better steeped in the nature and problems of the specific industries they served.

Recruiting

Recruiting was another important function that was overseen by a partner and that demanded considerable time from the senior professionals in the office. Recruiting concentrated on local schools, although all the recruiting was done for the firm at large and not just for the Charlotte office. Recruiting was done at both the undergraduate and master's levels.

Supporting the Operations

The professionals in the Charlotte office were supported handsomely by both technology and specialized staff. Everyone was tied into the Andersen computer network that enabled easy access to contacts and expertise within the firm and specialized sources of information such as Andersen's Global Best Practices database or CDs to aid audit research. Maintaining this information were computer experts and a librarian.

The office had its own graphic designer and document production staff to help generate reports and a print shop to produce finished documents and proposals for clients. There were even two travel agents to help arrange travel to client premises.

The Manager's Life

Managers organized and oversaw the operations of each audit engagement. It was their job to assemble and to coordinate the team of professionals for each engagement, to see that the audit was done well and on time, and to assess whether the fee level was appropriate. They were responsible for developing the staffing plan and budget for the engagement and for billing and collecting from the client. Managers wanted to avoid any surprises on an engagement, and thus it was in their interest to have seniors and staff who could be trusted and whose competence and capabilities would be unquestioned.

Managers spent a good deal of their time outside the office—perhaps 55 to 65 percent. Most of that time was spent at existing clients, attending to their needs and solving any problems that had cropped up. About 20 to 25 percent of the manager's time was spent with administrative chores. And because managers were partners-in-training to a large degree, they spent some of their time developing new clients and new business for the firm.

In the main, managers were pleased with their lives at Arthur Andersen. Their jobs were viewed as challenging, motivating, and educational, and the partners gave them a good deal of autonomy. The partners were also regarded as fair, and the up-or-out nature of the business was not unduly confining because the managers felt that they could easily leave the firm for attractive jobs elsewhere.

The Partner's Life

Many duties fell on the partners in the Charlotte office. The typical partner incurred about 1000 hours each year that were charged to the engagements on which he was the senior member. Of that time, perhaps two thirds was spent at the client, discussing the client's business and supervising the audit there. Other chargeable hours were spent in the planning phase and final report phases of the actual audit. As an accountant and auditor, the partner was responsible for solving problems, for analyzing risk, and for monitoring quality.

The other 1400 to 1500 hours of a partner's year were spent in many different activities: recruiting; training, including teaching the junior people; practice development, which was the marketing and sales function for generating new business; personnel matters, such as counseling junior professionals and reviewing their progress; and providing counsel to other Arthur Andersen professionals on matters of the partner's own expertise (e.g., the Charlotte office was viewed as the firm's source of expertise for textiles).

Partners were well compensated. Their high incomes were a motivation for many of the junior people. There were two classes of partner. One could be a U.S. partner or a partner of Arthur Andersen & Co., SC—the Geneva-based "société coopérative" within the Arthur Andersen Worldwide Organization—and it was increasingly the norm that a manager was first promoted to be a U.S. partner, and then, later, an SC partner. SC partners were paid by splitting the worldwide profits of the company according to how many "units" they held. Each unit was stated in U.S. dollars. All partners started with a fixed quantity of units, and over time, these units were added onto, based upon seniority and merit. In keeping with the no-secrets aspect of the firm, files were kept on all partners, and all partners knew what everyone else in the firm made.

A manager was not promoted to partner based solely on the evaluations of the office in which he or she served. There were uniform standards for the promotion to partner that were overseen by a firm-wide committee. Upon becoming SC partners, managers were required to contribute some capital to the firm, but this was a rather modest amount relative to the income the partner made.

PART TWO: DISCUSSION

Arthur Andersen is in no way responsible for the following views and presentation. They remain solely the responsibility of the author.

The Flow of the Process and of Information

Figure I4 is a very rough process flow diagram of the audit process. It shows the degree of involvement by the various levels comprising the engagement team. This process flow also includes the proposal stage and the selection and scheduling stage for the development of the audit team. The diagram depicts only the major phases of the audit process. One could, of course, develop a more detailed schedule of the work for any engagement, but that detailed schedule would be very particular to the client, and complex as well. It would include many of the work elements of Arthur Andersen's audit procedures; as such it is beyond the scope of this service tour.

Similarly, constructing a diagram of the information flow in a process like auditing is well-nigh impossible. The flows of information are so numerous and so idiosyncratic to the client and to the needs of the engagement team itself that it is not worth characterizing here. A Big Six accounting organization simply lives on information, and that information flow must be swift, it must involve all layers of the company, and it must carry differing quantities of information.

There are no real distinctions in either the process or information flows during peak versus nonpeak times. During peak times, of course, lots of overtime is put in, and people are perhaps more charged-up about work, but all of the steps must still be done, and all of the information must still flow as it does at nonpeak times.

FIGURE I4 Rough process flow diagram for auditing services at Arthur Andersen & Co.–Charlotte.

	Proposal Writing	Engagement Team Selection and Scheduling	Planning Phase	Specific Risk Analysis Phase	Final Audit Phase
Senior Members of the Engagement Team (Partners and Managers)	High involvement with client and among themselves	High involvement, especially by managers. Scheduler is very much involved	High involvement	Little involvement by partner(s), except for periodic troubleshooting and for quality reviews Day-to-day involvement by manager	High involvement
Junior Members of the Engagement Team (Seniors and Staff)	Little or no involvement	Some preferences for work are stated	Little involvement by staff. High involvement by seniors	High involvement. Much work done at client	High involvement

Demands of the Process on the Workforce

The workforce at Arthur Andersen is composed of the salaried professionals (managers, seniors, staff) and the less numerous support people. The process demands on them are essentially a high degree of training and a tremendous amount of flexibility. The firm's accountants have to move from job to job, to put in long hours when called upon, and to be out in the field for, perhaps, long stretches of time. Some of the work is tedious, although much of the work can be challenging and rewarding.

The firm's accountants, at all levels, must make decisions all the time. Even in the preliminary phase of an audit, there are decisions to be made and many issues that need to be resolved. Thus the members of an engagement team have to be constantly on the lookout for problems or opportunities (e.g., add-on business) that they should surface to the senior members of the engagement team for resolution. This is one reason why so much continual training is required to keep everyone fresh and knowledgeable as times and clients change.

Accountants must also face the up-or-out nature of advancement within the firm. Happily, the alternatives to employment are generally good. Arthur Andersen accountants are typically in high demand by client companies and others. The care with which advancement decisions are made and the counsel given accountants through this process help to ease any stress that this kind of advancement places on the accountants proceeding through the ranks.

The Pyramid [1]

Let us now depart from the organizational structure of Arthur Andersen to examine in more general terms the nature of the professional pyramid (Figure I5) as it applies in all sorts of professional service firms. For the sake of simplification, consider only three ranks of professionals: partner, manager, and junior. The partner is chiefly responsible for client relations and the running of the firm itself. The manager is the one responsible for the day-to-day activities of the project (en-

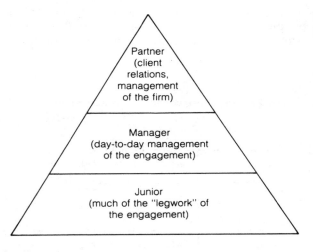

FIGURE I5 The professional pyramid.

---

[1]Much of the discussion is based upon David Maister, "Balancing the Professional Service Firm," *Sloan Management Review* (Fall 1982): 15–29.

gagement)—what there is to do, how it is to be done, and whether it is being done properly, on schedule, and within budget. The junior professional is assigned many of the tasks that constitute the "legwork" of the project. This dispersion of responsibility among partners, managers, and juniors has led some wags to term this hierarchy one of "finders, minders, and grinders."

What determines the shape of the pyramid—whether it is broad or narrow? There are two major determinants of the pyramid's shape:

1. The composition of work on the projects undertaken.
2. The utilization rates of the firm's professionals.

Let's explore these factors in greater detail. Assume, for example, that a typical project of 600 hours required certain time commitments from the firm's professionals and that the professionals were used on projects to the degree shown in the following table.

Professionals	Typical Time Commitment[a] (Hours)	Utilization Rate[a] (Percent)
Partner	60	50
Manager	140	70
Junior	<u>400</u>	85
	600	

[a]These are meant to be illustrative and do not reflect figures for Arthur Andersen.

The utilization rates reflect the facts that other things take up professionals' time (training, recruiting, scheduling, counseling, soliciting new business) and that these other activities are relatively more demanding of the senior professionals in the firm. Given a planning figure of 2000 hours of work per person per year, one partner could sustain supervision of 16.67 average projects (calculated as 1000 hours of partner time available for projects divided by 60 hours of time per typical project, or 16.67 projects per year). A manager, on the other hand, could sustain direction of 10 projects (1400 hours available and 140 hours average for each project). Thus for the firm to be balanced, for every partner there have to be 1.67 managers. Similarly, a junior can work on 4.25 projects each year (1700 hours available and 400 hours for each project). In this way, the pyramid's shape is determined: Every partner supports 1.67 managers and 3.92 juniors.

The shape of the pyramid, in turn, largely determines the rate at which professionals can be advanced and how selective that advancement has to be. Assume, for example, that juniors are 6 years in rank and that managers are 4 years in rank. If there are 10 partners, the pyramid would look as in Figure I6. Suppose that every year a partner has to be added, either to sustain the growth of the firm or to replace a partner who retires or otherwise leaves the firm. Every year, then, a manager has to be made a partner in order for the pyramid to be in balance. If, on average each year, 4 of the 17 managers are in the fourth year, the advancement rate has to be 1 in 4. Similarly, if during any year, 4 new managers are required and there are 7 juniors in their final sixth year, then roughly half of the juniors can be promoted to manager status. In this way, the pyramid sustains itself. Of the 11 juniors and managers in their last year, 1 becomes a partner, 4 become managers, and 6 leave the firm. Of the 7 new recruits, only 1 can expect to make partner after 10 years.

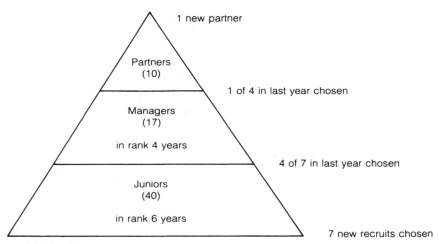

FIGURE 16 The pyramid and advancement.

Demands of the Process on Management

The partners in a professional firm like Arthur Andersen have a number of responsibilities that they alone must shoulder. Many of these responsibilities relate to the workforce. Managing the pyramid well, as discussed earlier, is an absolute requirement. Partners must take the lead in recruiting new accountants, in training them, and in managing their advancement through the firm. These activities take up tremendous chunks of partner time.

Partners must also use that pyramid well in order to make money. Thus the assignment of accountants to engagements and the scheduling of those accountants are important areas of partner concern. Even though the actual schedule itself is accomplished by a manager level professional, the partners must develop the strategy underlying the schedules developed.

Partners are also primarily responsible for procuring new business. They are the ones who must contact the clients, develop proposals, and establish fees. And, of course, the partners must be, in themselves, excellent accountants. They must be intimately involved in the general risk analysis and the final phase of each audit. They are called on to troubleshoot and to review the quality of any audit through all its phases, particularly the preliminary phase. In addition to this line management authority, they are also called on by others in the firm as experts in certain areas (e.g., industries and certain accounting practices). Thus partners must wear many hats and are pulled in many different directions.

Questions

1. What advantages do you see to the hierarchical structure of an accounting firm like Arthur Andersen? Do you see any disadvantages?
2. What kinds of factors do you suppose would affect the fee schedule advanced in a proposal to a client?
3. In a partner-manager-junior type of organization, as described in the discussion to this service tour, suppose the time commitments were changed from a 60–140–400 breakdown to one of 100–200–300. Assuming the same utilization rates, how would the pyramid change, if it were to remain perfectly balanced?

4. What benefits and costs are involved in increasing the average chargeable hours in the office from its current level of 1400 to 1500 hours per year?

5. What kinds of trade-offs are the hardest for the office's scheduler? What kinds are the easiest?

6. What are the characteristics you would look for in the typical recruit for a staff accountant position?

Situation for Study I-1
Johnson and Trotter Advertising

The Johnson and Trotter Advertising Agency (J&T) was a large, New York–based agency with a wide variety of clients. J&T was organized into six functional departments: account management, research, creativity, production, media, and legal. The account management department was charged with client relations and was responsible for coordinating the efforts of all of the other departments on the client's behalf. The research department was responsible for uncovering useful facts about the products and services advertised that may be of use in developing new ads, and they were also charged with substantiating the advertising claims made by the ads. The creativity department was the lead department in developing new ideas and the means by which the client's products and services could be advertised. The production department was responsible for making the print, radio, and TV ads that had been conceived by the creativity department. The media department interacted with all of the media in which the agency's clients advertised, while the legal department handled any legal issues raised by the agency's efforts.

The agency accomplished its work in teams. Members of the various departments generally worked on more than one account at the same time except for the account executive, who was charged with keeping all members of the product team informed about such things as the client's situation, research findings, creative ideas, production status, and any other information on the account. The account executive was also charged with keeping the entire effort on the established timetable and within budget. Members of each product team could expect to spend several years working for a client, before being rotated off. Any differences of opinion were generally dealt with by compromise within the product team. Account executives did not have the authority to overrule a specialist on a question involving that specialist's realm of expertise. If a difference of opinion persisted, the team could take its dispute to its superiors within each department, where it was usually resolved.

There were three quality control mechanisms at J&T: a strategy review board, a creative review board, and a media review board. At key stages of the firm's process, these quality control mechanisms could be invoked.

Promotion for the professionals of the agency came from within each department. For example, within account management, one typically started as an assistant account executive, moved up to account executive, then, on to account supervisor, management supervisor, and then executive vice-president for client services. A general manager oversaw all of the six functional groups.

1. What strengths do you see in the organization of Johnson and Trotter?

2. What potential disadvantages exist with this operation?

TOUR J

A Project

Geupel DeMars, Inc.
Indianapolis, Indiana

(Courtesy of Geupel DeMars, Inc., Indianapolis, Indiana)

Geupel DeMars, a subsidiary of the DeMars Corporation, was an Indianapolis-based construction management firm for industrial and commercial properties. The company was formed in 1927 and first worked on department store construction. Since that time it had gradually broadened its client base. During the time period captured by this tour, the firm employed about 250 people. See the organization charts in Figure J1.

Geupel DeMars (GDI), as a construction management firm, acted as the agent for an Owner. It did no actual construction itself, but rather planned for the construction of the building, arranged for Owner-held contracts for the different

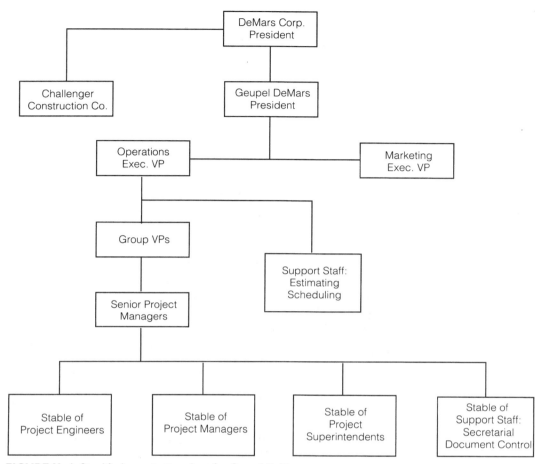

FIGURE JI A. Simplified organization chart for Geupel DeMars.

aspects of the job, oversaw the work, and reported to the Owner. For its effort, the Owner paid Geupel DeMars a fee to cover the salaries and benefits of its employees on the job, plus a percentage markup.

As a construction management firm, Geupel DeMars was distinct from (1) an architectural/engineering (A/E) firm that designs buildings and does the engineering required to translate the design into documents that serve as the basis of contractor bids on the project; (2) a design/build firm that combines the design, engineering, and construction of a building into a single one-stop package for the Owner; or (3) a contractor that only builds.

The workings of a construction management firm are best seen by examining a particular project. For this tour, the project is the construction of Research Building No. 48 for Eli Lilly & Company. This building (see Figure J2) of 550,000 square feet, had its "date of substantial completion" (when the architect certifies that the owner may occupy the building to do the work it was designed to perform) in November 1993 at a total cost of $139.5 million. The building was of four stories, laid out in three wings (Biology, Chemistry, and Animal) tied to a central administrative section. The nature of the building called for features that were distinct from typical office buildings: special ventilation for the 162 labs, greater ca-

FIGURE J1 B. Organization chart for the project.

pacity HVAC (heating, ventilation, and air-conditioning), purified water sources, and special drainage systems, among others.

PART ONE: PROCESS DESCRIPTION

Project Organization and Timetable

Research Building No. 48 took three years and nine months to build from groundbreaking to completion. Prior to that time, considerable planning had to be done. Geupel DeMars became involved with the project about two years before construction began. The nature of its involvement in the project changed over time. To wit:

YEAR ONE, 1988

Personnel: 0 in field; 2 in the office.

Tasks: Gather data; estimate costs and constructability; develop overall schedule.

When Geupel DeMars entered the project, Lilly had already engaged the architectural/engineering firm (CUH2A of Princeton, New Jersey) and the building's design was proceeding. Although the location for the building was set, there was still considerable fluidity to the design: how many stories, how stretched out, how the various research wings would be connected. Geupel DeMars's role in this conceptual phase of the project involved the following tasks:

FIGURE J2 Floor plan for Research Building 48's first floor.

- Reviewing the plans and estimating the costs of various alternative designs.
- Reviewing the constructability of the building and identifying the cost-feature trade-offs that the Owner (Lilly) would have to make, tasks known as value engineering.
- Identifying schedule parameters and inputs. Preparing and presenting alternative schedule strategies for delivery of the project.

In this conceptual phase, GDI provided cost estimates to the Owner with an accuracy of within 10 to 20% of actual costs for each of the building configurations seriously considered. These estimates were based on costs per square foot of interior space, costs per square foot for the face of the building (stone, glass, concrete), and costs for HVAC, plumbing, electrical requirements, and so on.

YEAR TWO, 1989

Personnel: 0 in the field; 2 in the office.

Tasks: Continue Year One tasks but with further refinement, establish budget.

The second year of the project continued the tasks begun in Year One. Over time, decisions were made that refined the project more and more. The project moved from "conceptual drawings" of the building to "schematic drawings," which were half to two-thirds complete in nature and on which materials began to be specified. These schematic drawings required renewed cost estimation and value engineering.

The character of Geupel DeMars's value engineering could include the following types of suggestions:

- *Selection of materials.* The choice of materials can often affect the cost of the project by 5 to 10 percent. Such choices can include the use of concrete versus structural steel, the type of roofing materials to use, the choice of pipe materials for purified water systems, and the like.
- *Design modifications.* The construction manager can suggest which design details are likely to be expensive to render and which are not. Examples include roofing details such as flashings and eaves, structural concrete details on how the concrete is to be formed, and finish details such as door jambs and lighting fixture wiring systems.

The schematic drawings were followed by the even more specific "design development drawings" and the first of the "construction documents" upon which supplier and contractor bids could be made.

YEAR THREE, 1990

Personnel: 1 in the field; 4 in the office.

Tasks: Supervise excavation and initial construction; begin bidding procedures for contractors; establish procedures for scheduling, quality control, and cost control.

Excavation of the site began in February 1990. During the rest of that year, the foundations were poured and the erection of the steel superstructure for the building was started. One superintendent in the field oversaw this work.

This year also saw the start of what was termed the "fast-track construction design." This process called for the identification of sequential "bid packages" of work, the scheduling of the design process to support this sequence, bidding, the award of initial contracts, and the subsequent commencement of work. The development and awarding of bid packages was done on a rolling basis and would continue for a year and a half. Major parts of the construction were treated in this way: excavation, foundation, concrete, structural steel, enclosure packages (skin, roof, doors); elevators, mechanicals (HVAC, fire protection, plumbing); electricals; and various interior finishes (painting, flooring, carpeting, ceiling, partitions, wall coverings, etc.). Likewise, as part of this process, came the purchase of equipment for the building by the Owner.

This was also the year to establish the balance of the procedures that would govern the construction of the project as time went on. These procedures were essential to the control of the project (schedule, cost, quality) so that the Owner actually received what was designed and specified. These controls are explained in more detail later.

YEAR FOUR, 1991

Personnel: 5 in the field; 9 in the office.

Tasks: Continue construction supervision; continue the development and award of bid packages; monitor project schedule, costs, and quality and report to the Owner.

In this year, the building took shape and the need for field monitoring and supervision escalated dramatically. Bid packages continued to be assembled, bid, and awarded.

The year also saw more "administration and management" of the project as opposed to the earlier planning and estimating work that dominated the efforts of Geupel DeMars. This "management" essentially consisted of pursuing the control procedures that had been laid out in the previous year, reporting on progress to the Owner, and dealing with the myriad field questions and problems, both large and small, that inevitably accompanied the work of the contractors as they actually built the research building and as procurement proceeded.

YEAR FIVE, 1992

Personnel: 8 in the field; 10 in the office.

Tasks: Continue supervision of the construction; continue management of the project; start-up of major systems.

YEAR SIX, 1993

Personnel: 8 in the field; 10 in the office.

Tasks: Continue supervision of the construction; continue management of the project; continue the start-up of major systems.

YEAR SEVEN, 1994

Personnel: 3 in the office.

Tasks: Close out the project for the Owner; interact with the Lilly researchers occupying the building and try to incorporate their ideas for improvements.

Although the construction was completed in late 1993 and the Owner had begun to occupy the building then, the project was not closed out until June 1994. Closing out a project meant several things.

- All contractors had completed their work, including their "punch lists" (i.e., the lists of repairs and inadvertent omissions that are identified prior to an Owner taking possession).
- The contractors had supplied the "as built" drawings, warranties, and guarantees.
- All paperwork had been finished, including all letters answered and items resolved.
- The project file was completed, including all copies of correspondence, all shop drawings (the detailed drawings from the contractors of which there were thousands of pages), all as-built drawings, all quality control documents, and all test reports.

The Manual and Its Controls

Prior to the start of construction, Geupel DeMars and Lilly prepared a procedures manual that outlined the specific duties of each party. This manual was the basic control document for the project. In it, procedures were described for such items as bidding, materials substitutions, submittals, quality control, requests for information (usually from a contractor to the A/E firm and the Owner), design changes, and progress payments to the contractors.

Submittals were a particularly important point of control. A submittal was the contractor's submission for review of any of several types of documents:

- Catalog and performance data for the materials to be used
- "Shop drawings"—the contractor's drawings detailing what actually was to be done
- Guarantees
- Job standards, consisting of certifications or approved samples that could be of use as field examples

- Maintenance data and operating instructions
- Installation instructions
- Physical samples of material and assemblies

Once the submittals were reviewed and approved by the A/E, the contractor could procure and install the material and equipment. Submittals thus led to the approval of materials, and materials were seen as driving both the schedule and the budget. Geupel DeMars was insistent that contractors follow a submittal schedule so that they performed on time with the proper information.

Substitutions were another important item to control. Substitutions of materials were usually made to reduce cost, to provide a better product (perhaps as a result of value engineering), or to speed up an aspect of the project that had fallen behind schedule. Substitutions required the approval of the Owner and the A/E firm.

There were a host of other controls on quality. For example, the superintendents completed reports each day on the work accomplished. There were reports on nonconforming work, which typically would necessitate repair. Independent tests were made to verify that items such as the soil, concrete, structural work, roofing, HVAC, and high voltage met design requirements. A periodic report was distributed to the Owner on (1) the construction progress, (2) the topics at morning meetings, and, (3) most importantly, a listing of "open issues."

Contractor Bidding

Geupel DeMars did no real construction on Building No. 48, acting only as the agent for the Owner. A major task for the company was to assist the Owner in assembling the best available stable of contractors who (1) had the expertise, (2) met the Owner's financial requirement, and (3) were aware of the Owner's high quality standards. Working from the plans and engineering specifications of the architectural/engineering firm, Geupel DeMars assembled a total of about 30 bid packages for the diverse pieces of the construction. A bid package contained (1) a summary of work that spelled out all that the contractor was to do; (2) a manual detailing procedures used by Geupel DeMars and Lilly; and (3) the applicable construction drawings and technical specifications by the A/E firm. A bid package took about a week to assemble. Once assembled, the bid package was sent to between four and six contractors that had been invited to bid on the job. These contractors were generally well known to Geupel DeMars either from past work or from the formal approval process, and were all considered to be capable of performing quality work of the scale required. (Often, the Owner would have its own preferred list.) New or previously unknown contractors would be visited and their operations and financial conditions reviewed.

After the bidding documents were out for two weeks, Geupel DeMars held a pre-bid meeting with the invited contractors. At this meeting, GDI reviewed the manual and the summary of work and then, with the assistance of the A/E and the Owner, answered questions. Following the meeting, an addendum with meeting minutes and revisions was issued.

It took the contractors between three and six weeks to prepare their bids. After review of the bids, the apparent low bidder was invited to attend a pre-contract meeting between the contractor, the Owner, the A/E (if necessary), and GDI. This was a technical meeting that sometimes involved Geupel DeMars's field superintendents. If all issues were resolved, the Owner then signed a contract with the successful bidder. Construction then began on that contracted work.

Dealing with Contractors on the Job

Once construction began, Geupel DeMars passed on information between contractors and the Owner and the A/E firm. (The Lilly team for this project numbered about 10 people. The A/E firm, at one point, had as many as 300 on the design effort, with about 10 on the continuing supervisory team.) Sometimes, the contractor would have questions about particular details of the construction, questions that were generally overlooked by all parties before then. These questions triggered a formal RFI (Request for Information). Geupel DeMars's role was (1) to follow up on the RFI, (2) to distribute the information to the appropriate people, and (3) to communicate any decided changes to the scope of work.

Geupel DeMars felt that it had failed if any major problems occurred. The company was always looking ahead to such things as the schedule of submittals, approved materials, and test results. Fortunately for all concerned, there were few problems of any magnitude with the Research Building No. 48 project.

Field Supervision

As the building progressed, more and more attention was devoted to planning and supervising the daily construction activities. This was the responsibility of the field's construction superintendents and field engineers. Initially, there was only one to supervise the excavation and foundation work. As the superstructure was set in place, more superintendents joined the project and a greater division of labor ensued. For Research Building No. 48, there were different superintendents for each of the major trades represented by the contractors (e.g., structure, mechanicals, electricals).

The superintendents oversaw the quality of work being done, any testing of materials, and the coordination of the contractors' work. They reviewed requests for information. They also determined the percentage completion of various aspects of the job, which affected scheduling and the progress payments Lilly made each month.

Scheduling

After quality control in importance came the control of the project's schedule. The schedule affected both quality and cost. Although keeping on schedule was everybody's concern, there was a scheduler whose task was to document the schedule and the project's conformance to that schedule.

The schedule was derived in backward fashion. The Owner typically had a completion date in mind. From that date the scheduler worked back to the relevant start dates.

The raw data for the schedule were the numerous activities that had to be accomplished. Some of these activities had to precede others, although many activities could be accomplished simultaneously. For the most part, the activities comprising the schedule followed the various bid packages. The contractors responsible for each bid package detailed their construction schedules, floor-by-floor, and this information served as a basis for the schedule. Geupel DeMars then applied its own experience and its knowledge of supplier timetables, especially for long lead-time items.

A computer program, Primavera Primavision, was used to document, monitor, and make changes to the schedule. Primavera kept track of all the designated activities, their expected times-to-completion, and their relationships to each other. The input to Primavera was built up bit-by-bit as GDI developed each bid package. The program's input began shortly after excavation was begun. By the end of the project, it was expected that 2000 activities would be captured. Of those 2000 activities, for example, 640 would pertain to mechanical and electrical installations. Only about 20 percent of the activities pertained directly to actual installation; the other 80 percent referred to various reviews, approvals, bidding, comments, documentation, and the like.

Primavera Primavision generated several documents that helped with the project's scheduling:

1. *Gantt charts.* Figure J3 is a Gantt chart generated by Primavera. Gantt charts are simply bar charts that plot time for each activity. They show expected start and stop times, and the bars could be filled in to show the extent of actual progress at each point in time. Note that in Figure J3 the project is up to date. All of the activities that should have been accomplished by the time of the chart's date, April 1991, have indeed been accomplished.

The solid color bars represent activities that are designated as "critical." More formally, these are activities that lie on the so-called "critical path." Activities on the critical path are those which, if delayed, will delay the entire project. For them, there is no spare catchup time available to be used. They must be accomplished on time or the project gets delayed.

Sometimes, of course, an activity might be hurried up in order to put a delayed project back on track. Often, such hustling costs money in addition to the extra effort of those involved. This hustling was typically termed "crashing" an activity. For example, for Research Building No. 48, the erection of the curtain wall began seven weeks late. The contractor, however, captured back some of the lost time by putting more people on the task than was originally planned.

2. *Time logic diagrams.* Another output of Primavera is a time logic diagram, such as depicted in Figure J4. This diagram depicts the precedence relationships among activities. In the diagram and the accompanying sheet of detail, the ties between activities become clear. For example, Figure J4 relates to Bid Group VII-2 (fire protection), and among its first set of activities, there are these ties to other activities:

Activity 1110	The bidding was due on December 12, 1990. Prior to the bidding, two things had to happen: Lilly had to sign the Phase II construction documents (Activity 1024), and GDI had to prepare the bidding documents themselves (Activity 1026). These two things were completed in October. The successor activity (1112) was the awarding of the contract. The expected duration of the activity, 37 days, is given in the ORIG DUR (Original Duration) column.
Activity 1112	This is the successor activity to Activity 1110. It was accomplished by 1/11/91. We know this is so for several reasons: the progress shown on the chart's bar, the 100 percent completion shown in the PCT column, the "0" in the REM DUR (Remaining Duration) column, and the "A," for Actual, after the early start and early finish dates. Activity 1112 has two successor activities: preparing a preliminary design and working up fire protection coordination drawings.
Activity 1115	This activity is one of the successors to Activity 1112. It is on schedule, but it has not yet reached its conclusion. The percentage completion is 33 percent, with 40 of the expected 60 days' worth of work remaining. It has one successor activity, installing the fire protection pipe supports in the B-wing, slated to begin on August 12, 1991.

FIGURE J3 A portion of the project schedule for Research Building 48——Gantt chart.

227

ACTIVITY ID	ORIG DUR	REM DUR	PCT	CODE	ACTIVITY DESCRIPTION	EARLY START	EARLY FINISH	LATE START	LATE FINISH	TOTAL FLOAT
VII-2 FIRE PROTECTION										
1110	37	0	100	44	BIDDING DUE - FIRE PROTECTION 12/12	23OCT90A	12DEC90A			
1112	22	0	100	44	AWARD CONTRACT - FIRE PROTECTION 1/11	13DEC90A	11JAN91A			
1114	75	5	93	44B	PREP PRELIMINARY DESIGN F.P. 3/29	14JAN91A	26APR91		26APR91	0
1115	60	40	33	44B	FIRE PROTECTION COORDINATION DRAWINGS 6/14	25MAR91A	14JUN91		14JUN91*	0
1116	10	10	0	44B	OWNER REVIEW PRELIM DESIGN 5/10	29APR91	10MAY91	29APR91	10MAY91	0
1118	25	25	0	44B	REVISE & RESUBMIT F.P. SHOPS 6/14	13MAY91	14JUN91	13MAY91	14JUN91	0
1120	15	15	0	44B	OWNER REVIEW REVISED SHOPS 7/5	17JUN91	5JUL91	17JUN91	5JUL91	0
1122	25	25	0	44B	FINALIZE DESIGN FOR INSURANCE REVIEW 8/9	8JUL91	9AUG91	8JUL91	9AUG91*	0
1150	25	25	0	44 BB	INSTALL F.P. PIPE SUPPORTS B-WING 9/13	12AUG91	13SEP91	12AUG91	13SEP91	0
1124	25	25	0	44B	PROCURE & FAB PIPING B-WING 9/13	12AUG91	13SEP91	26AUG91	18OCT91*	25
1160	100	100	0	44	PROCURE F.P. EQUIPMENT 12/27	12AUG91	27DEC91	26AUG91	10JAN92	10
1152	25	25	0	44 CC	INSTALL F.P. PIPE SUPPORTS C-WING 10/18	16SEP91	18OCT91	16SEP91	18OCT91	0
1128	25	25	0	44C	PROCURE & FAB PIPING C-WING 10/18	16SEP91	18OCT91	21OCT91	22NOV91*	25
1154	25	25	0	44 AA	INSTALL F.P. PIPE SUPPORTS A-WING 11/22	21OCT91	22NOV91	21OCT91	22NOV91	0
1132	25	25	0	44A	PROCURE & FAB PIPING A-WING 11/22	21OCT91	22NOV91	25NOV91	27DEC91*	25
1126	65	65	0	44 BB	INSTALL F.P. MAINS & BRANCH PIPING B-WING 1/31	4NOV91*	31JAN92	4NOV91	31JAN92*	0
1156	25	25	0	44 HH	INSTALL F.P. PIPE SUPPORTS H-WING 12/27	25NOV91	27DEC91	25NOV91	27DEC91*	0
1136	25	25	0	44H	PROCURE & FAB PIPING H-WING 12/27	25NOV91	27DEC91	30DEC91	31JAN92*	25
1130	65	65	0	44 CC	INSTALL F.P. MAINS & BRANCH PIPING C-WING 2/28	2DEC91*	28FEB92	2DEC91	28FEB92*	0
1162	100	100	0	44	INSTALL F.P. EQUIPMENT 5/15	30DEC91	15MAY92	13JAN92	29MAY92*	10
1134	65	65	0	44 AA	INSTALL F.P. MAINS & BRANCH PIPING A-WING 4/3	6JAN92*	3APR92	6JAN92	3APR92*	0
1135	0	0	0	44 BB	B-WING MOCK-UP ROOM 01/15	15JAN92*	15JAN92	15JAN92	15JAN92*	0
1138	65	65	0	44 HH	INSTALL F.P. MAINS & BRANCH PIPING H-WING 5/1	3FEB92*	1MAY92	3FEB92	1MAY92*	0
1137	0	0	0	44 CC	C-WING MOCK-UP ROOM 02/12	12FEB92*	12FEB92	12FEB92	12FEB92*	0
1164	40	40	0	44 BB	TEST DROPS & HEADS B-WING 7/24	1JUN92*	24JUL92	1JUN92	24JUL92	0
1166	45	45	0	44 CC	TEST DROPS & HEADS C-WING 9/25	27JUL92	25SEP92	27JUL92	25SEP92*	0
1168	45	45	0	44 AA	TEST DROPS & HEADS A-WING 10/23	24AUG92	23OCT92	24AUG92	23OCT92*	0
1170	50	50	0	44 HH	TEST DROPS & HEADS H-WING 11/27	21SEP92	27NOV92	21SEP92	27NOV92*	0
1172	25	25	0	44	TEST F.P. SYSTEMS 1/1	30NOV92	1JAN93	30NOV92	1JAN93*	0

FIGURE J3 (continued)

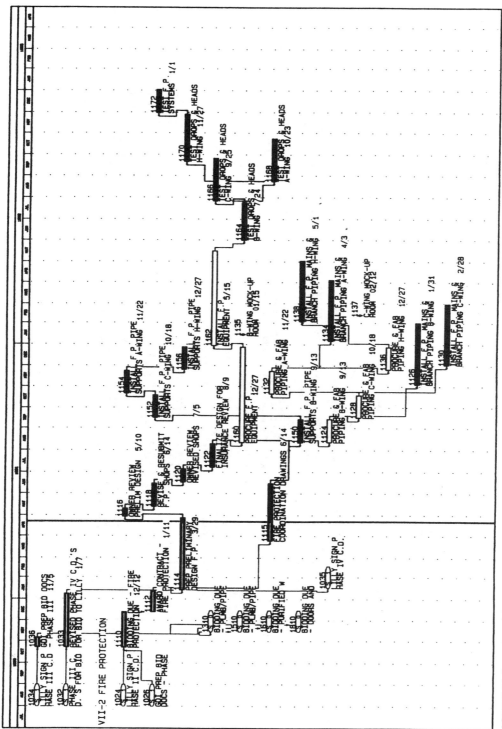

FIGURE J4 A portion of the project schedule for Research Building 48—Activity descriptions.

VII-2 FIRE PROTECTION

ACTIVITY ID	ORIG DUR	REM DUR	PCT	CODE	ACTIVITY DESCRIPTION	EARLY START	EARLY FINISH	LATE START	LATE FINISH	TOTAL FLOAT
1110	37	0	100		44 BIDDING DUE - FIRE PROTECTION 12/12	23OCT90A	12DEC90A			
1024	10	0	100	PRED	6 LILLY SIGN PHASE II C.D.'s 10/12	9OCT90A	12OCT90A			
1026*	10	0	100	PRED	GDI PREP BID DOCS - PHASE II 10/22	9OCT90A	22OCT90A			
1112*	22	0	100	SUCC	C AWARD CONTRACT - FIRE PROTECTION 1/11	13DEC90A	11JAN91A			
1112	22	0	100		44 AWARD CONTRACT - FIRE PROTECTION 1/11	13DEC90A	11JAN91A			
1110*	37	0	100	PRED	BIDDING DUE - FIRE PROTECTION 12/12	23OCT90A	12DEC90A			
1114*	75	5	93	SUCC	PREP PRELIMINARY DESIGN F.P. 3/29	14JAN91A	26APR91		26APR91	0
1115	60	40	33	SUCC	FIRE PROTECTION COORDINATION DRAWINGS 6/14	25MAR91A	14JUN91		14JUN91*	0
1114	75	5	93		44 PREP PRELIMINARY DESIGN F.P. 3/29	14JAN91A	26APR91		26APR91	0
1112*	22	0	100	PRED	AWARD CONTRACT - FIRE PROTECTION 1/11	13DEC90A	11JAN91A			
1116*	10	10	0	SUCC	OWNER REVIEW PRELIM DESIGN 5/10	29APR91	10MAY91	29APR91	10MAY91	0
1115	60	40	33		44 FIRE PROTECTION COORDINATION DRAWINGS 6/14	25MAR91A	14JUN91		14JUN91*	0
1112*	22	0	100	PRED	C 50 AWARD CONTRACT - FIRE PROTECTION 1/11	13DEC90A	11JAN91A			
1150*	25	25	0	SUCC	C 40 INSTALL F.P. PIPE SUPPORTS B-WING 9/13	12AUG91	13SEP91	12AUG91	13SEP91	0
1116	10	10	0		44 OWNER REVIEW PRELIM DESIGN 5/10	29APR91	10MAY91	29APR91	10MAY91	0
1114*	75	5	93	PRED	PREP PRELIMINARY DESIGN F.P. 3/29	14JAN91A	26APR91	29APR91	26APR91	0
1118*	25	25	0	SUCC	REVISE & RESUBMIT F.P. SHOPS 6/14	13MAY91	14JUN91	13MAY91	14JUN91	0
1118	25	25	0		44 REVISE & RESUBMIT F.P. SHOPS 6/14	13MAY91	14JUN91	13MAY91	14JUN91	0
1116*	10	10	0	PRED	OWNER REVIEW PRELIM DESIGN 5/10	29APR91	10MAY91	29APR91	10MAY91	0
1120*	15	15	0	SUCC	OWNER REVIEW REVISED SHOPS 7/5	17JUN91	5JUL91	17JUN91	5JUL91	0
1120	15	15	0		44 OWNER REVIEW REVISED SHOPS 7/5	17JUN91	5JUL91	17JUN91	5JUL91	0
1118*	25	25	0	PRED	REVISE & RESUBMIT F.P. SHOPS 6/14	13MAY91	14JUN91	13MAY91	14JUN91	0
1122*	25	25	0	SUCC	FINALIZE DESIGN FOR INSURANCE REVIEW 8/9	8JUL91	9AUG91	8JUL91	9AUG91*	0
1122	25	15	0		44 FINALIZE DESIGN FOR INSURANCE REVIEW 8/9	8JUL91	9AUG91	8JUL91	9AUG91*	0
1120*	15	15	0	PRED	OWNER REVIEW REVISED SHOPS 7/5	17JUN91	5JUL91	17JUN91	5JUL91	0
1150*	25	25	0	SUCC	INSTALL F.P. PIPE SUPPORTS B-WING 9/13	12AUG91	13SEP91	12AUG91	13SEP91	0
1160*	100	100	0	SUCC	PROCURE F.P. EQUIPMENT 12/27	12AUG91	27DEC91	26AUG91	10JAN92	10
1150	25	25	0		44 INSTALL F.P. PIPE SUPPORTS B-WING 9/13	12AUG91	13SEP91	12AUG91	13SEP91	0
1115*	60	40	33	PRED	C 40 FIRE PROTECTION COORDINATION DRAWINGS 6/14	25MAR91A	14JUN91		14JUN91*	0
1122*	25	15	0	PRED	FINALIZE DESIGN FOR INSURANCE REVIEW 8/9	8JUL91	9AUG91	8JUL91	9AUG91*	0
1152*	25	25	0	SUCC	INSTALL F.P. PIPE SUPPORTS C-WING 10/18	16SEP91	18OCT91	16SEP91	18OCT91	0
1124	25	25	0		44 PROCURE & FAB PIPING B-WING 9/13	12AUG91	13SEP91	16SEP91	18OCT91*	25
1122*	25	15	0	PRED	FINALIZE DESIGN FOR INSURANCE REVIEW 8/9	8JUL91	9AUG91	8JUL91	9AUG91*	0
1126*	65	65	0	SUCC	INSTALL F.P. MAINS & BRANCH PIPING B-WING 1/31	4NOV91*	31JAN92	4NOV91	31JAN92*	0
1128*	25	25	0	SUCC	PROCURE & FAB PIPING C-WING 10/18	16SEP91	18OCT91	21OCT91	22NOV91*	25
1160	100	100	0		44 PROCURE F.P. EQUIPMENT 12/27	12AUG91	27DEC91	26AUG91	10JAN92	10
1122*	25	15	0	PRED	FINALIZE DESIGN FOR INSURANCE REVIEW 8/9	8JUL91	9AUG91	8JUL91	9AUG91*	0
1162*	100	100	0	SUCC	INSTALL F.P. EQUIPMENT 5/15	30DEC91	15MAY92	13JAN92	29MAY92*	10
1152	25	25	0		44 INSTALL F.P. PIPE SUPPORTS C-WING 10/18	16SEP91	18OCT91	16SEP91	18OCT91	0
1150*	25	25	0	PRED	INSTALL F.P. PIPE SUPPORTS B-WING 9/13	12AUG91	13SEP91	12AUG91	13SEP91	0
1154*	25	25	0	SUCC	INSTALL F.P. PIPE SUPPORTS A-WING 11/22	21OCT91	22NOV91	21OCT91	22NOV91	0

FIGURE J4 (continued)

Observe that not all of the activities noted in the diagram have bars shown. The complexity of the relationships has forced Primavera to show them on a different sheet. This diagram is useful for depicting the relationships. Also observe that some of the forthcoming activities are colored solid, indicating that they are critical activities, but that some are not filled in. These latter activities are not on the critical path and thus have some slack associated with them.

Primavera was capable of generating other useful documents and of sorting the activities in different ways. Sorts could be done by contractor or by floor of the building. By examining the scheduled activities in these ways, conflicts among contractors, and any subsequent rescheduling, could be held to a minimum.

Weekly meetings were held to track the schedule. Data for the schedule monitoring was provided by the superintendents on the site and by the GDI project engineers who followed the submittals and other paperwork. Every two weeks a rolling four-week summary schedule was generated.

Budgeting

The budget's major components included the following:

	Budget (in millions)
Construction (building materials, labor, Owner furnished equipment . . .)	$110.6
Engineering (Owner's cost, A/E firm, GDI)	28.9
	$139.5

Geupel DeMars monitored these costs and managed the construction costs and its own costs closely.

PART TWO: DISCUSSION

Geupel DeMars, Inc. is in not way responsible for the following views and presentation. They remain solely the responsibility of the author.

The Flow of the Process and of Information

Figures J5 and J6 display process flow and information flow diagrams for a project like the construction of Building No. 48. The diagrams are fairly general and include numerous entries that can be repeated. For example, there is a whole sequence of the process flow diagram that repeats for each of the 30 bid packages. With the information flow diagram, the interactions of RFIs, submittals, and approvals are repeated almost a countless number of times as the project continues. Geupel DeMars is really the "man in the middle" for a lot of these transactions, filtering information, monitoring progress and costs, making recommendations to the various parties, and so on. Coordination and communication are essential to the smooth running of the project.

This is an example of so-called "fast track" construction that is completely analogous to concurrent engineering in a factory setting dealing with new product development. Fast track construction overlaps the phases of construction so that detailed design aspects of the building proceed even as the initial construction is being done. Such management of the process calls for a great deal of coordination among the players, and that is just what Geupel DeMars provides.

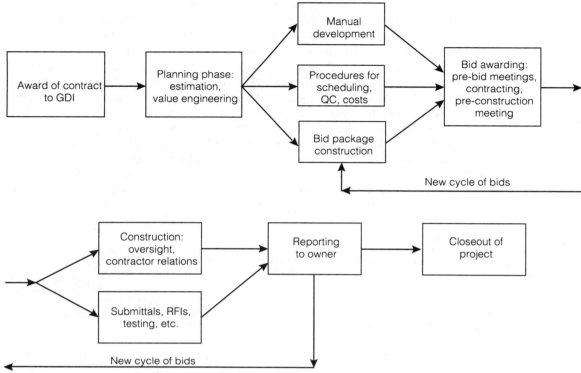

FIGURE J5 Process flow diagram for Geupel DeMars project.

Features of the Process

There are a number of interesting and distinctive aspects of the project that differentiate it from the other processes investigated in this book:

1. The staffing of this process is constantly changing. Not only are there varying numbers of construction workers on site, but there are variable numbers of architect/engineers and, importantly, varying numbers of GDI workers as well. There is

FIGURE J6 Information flow diagram for Geupel DeMars project.

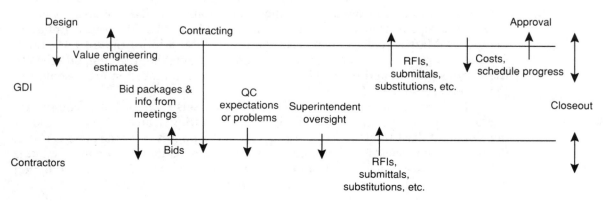

a constant ebb and flow of people of various skills and in various quantities as the project progresses.

2. A variety of specialized talents are called for. Again, these are talents not only in the architecture/engineering and construction trades themselves, but also with GDI itself as it manages the project. GDI, for example, needs specialists for construction superintendents, cost estimation, scheduling, and contractor and A/E firm relations.

3. Projects take a significant degree of up-front planning in order to be carried out well. The budget for Building No. 48 reveals this degree of planning. So much of the project involves one-of-a-kind design that such planning cannot be avoided.

4. Constant coordination is required among the parties.

5. The means by which resources can be husbanded is generally by stretching out the timetable. The contractors do this to save costs, and only when forced by slips in the schedule do they apply more labor or equipment to "crash" an activity. It is the same for GDI. Not all of the bid packages are prepared at the same time or bid on at the same time. Rather, because the job does not require it, and because it would tax GDI too much at the same time, the schedule of bid packages is spaced out. Such smoothing out of the work helps all concerned.

Demands of the Process on Management and the Workforce

At GDI management and the workforce are almost indistinguishable, as one could look at the project engineers as lower levels of management. For everybody, the demands of the process are quite similar. The process demands extraordinary planning skills of its workforce as well as tremendous attention to detail. The days of nearly everyone at GDI are filled with the follow-up and communication of details and, when called upon, the development of future needs and controls of all sorts. People live by their calendars, beepers, voice mail, faxes, and their ilk.

Planning and Control

The project lives and dies by the excellence of the planning that has gone into it and by the efficiency and thoroughness of the controls it has in place. All of these controls have to be planned for in advance, so that all parties are clear about what is required of them. The chief controls are on:

- Quality (knowing in advance what the requirements of the job are and what constitutes satisfactory accomplishment);
- Schedule (knowing when the job has to be started and stopped);
- Cost (knowing what the flow of expenses is); and
- Documentation (keeping a trail of paper about everything decided, everything accomplished, and everything changed).

The planning and control for the project outdoes that of the job shop and other kinds of processes. Similar kinds of documentation are kept: drawings, process and routing sheets (or their equivalents), tests of materials, change documents, quality documents, and schedules, but the quantities of them and the care with which they are handled are typically extraordinary. After all, with a project you only get one shot at it, and it better be right the first time, or other projects are not likely to be coming your way.

Drawings are an example. Consider the different kinds that are maintained: conceptual drawings, schematics, shop drawings, and as-built drawings. Everything about the building's construction is captured in these drawings. Everybody pores over them, communicates through them, and formally approves or changes them. And, they come by the hundreds and thousands.

Questions

1. Why does Geupel DeMars, Inc.'s organization chart look the way its does?
2. What are the differences between Figures J3 and J4?
3. Describe your concept of a typical working day for a GDI project engineer.
4. Describe the relationship between project quality, cost, and schedule.

TOUR SUMMARY

A Comparison of Production and Service Processes

In the tours, 10 different production and service processes were introduced and their key features described. There were threads in common among some of them as well as some sharp differences. The purpose of this chapter is to tie together the common threads and expose the sharp differences by comparing the processes described. Part One of this summary chapter deals with manufacturing and Part Two deals with services.

PART ONE: MANUFACTURING

Trends

First we should recognize that there are some clearly discernible trends among the six manufacturing processes introduced. The trends become evident when the processes are arrayed in the following order, a sort of "spectrum" of production processes:

- Job shop (example: Norcen Industries)
- Batch flow (example: Jos. A. Bank)
- Worker-paced line flow (example: Burger King Restaurant, Noblesville, Indiana)[1]
- Machine-paced line flow (example: Carrier Corporation, Indianapolis)
- Continuous flow (example: International Paper, Androscoggin Mill)

The hybrid process represented by the Stroh brewery at Winston-Salem, which displayed aspects of both a batch flow and a continuous flow process, is somewhat more difficult to place since it is not as pure an example as the others.

Analyzing the Trends

To provide some cohesion and organization, this discussion of process trends is divided into six parts, each part devoted to a comparison and analysis of some specific features: (1) product features, (2) general process features, (3) materials-oriented features, (4) information-oriented features, (5) labor-oriented features, and (6) management features. These six features will be addressed in turn.

---

[1]The Burger King restaurant can be viewed usefully as both a manufacturing process (a burger factory) and a service process (a fast-food restaurant). For this reason, it is included in both parts of this chapter. The project, represented by Geupel DeMars, is so unique that it is not included in these comparisons.

Product Features   Arrayed as they have been here, the different processes introduced demonstrate some distinct trends involving the types of products manufactured and how those products compete against others. Specifically, the more one goes from a job shop toward a continuous flow process, the more it is generally the case that:

1. The number of different kinds of products made declines.
2. Product volumes increase to the point where the continuous flow process is essentially producing a commodity for the mass market.
3. Product customization declines and product standardization increases.
4. New product introductions become less frequent and are more costly.
5. Competition is more likely to center on price.
6. Competition, at least in the middle ranges of the array, is more likely to emphasize aspects like workmanship, product performance, and product reliability; but as the process becomes more and more a continuous flow, these differences between rival products become narrower and narrower.

General Process Features   There are complementary trends in some general process features as well. For example, as one progresses down the array of processes from job shop to continuous flow, it is generally true that:

1. The pattern of the process becomes more rigid, and the routing of products through their various process steps becomes less individual, less unprescribed, and better defined.
2. Process segments become more tightly linked together.
3. Equipment becomes more specialized.
4. The operation becomes huge, and economies of scale are possible.
5. More, and generally larger, equipment is part of the process.
6. Equipment is less likely to be idle. Pieces of equipment become better balanced in size and speed to one another.
7. Equipment setups are fewer and run lengths are longer.
8. The pace of the process is determined largely by machine capabilities or regulated by machines or conveyors.
9. The pace of production keeps increasing.
10. The notion of capacity becomes less ambiguous and more measurable in physical, rather than dollar, units.
11. Additions to capacity come in large chunks, and incremental additions to capacity become less viable.
12. Bottlenecks become less and less movable and thus better understood.
13. Incremental change to the nature of the process itself becomes relatively more frequent and routine, but the impact of radical change to the process is likely to be more sweeping and thus scarier to contemplate.
14. Process layouts, with like machines grouped together, give way to line flow layouts.

Materials-Oriented Features   Again, keeping the array of different processes ordered from job shop through continuous flow process, some general trends in materials-oriented features can be observed. For example, as the process becomes more and more a continuous flow, it becomes more and more the case that:

1. The span of the process (vertical integration) becomes broader. A plant is more and more likely to start with "very raw" raw materials and transform them into products that may need little or no "finishing" before consumers purchase them.

2. Most processes take uniform materials and make differentiated products from them. Norcen Industries takes uniform blocks, bars, or rods of steel and machines a multitude of different parts from them. Jos. A. Bank uses the same materials to produce suits in different styles and sizes. The components that go into the various models of furnaces that Carrier produces are often very much the same. Such is not the case with many continuous flow processes. Often these processes take differentiated raw materials and make uniform products from them. One log of timber may not be the same as the next log, and so pulp and paper mills are constantly monitoring their raw materials and adjusting them so that the finished product, be it publication gloss or newsprint, looks exactly the same at the end of the roll as it does at the start. Similarly, steel plant blast furnaces make constant changes to their raw materials input mix.

3. As the time of actual production draws closer, materials requirements are generally known with more certainty.

4. Raw materials requirements are large, but their purchase and delivery can be made steady.

5. Supplier ties are long term, with frequent deliveries.

6. Because of large production volumes and steady purchases, control over suppliers for price, delivery, quality, design, and the like is great.

7. Control over the delivery time of the finished product becomes greater.

8. Work-in-process inventories, because of process design, become scant. Queues of work cease to exist.

9. Finished goods inventories are larger (relative to other inventories).

10. Finished goods are sold through formal distribution channels and can sometimes be forced down those channels for the sake of keeping production running smoothly.

Importantly, however, the batch/continuous flow hybrid process does not follow all of these trends. There is a definite work-in-process inventory situated between the batch flow portion of the process and the continuous flow portion. At least some of the raw materials are inventoried as a buffer stock to be drawn down in perhaps unexpected or haphazard fashion, while other raw materials are purchased to coincide with the production plan.

Information-Oriented Features   A number of trends are evident as well for many information-oriented features of the various production processes. As the process changes from job shop to continuous flow, generally it is more and more likely that:

1. Production has not been instigated by a bidding procedure.

2. Longer-term sales forecasts are used, and orders are "frozen" long before production is scheduled to start.

3. The corporation outside the plant is an integral part of the plant's scheduling and materials movement tracking.

4. Order scheduling is done on a very sophisticated basis.

5. A finished goods inventory is managed.

6. The flow of information and paperwork between management and workers is less.

7. Quality control measures become formal.

8. Inventory adjustments become important in responding to seasonal or business cycle changes in demand.

9. The process is less flexible in making swift adjustments to demand changes, and so production must be carefully planned in advance.

Labor-Oriented Features   Again, trends are evident across the spectrum of production processes explored, this time concerning labor issues. Progressing from job shop to continuous flow process, it is more likely that:

1. The labor content of the product becomes smaller and smaller, relative to the product's value.

2. Job contents diminish, although "art" is more likely to be found at either end of the process spectrum.

3. Labor is paid by the hour rather than by some incentive system. In fact, the progression of wage payment schemes tends to go from hourly or individual incentive rates for the job shop, through individual and then group incentive schemes, and then on to hourly rates.

4. The importance of setting standards for labor remains high. The mechanization of the continuous flow process, however, means that such standards are useful less to define the process and its capacity than to assign the workforce to the equipment.

5. As production moves more and more to mechanical or technological pacing, the scramble to complete a lot of production to meet monthly goals or billings becomes less and less prevalent.

6. The path of worker advancement becomes better defined and even formal.

Management Features   Finally, some trends can be identified as well for several aspects of the management of these diverse production processes. Progressing from job shop to continuous flow process, it is more and more the case that:

1. Staff operations concerning such topics as materials movement, scheduling, capacity planning, new technology planning, and quality control become more important relative to line operations.

2. The size of the plant's management (line and staff) is often larger relative to the size of the workforce both because the capital intensity of the operation is greater and because staff operations are more important. Table TS1 uses statistics from the processes we have discussed to show the ratio of management staff to total employees.

3. Given that the plant involved is part of a multiplant company, the involvement of managers situated at the corporate offices (rather than at the plant itself) becomes greater. The corporation's influence may extend to operations as well as to capital planning and spending.

4. The operation is controlled more as a cost center, as opposed to a profit center.

5. The major challenges that management faces are significantly altered, largely shifting from day-to-day operational considerations to very long-term, high-expense items.

TABLE TS1 Ratio of management staff to total employment

Company	Process	Management Staff/ Total Employment
Norcen Industries	Job shop	7/39 = 0.179
Jos. A. Bank	Batch flow	23/478 = 0.048
Burger King, Noblesville	Worker-paced line flow	7/52 = 0.135
Carrier, Indianapolis	Machine-paced line flow	N/A
Stroh, Winston-Salem	Batch/continuous flow hybrid	70/500 = 0.140
International Paper, Andoscoggin	Continuous flow	175/1300 = 0.135

The Process Spectrum

By comparing these trends, it is fairly plain that entire lists of characteristics hang together to describe particular processes. Table TS2 is an effort to compile just such lists for the range of production processes that have been introduced. Note that the batch/continuous flow hybrid, exemplified by the Stroh brewery, has been segregated from the others so that the process spectrum stretching from job shop through to continuous flow process remains as pure as we can reasonably expect.

Table TS2 offers some generalizations about particular types of production processes, drawing mainly from the processes discussed in the plant tours. Not all of the generalizations may ring true for all of the production processes one may conceivably classify in each category from job shop to continuous flow process. Most of the generalizations, however, are representative of a typical production process in each category.

TABLE TS2 Comparing processes of different types

Features	(1) *Job Shop (Example: Norcen Industries)*	(2) *Batch Flow (Example: Jos. A. Bank)*	(3) *Worker-Paced Assembly Line (Example: Burger King Restaurant, Noblesville)*	(4) *Machine-Paced Assembly Line (Example: Carrier Corporation, Indianapolis)*	(5) *Continuous Flow (Example: International Paper, Androscoggin Mill)*	(6) *Batch/Continuous Flow Hybrid (Example: Stroh Brewery, Winston-Salem)*
			Product Features			
Product mix	Generally custom products	Lots of generally own-designed products	Mostly standard products; some opportunities for selected options	Same as for 3	Standard products with little or no customization possible; not produced in discrete units, so has to be measured in tons, barrels, and so on	Same as for 3 and 4
Products compete largely on:	Speed of delivery, product customization, new product introduction	Product performance, product reliability and workmanship, delivery reliability, new product introduction, flexibility to produce either low or high volumes	Product performance, price, product reliability and workmanship, delivery reliability	Product performance, price, product reliability and workmanship, delivery reliability	Price	Product reliability and workmanship, price
Products unlikely to compete on:	Price				New product introduction, product customization	
New product introduction	All the time; easy	Frequent; routine	Sometimes	Sometimes; generally expensive	Hardly at all; very costly	Infrequent; expensive

Process Features

	1	2	3	4	5	Hybrid
Process pattern	No rigid pattern; product can be routed anywhere; sometimes a dominant flow	Not all procedures performed on all products; product can be routed many ways; often a dominant flow	Clear pattern, though special treatment of some products sometimes permitted	Clear, rigid pattern, though some off-line work possible	Clear, very rigid pattern	Same as for 5
Linking of process segments	Very loose	Loose, but "cells" can be created	Between tight and loose; tighter if JIT followed	Tight, especially if JIT followed	Very tight	Loose link between different process types
Type of equipment	General purpose	Mostly general purpose	Specialized	Same as for 3	Same as for 3	Same as for 3, 4, and 5
Balance of equipment	Balance of speed and time done in only the grossest, long-run terms. At any one time, an imbalance is likely to exist	Balance likely to be imperfect between segments of process but better coordinated than typical job shop	Machinery speed and size in good balance with peak needs	Speed and size of equipment very well balanced. Capable of being adjusted together over small changes in line speed	Good balance of speed and size. Any excess capacity often placed in latter portion of process to provide insurance against breakdowns or unusual order requests	Same as for 5
Type of layout	Process layout; similar machines grouped together	Process layout; similar tasks and equipment grouped together	Line flow layout; distinct for product produced	Same as for 3	Same as for 3	Two distinct layouts, one for batch and one for the continuous flow
Capital use	Labor intensive; machines frequently idle	Labor intensive, although less machine idleness	Although equipment is specialized, it is fairly cheap; labor still a big item	Capital intensive	Very capital intensive; machines nearly always used	Same as for 5
Typical size of operation	Generally small	Generally medium-sized	Variable	Large	Mammoth	Same as for 4
Economies of scale	None	Few, if any	Same as for 2	Some, perhaps	Yes	Same as for 5
Yields	Often dependent on setup and product complexity	Often dependent on workers; yields usually high	Same as for 2	Often dependent on both workers and equipment function; yields usually high	Often dependent on raw materials; yields can be variable	Can vary depending on type of hybrid

(continued)

Features	(1) Job Shop (Example: Norcen Industries)	(2) Batch Flow (Example: Jos. A. Bank)	(3) Worker-Paced Assembly Line (Example: Burger King Restaurant, Noblesville)	(4) Machine-Paced Assembly Line (Example: Carrier Corporation, Indianapolis)	(5) Continuous Flow (Example: International Paper, Androscoggin Mill)	(6) Batch/Continuous Flow Hybrid (Example: Stroh Brewery, Winston-Salem)
Notion of capacity	Very fuzzy; definable vaguely in dollar terms; useful only in long run	Fuzzy; product mix implies a dollar definition only	Increasingly clear; some physical unit measures possible	Clear; physical unit measures	Same as for 4	Same as for 4 and 5
Additions to capacity	Incremental over full range of possible capacity	Larger increments possible, but over full range of possible capacity	Same as for 2	Changes can be made, but costly to do so because capacity comes in large chunks; otherwise, mild fluctuations possible within relatively narrow limits (such as line rebalance)	Only modest range for incremental change; otherwise, huge chunks of capacity required	Comparatively modest range for incremental change; then huge chunks of capacity required
Speed of process (dollars of output/unit of time or dollars of output/dollars of input/unit of time)	Slow	Reasonably slow	Increasingly fast	Fast	Fast, sometimes astounding	Same as for 5
Pacing	Worker discretion key	Worker-paced	Worker-paced but set within some bounds by management action (such as line balance)	Machine-paced but can be a management goal as well (such as line balance)	Determined technologically; built into equipment	Generally determined technologically but some leeway available
Bottlenecks	Movable; frequent	Movable, but often predictable	Occasionally movable, but often predictable	Generally known and stationary	Known, stationary	Same as for 5

Nature of process change	Incremental	Mostly incremental; some significant radical changes possible	Mostly routine (rebalance); sometimes radical (equipment)	Same as for 3	Most change incremental but radical change possible; means big bucks and sweeping conversions	Sometimes radical; sometimes incremental
Place of technological change in process itself	Little impact; unlikely to be revolutionary	Important once in a while; usually incremental	Increasingly important; embodied in equipment	Important; embodied in equipment	Far-reaching; surprisingly regular	Same as for 4
Setups	Many; varied expense	Some setups needed, but generally easy to do	Same as for 2	No setup required; line already set up	Few and expensive, if any; process organized to simplify most kinds of setups	Little or no setup required; process simplifies need for most kinds of setups
Run lengths	Short	Medium	Some long, some short	Long	Very long	Same as for 5
Materials-Oriented Features						
Materials requirements	Uncertain	Can often be placed statistically within reasonably narrow bounds	Known statistically within fairly close limits	Certain once production plan established	Same as for 4	Some aspects certain, others known statistically
Character of materials	Set bill of materials; uniform quality; can adapt to nonstandard types	Set bill of materials; uniform quality; often many types possible	Set bill of materials; uniform quality; can adapt to nonstandard types	Same as for 3	Sometimes variable bill of materials; variable quality, since often processes are agricultural/mining extracts	Sometimes variable quality, sometimes uniform quality
Vertical integration	None	Sometimes backward, sometimes forward	Same as for 2	Sometimes backward, often forward	Often backward and forward	Same as for 2 and 3

(continued)

TABLE TS2 (Continued)

Features	(1) Job Shop (Example: Norcen Industries)	(2) Batch Flow (Example: Jos. A. Bank)	(3) Worker-Paced Assembly Line (Example: Burger King Restaurant, Noblesville)	(4) Machine-Paced Assembly Line (Example: Carrier Corporation, Indianapolis)	(5) Continuous Flow (Example: International Paper, Androscoggin Mill)	(6) Batch/Continuous Flow Hybrid (Example: Stroh Brewery, Winston-Salem)
Inventories; raw materials	Small; most raw materials purchased to coincide with orders	Moderate; some purchased to coincide with orders and some purchased to provide buffer stock	Varies; often steadily purchased since material needs are generally known within reasonably narrow bounds	Varies; often steadily purchased to coincide with production plan	Often large, but can vary and be steadily purchased to coincide with production plan	Varies; some purchased for buffer stock and some purchased to coincide with production plan
Work-in-process	Large	Moderate	Little	Same as for 3	Very little	Inventory placed between batch and continuous flow segments of process; moderate batch WIP, little continuous flow WIP
Finished goods	Low, if any	Varies	Same as for 2	Can vary; often thrust down distribution channels	Varies; often thrust down distribution channels; safety stocks often required	Same as for 5
Control over suppliers	Low	Moderate	Great	Same as for 3	Same as for 3	Same as for 3, 4, and 5
Control over customers	Little or none	Same as for 1	Same as for 1	Same, as to delivery	Same as for 4	Same as for 4 and 5
Supplier ties	Informal; spot buys	Some spot buys, some longer term contracts	Contracts increasingly long term	Formal; long term	Formal; generally long term	Same as for 5
Customer ties	Informal; repeat business encouraged, however	Some informal, some formal distribution	Can be informal or formal	Formal distribution channels	Same as for 4	Same as for 4 and 5

Information-Oriented Features

Order handling and sales	Often bid for sales are to order	Varies; some to order, and some from stock with lagged adjustments to that stock	Same as for 2	Sales well established ahead of time or from finished goods inventory; lagged adjustments to stock	Sales well established ahead of time or from finished goods inventory	Same as for 5
Degree of information coordination outside factory	Needed only for bids, receipt of any supplied materials, and to initiate supplies	Needed only to monitor sales and to initiate supplies	Needed to monitor sales and to place orders for supplies; sometimes for order scheduling	Elaborate order scheduling, materials tracking; various levels of forecasts; great deal of corporate communication	Elaborate order scheduling, materials tracking, forecasting; great deal of corporate communication	Monitoring sales, placing supply order; little corporate communication on day-to-day operations
Information systems within factory	Elaborate, viewed as central; lots of flow between factory workers and management, lots of paperwork	Less elaborate but still considerable; less feedback required, considerable paperwork	Little information needed, basically just to communicate order; flow from management to workers. Opposite flow used primarily to signal breakdowns; generally more informal; little paperwork	Same as for 3	Little information needed, basically just to communicate product change; flow from management to workers. Opposite flow used primarily to signal breakdowns; generally more informal	Same as for 5
Trigger for production	Order itself; expediting common	Could be order or level of finished goods inventory; some expediting	Level of finished goods inventory, longer term forecasts, or "frozen" orders; little expediting	Level of finished goods inventory, longer term forecasts, or "frozen" orders; no expediting possible	Same as for 4	First portion of process triggered by forecasts; second portion triggered by "frozen" orders
Scheduling	Uncertain, flexible; always subject to change	Flexible, but not as uncertain; less subject to change	Process designed around fixed schedule	Same as for 3	Easy to group similar jobs or orders; fixed schedule often set technologically and well in advance	Similar jobs or orders grouped together; fixed schedule set in advance, at least for second portion of process

(continued)

TABLE TS2 (Continued)

Features	(1) Job Shop (Example: Norcen Industries)	(2) Batch Flow (Example: Jos. A. Bank)	(3) Worker-Paced Assembly Line (Example: Burger King Restaurant, Noblesville)	(4) Machine-Paced Assembly Line (Example: Carrier Corporation, Indianapolis)	(5) Continuous Flow (Example: International Paper, Androscoggin Mill)	(6) Batch/Continuous Flow Hybrid (Example: Stroh Brewery, Winston-Salem)
Quality control	Informal, by each worker; spot checks; machine capabilities can be determined	Can be more formal, though often is not	Some on-line checks, some postassembly checks; process capability can be monitored	Same as for 3	Essentially done by process control people; designed into process; periodic sampling often done and process capability monitored	Much of quality designed into process; periodic sampling often done and process capability monitored
Response to cyclicality in demand	Overtime, shift work, some subcontract, hire/fire	Overtime; adjustments can be made by building and depleting inventory, shift work, and hire/fire	Overtime work or closing line early; some adjustments can be made by building and depleting inventory, rebalance, and closing down shift or plant	Same as for 3	Inventory adjustments; otherwise, shift or plant is shut down	Same as for 5
Worker payment	Hourly; piece rate or other incentive wage	Often piece rate or other incentive wage	Hourly base; sometimes also tied to percentage of standard that crew achieves	Hourly	Same as for 4	Same as for 4 and 5
End-of-month syndrome (more produced at end of month for billing than at beginning)	Inevitable	Often happens	Close to nonexistent	Same as for 3	Nonexistent	Same as for 5

Labor-Oriented Features

Advancement for worker	Knowledge of more and more machinery and machine capabilities. With more skills and/or seniority acquired, greater pay and responsibilities given, such as "lead worker." Seniority can lead to change in shift assignment	Knowledge of more and more machinery and machine capabilities. With more skills and/or seniority acquired, greater responsibilities given, such as "lead worker." Seniority can lead to change in shift assignment or department	With more skills and/or seniority acquired, greater responsibilities given, such as "lead worker" or "group leader." Seniority can lead to change in department or shift assignment	Seniority can lead to change in department or shift assignment	Seniority can lead to change in shift or, sometimes, department assignment	Same as for 5
Labor content per $1 of product value	Very high	High	Medium	Low	Very low	
Job content	Large	Medium	Small	Same as for 3	Often small "push button" stuff; but can be "art" as well	Same as for 5
Importance and development of standards for labor	Key for scheduling planning growth; big purpose of information system; sometimes key for wage payment	Often key for wage payment; needed also for scheduling product mix	Crucial for process design	Same as for 3	Important largely for assigning workforce to equipment	Same as for 5

(continued)

TABLE TS2 Comparing processes of different types

Features	(1) Job Shop (Example: Norcen Industries)	(2) Batch Flow (Example: Jos. A. Bank)	(3) Worker-Paced Assembly Line (Example: Burger King Restaurant, Noblesville)	(4) Machine-Paced Assembly Line (Example: Carrier Corporation, Indianapolis)	(5) Continuous Flow (Example: International Paper, Androscoggin Mill)	(6) Batch/Continuous Flow Hybrid (Example: Stroh Brewery, Winston-Salem)
Management Features						
Staff-line needs	Small staff (information, quotes, and new product development). Much line supervision needed	Small staff (generally methods related). Line supervision more critical	Large staff for process redesign, methods, forecasting, capacity planning, and scheduling. Line supervision and troubleshooting still critical	Same as for 3	Large staff for technology and capacity planning, and scheduling. Line supervision less crucial; maintenance key	Same as for 5
Degree of corporate influence on operations, if plant within a multiplant company	Modest	Same as for 1	Same as for 1	Great, for both operations and capital expenditures	Same as for 4	Variable; more likely that corporate influence is with capital expenditures than with day-to-day operations
Means of control	Usually a profit center	Can be either a profit center or a cost center	Same as for 2	Usually a cost center	Same as for 4	Same as for 4 and 5
Challenges to management	Scheduling, bidding, information flows, expediting product innovation, shifting bottlenecks	Order processing, labor issues and pay, handling cyclicality	Balance (process design), product design, managing workforce, technological advances, capacity planning, materials management	Same as for 3	Capital needs, maintenance, site, technological change, vertical integration, raw materials sourcing	Same as for 5

PART TWO: SERVICE OPERATIONS

Comparison of Services

The characterization of services as service factories, service shops, mass service, and professional service can be used as well for comparing service processes in much the same way that Table TS2 compared manufacturing processes. This is accomplished in Table TS3. The various features compared there are placed into various groups: service, process, customer-oriented, labor-related, and management. These features undergird the challenges for management that were introduced earlier.

TABLE TS3 A service comparison

Features	Service Factory (Example: Burger King Restaurant)	Service Shop (Example: Ogle–Tucker Buick)	Mass Service (Example: Lazarus–Castleton)	Professional Service (Example: Arthur Andersen)
	Service Features			
Mix of services	Limited	Diverse	Limited	Diverse
Products compete largely on:	Price, speed, perceived "warmth" or "excitement"	Wide choice, competence	Price, choice, perceived "warmth" or "excitement"	Competence, range of expertise
New or unique services introduced or performed	Infrequent	Routine	Limited experimentation	Routine
	Process Features			
Capital intensity	High	High	Low	Low
Pattern of process	Rigid	Adaptable	Rigid	Very loose
Ties to equipment	Integral part of process, little choice applies	Equipment important to process, but usually several options exist for its use	Limited ties to equipment, more tied to plant and layout	No close ties to plant or equipment
Importance of balance of tasks and any equipment to smooth process functioning	Balance critical	Balance often not critical	Balance not critical	Balance can be critical
Tolerance for excess capacity	Excess capacity abhorred	Excess capacity often not a problem	Excess capacity implies workforce adjustment that is fairly easily made	Excess capacity abhorred
Ease of scheduling	Sometimes tough to schedule, peak demand can be difficult	Scheduling more easily done	Scheduling easily done	Sometimes tough to schedule, peak demand can be difficult
Economies of scale	Some	Some—permits better equipment use and thus justification	Few, if any, except those related to any inventories	Few, if any, although some specialization can occur
Notion of capacity	Fairly clear-cut, sometimes definable in physical terms	Fuzzy, very dependent on mix of demands. Only definable in dollar terms	Not as fuzzy as with service shop. Limits are often due to plant, not processing time	Fuzzy
Layout	Line flow-like preferred	Job-shop or fixed position	Typically fixed position although layout may change frequently, customers move through layout	Job-shop frequently

Addition to capacity	Can be in variable increments, requires balance of capital and labor	Can be in variable increments, aspects of balance more murky	Often takes big changes to plant to enact. Processing can sometimes be sped up by adding some labor	Means adding primarily to labor in incremental fashion
Bottlenecks	Occasionally movable, but often predictable	Movable, frequent	Typically well known, predictable	Can sometimes be forecast, but otherwise are uncertain
Nature of process change	Sometimes routine (rebalance), sometimes radical (new equipment)	Occasionally radical (new equipment and procedures)	Process change seldom occurs, although it can be radical (such as big change to plant)	Mostly incremental
Importance of material flow to service provision	Both inventories and flow are important	Inventories important but not so much the flow	Inventories are often important and must be controlled	Incidental to most services
Customer-Oriented Features				
Importance of attractive physical surroundings to marketing of service	Can be critical	Often insignificant	Critical	Often insignificant
Interaction of customer with process	Little, brief	Can be great	Some	Typically, very great
Customization of service	Scant	Significant	Scant	Significant
Ease of managing demand for peaks and nonpeaks	Can be done through price	Some promotion of off-peak times can be done, but often difficult	Same as for service shop	Often very difficult to manage demand, may not be responsive to price
Process quality control	Can be formal, amenable to standard methods (such as control charts)	Can be formal. Checkpoints can easily be established. Training can be critical to quality	Mainly informal. Training critical to quality	Mainly informal. Training critical to quality

(continued)

TABLE TS3 (Continued)

Features	Service Factory (Example: Burger King Restaurant)	Service Shop (Example: Ogle–Tucker Buick)	Mass Service (Example: Lazarus–Castleton)	Professional Service (Example: Arthur Andersen)
		Labor-Related Features		
Pay	Typically hourly	Varies, could include individual incentive or commission schemes	Same as for service shop	Salary, often with bonus of some type
Skills levels	Generally lower skills	High skills	Variable, but most often lower skills	Very high skills
Job content	Small	Large	Often medium, but variable	Very large
Advancement	With more skills and/or seniority acquired, greater responsibility given. Seniority can lead to change in department or shift assignment	Often, worker is an independent operator of sorts and can exert some control on what he gives and gets from job; limited hierarchical progression	Often a hierarchy to progress upward through	Often a pyramid, up or out. Top of pyramid exerts leverage over bottom or pyramid
		Management Features		
Staff-line needs	Large staff for process redesign, methods, forecasting, capacity planning, and scheduling. Line supervision and troubleshooting still critical	Limited staff, mostly line operation	Some staff, often focused on personal issues	Limited staff; many line managers wear multiple hats
Means of control	Variable; can be cost or profit	Usually a profit center	Usually a profit center	Usually a profit center

Index

MAI

11-4-98